Europe's Auto Industry

Drawing on the analytical approaches of global production networks, global value chains, and spatial divisions of labor, this book investigates the changing automotive industry in Europe. Petr Pavlínek, a leading scholar of the automotive industry, focuses on its restructuring and geographic reorganization since the early 1990s to analyze the driving forces and regional development effects of these changes. Pavlínek explains the spatial profit-seeking strategies of large automotive firms and their role in the restructuring and increasing internationalization of Europe's automotive industry through foreign direct investment. He also considers how rapid growth in eastern Europe has affected western Europe, evaluates the relative position of countries in the European automotive industry, and examines the transition to the production of electric vehicles in eastern Europe. *Europe's Auto Industry* features original data, concepts and methods that may be applied in other disciplines. This title is also available as Open Access on Cambridge Core.

Petr Pavlínek is Professor of Geography at the University of Nebraska Omaha and Charles University. His previous books include *Economic Restructuring and Local Environmental Management in the Czech Republic* (1997), *Environmental Transitions: Transformation and Ecological Defence in Central and Eastern Europe* (with John Pickles, 2000), *A Successful Transformation? Restructuring of the Czech Automobile Industry* (2008) and *Dependent Growth: Foreign Investment and the Development of the Automotive Industry in East-Central Europe* (2017).

Development Trajectories in Global Value Chains

A feature of the current phase of globalization is the outsourcing of production tasks and services across borders, and the increasing organization of production and trade through global value chains (GVCs), global commodity chains (GCCs), and global production networks (GPNs). With a large and growing literature on GVCs, GCCs, and GPNs, this series is distinguished by its focus on the implications of these new production systems for economic, social, and regional development. This series publishes a wide range of theoretical, methodological, and empirical works, both research monographs and edited volumes, dealing with crucial issues of transformation in the global economy. How do GVCs change the ways in which lead and supplier firms shape regional and international economies? How do they affect local and regional development trajectories, and what implications do they have for workers and their communities? How is the organization of value chains changing and how are these emerging forms contested as more traditional structures of North–South trade complemented and transformed by emerging South–South lead firms, investments, and trading links? How does the large-scale entry of women into value-chain production impact on gender relations? What opportunities and limits do GVCs create for economic and social upgrading and innovation? In what ways are GVCs changing the nature of work and the role of labor in the global economy? And how might the increasing focus on logistics management, financialization, or social standards and compliance portend important developments in the structure of regional economies?

This series includes contributions from all disciplines and interdisciplinary fields and approaches related to GVC analysis, including GCCs and GPNs, and is particularly focused on theoretically innovative and informed works that are grounded in the empirics of development related to these approaches. Through their focus on changing organizational forms, governance systems, and production relations, volumes in this series contribute to on-going conversations about theories of development and development policy in the contemporary era of globalization.

Series editors

Stephanie Barrientos is Emeritus Professor of Global Development at the Global Development Institute, University of Manchester.

Gary Gereffi is Emeritus Professor of Sociology and Founding Director of the Global Value Chains Center, Duke University.

Dev Nathan is Visiting Professor at the Institute for Human Development, Delhi; Visiting Scholar at The New School for Social Research, New York; and Research Director at the GenDev Centre for Research and Innovation, Gurgaon.

John Pickles is Earl N. Phillips Distinguished Professor of Geography and International Studies at the University of North Carolina, Chapel Hill.

Jennifer Bair is Professor of Sociology and Associate Dean for Social Sciences in the College and Graduate School of Arts & Sciences at the University of Virginia.

Valentina De Marchi is Associate Professor in Sustainability Management at the Department of Society, Politics and Sustainability, ESADE Business School.

Joonkoo Lee is Associate Professor of Organization Studies at the School of Business, Hanyang University, Seoul.

Shengjun Zhu is Associate Professor in the College of Urban and Environmental Sciences, Peking University.

Titles in the series

Europe's Auto Industry

Global Production Networks and Spatial Change

PETR PAVLÍNEK

University of Nebraska Omaha
Charles University

CAMBRIDGE
UNIVERSITY PRESS

CAMBRIDGE
UNIVERSITY PRESS

Shaftesbury Road, Cambridge CB2 8EA, United Kingdom

One Liberty Plaza, 20th Floor, New York, NY 10006, USA

477 Williamstown Road, Port Melbourne, VIC 3207, Australia

314–321, 3rd Floor, Plot 3, Splendor Forum, Jasola District Centre,
New Delhi – 110025, India

103 Penang Road, #05–06/07, Visioncrest Commercial, Singapore 238467

Cambridge University Press is part of Cambridge University Press & Assessment,
a department of the University of Cambridge.

We share the University's mission to contribute to society through the pursuit of
education, learning and research at the highest international levels of excellence.

www.cambridge.org
Information on this title: www.cambridge.org/9781009453233

DOI: 10.1017/9781009453196

First published 2025

Cover image: Cover photograph: A finished car starts up for the first time at the Skoda Auto
factory located in Czechia © Škoda Auto a.s. 2024.

A catalogue record for this publication is available from the British Library.

A Cataloging-in-Publication data record for this book is available from the Library of Congress

ISBN 978-1-009-45323-3 Hardback

Contents

Figures

Tables

Preface

This book investigates the changing European automotive industry from the perspective of economic geography by employing the analytical lenses of the global production networks (GPNs) and global value chains (GVCs) perspectives. It focuses on the restructuring and geographic reorganization of the European automotive industry since the early 1990s by analyzing the driving forces behind this transformation and the regional development effects of these changes.

From the geographical perspective, the biggest change in the European automotive industry during this period has been the integration of Eastern Europe into the Western European production and distribution networks, and the development of European transnational automotive industry production networks. These processes have been driven by the investment strategies of automotive industry firms. Both assemblers and suppliers heavily invested in Eastern Europe to benefit from potentially higher rates of profit than in existing locations in the rest of Europe. Potentially higher rates of profit in Eastern Europe were made possible by its location-specific advantages in production factors, resulting in lower production costs than in other European regions. At the same time, the rapid growth of the automotive industry in Eastern Europe had important consequences for the rest of the European automotive industry, especially in Western Europe, leading to its restructuring, and resulting in the finer spatial division of labor in the European automotive industry.

Theoretically and conceptually, this book draws on the GVCs/GPNs perspective (e.g., Sturgeon et al., 2008; Coe and Yeung, 2015, 2019; Gereffi, 2018; Kano et al., 2020; Coe, 2021). Although the GVC and GPN perspectives are distinct, they share their focus on the transnational organization of industries in value chains/production networks, power distribution in these networks, the role of various institutions in affecting the configuration and operation of GVCs/GPNs, and the impact of GVCs/GPNs on economic development within the context of the international division of labor (e.g., Pavlínek, 2018; 2022a). For the purposes of this book, I apply the GVC and GPN perspectives as one broad analytical approach to examine the changes in the European automotive industry, although in most cases I simply refer to this broad approach as the GPN perspective.

In this book, I am using the term Eastern Europe as an all-encompassing geographic term referring to the pre-1990 state-socialist countries in Central Europe (Czechia, Hungary, Poland, Slovakia and Slovenia), Southeastern Europe (Bulgaria, Croatia and Romania) and the Baltic states (Estonia, Latvia and Lithuania) that became European Union members. Eastern Europe also includes non-European Union member countries in Southeastern Europe (Serbia, Bosnia and Herzegovina, North Macedonia and Moldova) that have been integrated into the European automotive industry production system through investment and trade links. Russia, Ukraine and Belarus are excluded from the analysis and are beyond the scope of this book.

OVERVIEW OF THE BOOK

The automotive industry is a typical example of producer-driven GVCs/GPNs in which lead firms usually directly own and operate production facilities, including those in foreign locations. More specifically, the automotive industry is a typical example of captive GVCs (Gereffi et al., 2005) or a so-called quasi hierarchy (Humphrey and Schmitz, 2004), in which lead firms organize and regulate GVCs/GPNs through their corporate and market power. Investment in production facilities that are built in new locations and disinvestment in existing locations play a crucial role in the restructuring of automotive industry GVCs/GPNs because they affect the extended networks of component suppliers. Cross-border investment in the form of foreign direct investment (FDI) and disinvestment, especially in large assembly factories and component suppliers in the form of follow sourcing, therefore potentially have very significant long-term economic development effects in host countries and regions. Since it is important to understand these potentially long-term economic development effects of automotive industry FDI, Chapter 1 reviews FDI in less developed countries and critically evaluates both the mainstream and heterodox approaches to FDI.

Chapter 2 broadens the scope of this discussion on FDI's long-term economic development effects to the less developed (peripheral) regions of more developed countries. Since the 1960s, a high proportion of automotive industry FDI in Europe has been invested to develop the production capacity in peripheral regions to benefit from their lower production costs compared to more developed (core) regions. Chapter 2 identifies the different types and mechanisms of FDI in core and peripheral regions. It highlights the importance of linkages between foreign-owned and domestic firms and spillovers from foreign-owned to domestic firms in host regions to argue that, in the long run, FDI tends to benefit core regions more than peripheral regions.

Chapter 2 also critically evaluates the most important approaches to FDI in peripheral regions developed in economic geography since the 1970s, namely the branch plant economy and truncation, new regionalism, new international division of labor and spatial divisions of labor, and the GPN perspective.

Chapter 3 examines the regional development effects of FDI in what I call the integrated peripheries of the automotive industry by analyzing supplier linkages between foreign subsidiaries and domestic firms. It introduces the spatial concept of integrated peripheries in core-based macro-regional production networks to explain the rapid growth of the automotive industry in Europe's peripheral regions. Conceptually, it draws on Harvey's spatiotemporal fix and on the GPN concept of strategic coupling to investigate the mode of articulation of integrated peripheries into macro-regional production networks. Empirically, it examines the rapid growth of the automotive industry in Slovakia and its consequences for the domestic automotive industry by analyzing the quantity and quality of supplier linkages. The chapter demonstrates how the weak integration of domestic firms into foreign-controlled supplier networks limits the potential for technology transfer from foreign firms to the Slovak economy and for the development of a stronger domestic supplier industry.

Chapter 4 builds on the concept of integrated peripheries introduced in Chapter 3 to conceptualize the changing geography of the European automotive industry based on the spatial profit-seeking strategies of automotive firms. It explains the growth of the automotive industry in peripheral regions and its contemporaneous restructuring in existing locations. The empirical analysis is based on 2,124 restructuring events of large automotive industry firms in the European Union countries and Norway between 2005 and 2016, and on 91 interviews with foreign automotive industry subsidiaries conducted in Czechia and Slovakia between 2009 and 2015. Large differences in labor costs, corporate taxes and other production costs across the European Union explain the growth in the Eastern European integrated periphery and simultaneous restructuring in both traditional core regions and old integrated peripheries in Western Europe. The chapter demonstrates the increasing internationalization of the European automotive industry, which is driven by the investment strategies of global automotive lead firms and the decreasing role played by large domestic firms in the European automotive industry.

Chapter 5 investigates the core–semiperiphery–periphery structure of the European automotive industry between 2003 and 2017 by drawing on the GVCs/GPNs perspective and on the conceptual explanation of the spatial division of labor in transnational production networks in the automotive industry. It develops a methodology to empirically determine the relative position of countries in the core, semiperiphery or periphery and changes in their position over time. The methodology is calculated as "automotive industry power" of individual countries, which is a combination of trade-based positional power, ownership and control power, and innovation power in the automotive industry. The empirical analysis reveals a dominant position of Germany as a higher-order core. France and Italy are the only two additional countries positioned in the stable core of the European automotive industry. The periphery is mostly located in Eastern Europe, despite the rapid growth of the automotive industry there since the 1990s. Chapter 5 reveals that most countries kept a stable relative position in the core–semiperiphery–periphery structure of the European automotive industry transnational production system during the 2003–2017 period.

Chapter 6 develops an approach to measure value creation and value capture in regional production networks based on firm-level indicators to investigate how distinct tiers of firms contribute to value creation and value capture in the automotive industry. It investigates the relationships between the firm's position in GVCs/GPNs and its prospects for value creation and capture in the context of the Czech automotive industry. The empirical analysis suggests that the economic effects of the automotive industry largely depend on its capital intensity and that mostly foreign-owned higher-tier firms generate and capture greater value than lower-tier firms, which include the vast majority of domestic suppliers.

Chapter 7 analyzes the progress of the transition from the production of vehicles with internal combustion engines to the production of electric vehicles in Eastern Europe. It draws on the evolutionary economic geography perspective to contend that this transition is strongly embedded in and constrained by the previous FDI-dependent development of the automotive industry in Eastern Europe and its current integrated periphery position in the European automotive industry value chains and production networks. The chapter considers the consequences of the transition for the future position of Eastern European countries in automotive GVCs, GPNs and for the division of labor in the European automotive industry.

Chapter 8 summarizes basic points and arguments presented in the preceding chapters and discusses the important conceptual and methodological implications of the book.

Acknowledgments

Europe's Auto Industry draws on my six previously published articles in academic journals during the 2016–2023 period. All these original articles have been edited and where possible updated. Chapter 2 is based on Petr Pavlínek (2022) Revisiting Economic Geography and Foreign Direct Investment in Less Developed Regions. *Geography Compass* 16(4), e12617: 1–21, doi.org/10.1111/gec3.12617, published by Wiley. Chapter 3 was originally published by Taylor & Francis on behalf of Clark University as Petr Pavlínek (2018) Global Production Networks, Foreign Direct Investment, and Supplier Linkages in the Integrated Peripheries of the Automotive Industry. *Economic Geography* 94(2): 141–165, doi.org/10.1080/00130095.2017.1393313. Chapter 4 originally appeared as Petr Pavlínek (2020) Restructuring and Internationalization of the European Automotive Industry. *Journal of Economic Geography* 20(2): 509–541, doi.org/10.1093/jeg/lby070, published by Oxford University Press. Chapter 5 is based on Petr Pavlínek (2022) Relative Positions of Countries in the Core-Periphery Structure of the European Automotive Industry. *European Urban and Regional Studies* 29(1): 59–84, doi.org/10.1177/09697764211021882, published by SAGE Publications. Chapter 6 was originally published by SAGE Publications as Petr Pavlínek and Jan Ženka (2016) Value Creation and Value Capture in the Automotive Industry: Empirical Evidence from Czechia. *Environment and Planning A* 48(5): 937–959, doi.org/10.1177/0308518X15619934. Finally, Chapter 7 originally appeared as Petr Pavlínek (2023) Transition of the Automotive Industry towards Electric Vehicle Production in the East European Integrated Periphery. *Empirica* 50(1): 35–73, doi.org/10.1007/s10663-022-09554-9, which was published by Springer. I want to thank these publishers for their permission to use my previous work in this book. I also want to thank Jan Ženka for his permission to use the article "Value Creation and Value Capture in the Automotive Industry: Empirical Evidence from Czechia" he has originally coauthored for Chapter 6.

My gratitude goes to everyone who helped with the collection of data for the original articles used in this book. Pavla Žížalová, Jan Ženka, Pavol Hurbánek and Miroslava Poláková participated in organizing and conducting company interviews in Czechia and Slovakia. Jan Pulec and Tomáš Michl helped with the data extraction from the European Restructuring Monitor for Chapter 3. Monika Martišková extracted data from the ComExt database, calculated the positional power and conducted the cluster analysis used in Chapter 6. Inge Ivarsson and Claes Alvstam helped with finding R&D data for Sweden for Chapter 6. Karel Hostomský produced maps used in Chapters 2–3. Special thanks go to John Pickles for his encouragement to pursue the publication of this book.

I am grateful to the Czech Science Foundation for supporting the research presented in this book with three research grants over the years. The preparation of this book was supported by a research grant from the Czech Science Foundation (grant number: 23-07819S).

The biggest thanks go to my wife Gabriela and children Adam and Sára for their continuing love, support, patience and encouragement in my academic endeavors.

Abbreviations

BEV	battery electric vehicle
ERM	European Restructuring Monitor
EU	European Union
FDI	foreign direct investment
GM	General Motors
GPN	global production network
GVC	global value chain
PHEV	plug-in hybrid electric vehicle
PSA	Peugeot Société Anonyme Peugeot Citroën
R&D	research and development
TNC	transnational corporation
VW	Volkswagen
WWII	World War II

Foreign Direct Investment and Economic Development in Less Developed Countries

I.I INTRODUCTION

The importance of foreign direct investment (FDI) has rapidly increased in the world economy since the 1970s (Figure 1.1), reflecting its role in neoliberal approaches to economic development (Harvey, 2005a; Bohle, 2006; Gereffi, 2013). Since the 1960s, FDI-based development strategies have become increasingly important in less developed countries, where FDI levels varied and fluctuated during the twentieth century (Twomey, 2000; Amsden, 2001; Kohli, 2004; Dussel Peters, 2016). During the same period, similar strategies became popular in less developed regions of more developed countries, as we will see in Chapter 2 (Amin et al., 1994; MacKinnon and Phelps, 2001a). Since the 1990s, FDI played an increasingly prominent role in the economic development of Eastern Europe (Pavlínek, 2004; Drahokoupil, 2009), China (Chen, 2018) and in other less developed countries (Akyüz, 2017), where FDI-based strategies gradually replaced the import substitution strategies of economic development (Bruton, 1998; Rodrik, 2011), in which FDI played a limited role (Humphrey and Oeter, 2000; Narula and Driffield, 2012; Narula, 2018).

Consequently, the average global annual FDI inflows were sixty-three times higher during the decade of 2013–2022 (USD1.51 trillion) than in 1970–1979 (USD24 billion). The average annual FDI inflows to less developed countries grew 115 times (USD730 billion versus USD6.4 billion), while average inflows to more developed countries increased forty-one times (USD748 billion versus USD18 billion). As a result, the share of less developed countries making up total FDI inflows increased from the average of 26 percent during 1970–1979 to 49 percent during 2013–2021. FDI inward stock grew sixty-four times for the world as a whole, seventy-two times for more developed countries and fifty times for less developed countries between 1980 and 2022 (Figure 1.2) (UNCTAD, 2020). The 2020s are projected to be a decade of far-reaching

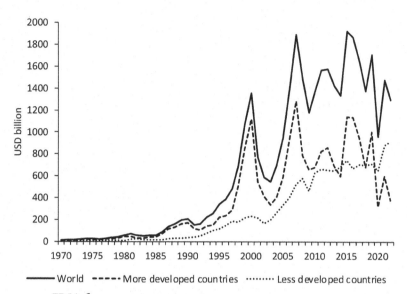

FIGURE I.I FDI inflows, 1970–2022
Source: author-based on data in UNCTAD (2023).

changes in the world economy that will strongly affect global FDI flows with potentially significant development implications for less developed countries (UNCTAD, 2020; Zhan, 2021). Uneven distribution and geographic concentration are the enduring structural features of FDI (Table 1.1) that contribute to global uneven development.

The significantly increased role of FDI in the world economy underlines the importance of analyzing and understanding the effects of FDI for host economies and its potential contribution to uneven development at various geographic scales, including in less developed countries. It is particularly compelling due to the fact that "the attraction of FDI constitutes a central component of the development strategies of most developing and emerging economies" (Jordaan et al., 2020: 2), while, at the same time, "FDI is perhaps one of the most ambiguous and least understood concepts in international economics" (Akyüz, 2017: 169) and "determining exactly how FDI affects development has proved remarkably elusive" (Moran et al., 2005: back cover).

The goal of this chapter is to review research on the development effects of FDI in less developed countries (what the world-systems approach labels as global periphery and semiperiphery).[1] I argue two main points. First, the

_____

[1] While the core–periphery terminology, which originated in the dependency and world-systems perspectives (UN, 1950; Wallerstein, 1979), is well established in economic geography (Friedmann, 1967; Aoyama et al., 2011; Pavlínek, 2022a), we need to keep in mind that the core, periphery and semiperiphery are slippery categories as the core–periphery processes operate

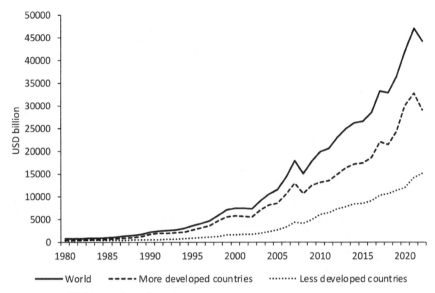

FIGURE 1.2 FDI inward stock, 1980–2022
Source: author-based on data in UNCTAD (2023).

empirical evidence points strongly towards very uneven and limited development effects of FDI in less developed countries. Second, mainstream and heterodox perspectives come to contrasting conclusions about the potential developmental effects of FDI in less developed countries and regions.

1.2 FDI IN LESS DEVELOPED COUNTRIES

I start with a brief overview of the history of FDI in less developed countries. Historically, FDI flows and stocks have been much smaller in less developed countries than in more developed countries (Figure 1.1) (Twomey, 2000) and there has been a great variation in the importance of FDI across less developed countries because of the high concentration of FDI in particular countries and macro regions (Table 1.1) (UNCTAD, 2023).

simultaneously at multiple geographic scales. Consequently, individual regions may occupy different positions in this spatial hierarchy at different geographic scales. For example, while Eastern Europe belongs to the global semiperiphery (Van Hamme and Pion, 2012), it is peripheral at the macro-regional scale of Europe (Pavlínek, 2018; 2020; 2022a). Moreover, cores, peripheries and semiperipheries can also be recognized at the scale of Eastern Europe and within individual countries (Zdanowska, 2021). Similar complex relationships exist in less developed world regions and countries with large metropolitan areas, being cores at national and macro-regional scales but being parts of the global periphery or semiperiphery at the same time, while the internal peripheries of core countries are still part of the global economic core.

TABLE I.I *FDI inward stock by world region in 2022*

	USD billion	Percent
Developed economies	29,093	65.7
Europe	15,604	35.3
North America	11,902	26.9
Other developed economies	1,587	3.6
Developing economies	15,160	34.3
Africa	1,053	2.4
Latin America and the Caribbean	2,580	5.8
Asia	11,495	26.0
East Asia	6,125	13.8
Southeast Asia	3,564	8.1
South Asia	650	1.5
West Asia	939	2.1
Central Asia	216	0.5
Oceania	32	0.1
World	44,253	100.0

Note: Totals exclude the financial centers in the Caribbean, Belgium/
Luxembourg, Iraq and the Netherlands Antilles. Other developed economies
include Australia, Bermuda, Israel, Japan and New Zealand.
Source: based on data in UNCTAD (2023).

In Latin America, FDI played an important role in economic development
from the beginning of the twentieth century, with Brazil recording the largest
FDI stock among less developed countries by World War II (WWII) (Kuczynski,
2003; Schneider, 2013). In East and Southeast Asia, Japan heavily invested in its
colonies before WWII, with the largest FDI stocks in Korea and Taiwan
(Amsden, 2001). In Africa, FDI concentrated in extractive industries but was
extremely low during the colonial period, with the exception of South Africa
(e.g., Twomey, 2000; Kohli, 2004). Overall, the value and importance of FDI in
less developed countries declined in the first half of the twentieth century
because of world wars and the Great Depression. The decline continued
following WWII due to the nationalization of extractive industries during
decolonization and anti-FDI policies in many less developed countries. For
example, foreign investment was eliminated in key manufacturing industries
in Asia after WWII (Twomey, 2000; Amsden, 2001; UNCTAD, 2007).

In the 1960s, FDI increased in Latin America (Thomas, 2011; Dussel Peters,
2016) but the political uncertainty in the wake of decolonization discouraged
FDI in Asia (Amsden, 2001). In Africa, FDI was low and concentrated in the
extractive industry and commodity exports after independence (Kohli, 2004).

FDI inflows in less developed countries more than doubled in the 1970s, more than tripled in the 1980s, grew six times in the 1990s, doubled in the 2000s and increased by only 10 percent in the 2010s (UNCTAD, 2023) (Figure 1.1). FDI stocks in less developed countries grew by 60 percent in the 1980s, tripled in the 1990s and again in the 2000s, and almost doubled in the 2010s (UNCTAD, 2023) (Figure 1.2). The efficiency-seeking FDI, especially access to cheap labor and other assets, is now the most important reason for FDI in less developed countries (Yamin and Nixson, 2016), although large national and regional differences exist (UNCTAD, 2023).

In Asia, despite the highest FDI stock in less developed countries (Table 1.1), FDI played a limited role in the rapid development of Japan (Paprzycki and Fukao, 2008) and once-peripheral Taiwan (Amsden and Chu, 2003), South Korea (Amsden, 1989) and most recently China (Lee et al., 2017). Instead, the growth and development in these countries depended on domestic firms, both private and state-owned, and strong industrial policies that actively supported their growth. Large domestic firms were then able to globalize through outward FDI (Amsden, 2001; Amsden and Chu, 2003; Farrell, 2008; Lee et al., 2014; 2017; Yeung, 2016; Taylor and Zajontz, 2020; Jo et al., 2023). The economic success of these countries thus primarily depended on the development of the strong and globally competitive domestic sector rather than FDI.

FDI stock has been low in Africa compared to other world regions (Table 1.1) despite its growth from USD32 billion in 1980 to USD1,053 billion in 2022 amid an increase in FDI inflows from USD926 million in 1970 and USD2.8 billion in 1990 to USD44.9 billion in 2022. The growth in FDI was mainly driven by the rising global demand for natural resources. However, Africa's share of global FDI inflows decreased from 7.1 percent in 1970 to 3.4 percent in 2022 and its share of global inward FDI stock dropped from 6.4 percent in 1980 to 2.4 percent in 2022 (UNCTAD, 2023). FDI has been heavily concentrated in extractive industries with limited effects on the broader economy and economic growth (Morrissey, 2012; Ndikumana and Sarr, 2019; Munyi, 2020) and it fueled capital flight during the 1970–2015 period (Ndikumana and Sarr, 2019). FDI did not have any significant effect on manufacturing during the 1980–2009 period (Gui-Diby and Renard, 2015) and it crowded out domestic investment in the 1990s (Agosin and Machado, 2005). The share of manufacturing of total FDI inflows declined from 46 percent in 2010 to 25 percent in 2017 (Munyi, 2020) and the future prospects of manufacturing development in Africa remain bleak (Gelb et al., 2020). Countries with weak industrial and FDI policies, such as Nigeria, failed to encourage the development of modern large-scale manufacturing despite relatively large FDI inflows and the strong FDI presence (Kohli, 2004). A recent rapid rise in Chinese FDI in resource extraction and infrastructure projects follows a familiar pattern of profit extraction and limited economic benefits for Africa (Taylor and Zajontz, 2020), which is also the case for increasing FDI in tourism (Murphy, 2019) and agriculture (Allan et al., 2013).

In other less developed world regions, such as Latin America, Eastern Europe, China and Southeast Asia, foreign firms developed modern manufacturing in selected industries (e.g., the automotive and electronic industries), which, however, remained mostly isolated from host economies and did not lead to the growth of the domestic-owned internationally competitive manufacturing. This has been the case of efficiency-seeking FDI in Mexico, Central America and the Caribbean, and resource-seeking FDI in Chile, Ecuador, Bolivia and Peru since the mid-1990s (Wionczek, 1986; Gallagher and Zarsky, 2007; Schneider, 2013; Dussel Peters, 2016). In Latin America as a whole, FDI crowded out domestic investment in manufacturing between 1971 and 2000 (Agosin and Machado, 2005), resulting in the negative effect of manufacturing FDI on economic growth (Nunnenkamp and Spatz, 2003).

As in Mexico, the growth of manufacturing in Eastern Europe since the 1990s has been driven by peripheral integration into macro-regional production networks through efficiency-seeking FDI (e.g., Pavlínek, 2017a). FDI inflows into manufacturing led to large increases in output and exports, created hundreds of thousands of jobs and contributed to GDP growth in both Eastern Europe (e.g., Pavlínek, 2020) and Mexico (South and Kim, 2019). In Mexico, however, despite large FDI inflows the average annual growth in GDP per capita was lower than in many Latin American and Asian countries between 1980 and 2012 (Dussel Peters, 2016).

The industrial development strategy of many countries in Latin America and Eastern Europe has increasingly relied on attracting manufacturing FDI but without a strategic industrial policy that would encourage the simultaneous development of strong, globally competitive domestic firms (Wionczek, 1986; Gallagher and Zarsky, 2007; Contreras et al., 2012; Pavlínek, 2016; 2017a; 2018; Yülek et al., 2020). As FDI crowded out domestic firms of most dynamic industries (Schneider, 2017; Pavlínek, 2020), the majority of domestic firms are small, possess low capabilities, are concentrated in lower-skill and lower-technology industries, and are often locked in dependent and captive trade relations with larger foreign firms. As a result, they have been unable to globalize at all or not to the same extent as domestic firms in the most successful Asian countries (Amsden, 2007; Pavlínek, 2020). It has been argued that this over-dependence on FDI for the industrial development in less developed countries without a more balanced growth of foreign-controlled and domestic sectors is unlikely to lead to a successful long-term economic development (e.g., Zhao et al., 2020).

Since the 1990s, China has been the largest recipient of FDI in less developed countries. Between 1990 and 2022, China attracted USD2.79 trillion (USD4.66 trillion including Hong Kong) and accounted for 20 percent (34 percent including Hong Kong) of total FDI inflows into less developed countries. By 2022, China's inward FDI stock stood at USD3.8 trillion (USD5.9 trillion including Hong Kong), accounting for 25 percent (39 percent including

Hong Kong) of less developed countries' total (UNCTAD, 2023). Inspired by the experience of other East Asian countries, China has followed a very careful and highly regulated FDI policy of gradual FDI liberalization, which was driven by national industrial development priorities and a strategic industrial policy (Chen, 2018). While it is generally assumed that FDI effects in China have been positive and strongly contributed to the rapid economic growth, no unequivocal conclusion can be made. For example, the removal of publication bias showed the actual effects of FDI to be statistically insignificant and ranging between "small" and "very small," along with insignificant spillovers at the aggregate level (Gunby et al., 2017). However, a different meta-analysis has found statistically significant backward technology spillovers in China (Fan et al., 2020).

Overall, the FDI experience across less developed countries has been highly uneven in terms of FDI distribution, national and regional effects of FDI, and government policies toward FDI. After reviewing FDI trends, I will critically assess how the mainstream and heterodox perspectives interpret FDI in less developed countries.

1.3 MAINSTREAM AND HETERODOX PERSPECTIVES OF FDI IN LESS DEVELOPED COUNTRIES

By its very nature, any theory of international production needs to employ the spatial perspective. It might therefore be surprising that the modern theory of international production was not originally developed by economic geographers but by economists in the 1960s and 1970s, who applied the spatial perspective to conceptualize the rapidly growing FDI in the world economy. Much has been written about Hymer's (1976 [1960]) seminal explanation of FDI based on the theory of the firm and industrial organization (e.g., Dunning and Rugman, 1985; Pitelis, 2006). Much has also been said about Hymer's recognition of the close relationship between FDI and uneven development, what he called the law on uneven development, in which the combination of vertical division of labor within transnational corporations (TNCs) with location strategies of TNCs tends to perpetuate spatial inequalities between core and peripheral regions (Hymer, 1972). In 1970, Hymer (1970: 448) envisioned the future consequences of growing TNCs and FDI in the world economy: "The coming age of multinational corporations should represent a great step forward in the efficiency with which the world uses its economic resources, but it will create grave social and political problems and will be very uneven in exploiting and distributing the benefits of modern science and technology."

Vernon (1966) introduced an explicitly locational dynamic to thinking about FDI by linking the internationalization of production to the product life cycle and recognizing different locational needs for the manufacturing of new, maturing and standardized products. As the product ages, the relative importance of the different factors of production changes and, consequently, an ideal location for its manufacturing shifts from developed to developing countries. Drawing on Hymer, Vernon and other theories of international trade and production, such as Caves (1971) and Buckley and Casson (1976), Dunning (1977) proposed what he originally called an "eclectic theory of international involvement" and later the "OLI (ownership-location-internalization) paradigm" in order to explain the rapidly growing role of FDI in the world economy (Dunning, 2000).

These modern approaches to FDI provide the basic conceptual framework within which the contemporary understanding of FDI and international activities of TNCs has developed in mainstream economics, international business and, to a large extent, also in economic geography (e.g., Iammarino and McCann, 2013). If we concentrate on FDI in less developed countries, we can recognize two main perspectives: the mainstream and heterodox (e.g., Jo et al., 2018). I also recognize the dependency/world-systems perspective on FDI as a distinct approach within heterodox approaches. These perspectives are summarized in Sections 1.3.1 and 1.3.2 and in Table 1.2.

1.3.1 The Mainstream Perspective

Mainstream economic approaches, which are closely associated with neoclassical economics and neoliberal approaches to economic development (Harvey, 2005a; Gereffi, 2018), view FDI as the engine of development and economic growth in less developed countries (e.g., Hirschman, 1958; UN, 1992; Klein et al., 2001; OECD, 2002; Jensen, 2003; Basu and Guariglia, 2007; WBG, 2019). FDI is considered "a powerful force of convergence across countries" (Brucal et al., 2019: 1) (Table 1.2). FDI-related inefficiencies and suboptimal performance in host countries are attributed to governmental intervention and regulation (e.g., Moran, 1999).

Along with the emphasis on free markets and the minimal role of the government for achieving the most efficient distribution and operation of FDI, this unambiguously positive view of FDI has been incorporated into the global ideology for economic development since the mid-1970s (Amsden and Chu, 2003; Gallagher and Zarsky, 2007; Yamin and Nixson, 2016; Chu, 2017; Sornarajah, 2017). Accordingly, the policy advice from international institutions such as the World Bank to less developed countries has been to liberalize FDI (e.g., Klein et al., 2001) because of its "transformative potential for development" (WBG, 2019: 1). Although some less developed countries began to liberalize FDI in the mid-1980s (Nunnenkamp, 2004), the trend of FDI liberalization has been the strongest since the 1990s (UNCTAD, 2013; 2023) (Figure 1.3).

This mainstream positive assessment of FDI has persisted despite the fact that depending on the data, research design and estimation method used,

TABLE 1.2 *Different perspectives on the role of FDI in less developed countries*

	Mainstream perspective	Heterodox perspective	Dependency and world-systems perspectives
Economic growth	FDI leads to economic growth	Economic growth attracts FDI rather than FDI leading to growth. Short-term benefits of FDI but potential long-term negative effects	FDI may lead to short- and medium-term growth but adversely affects economic growth in the long run
Development	FDI is the precondition for a successful development	FDI can be helpful if it is part of a well-crafted long-term development strategy. Dependence on FDI for development is unlikely to lead to a successful long-term development	FDI slows down development in the long run through the transfer of profits abroad, the destruction of domestic firms in the same industry and the suppression of their development
Role of government	Hands-off approach: governments should facilitate FDI but should not regulate or intervene	A targeted and performance-oriented approach: FDI regulation is necessary, strong industrial and FDI policies. Unregulated FDI is harmful for long-term development	Heavy regulation of FDI and limits on foreign ownership, such as foreign ownership ceilings
Spillovers	FDI generates technology and productivity spillovers that benefit the host economy	Spillovers are not automatic but depend on well-crafted industrial policies, performance requirements and the support of domestic firms to increase their absorptive capacity	Spillovers are minimal because FDI is isolated from host economies in foreign enclaves or export-processing zones with no or limited linkages to domestic firms

(*continued*)

TABLE 1.2 (*continued*)

	Mainstream perspective	Heterodox perspective	Dependency and world-systems perspectives
Jobs and wages	FDI creates "good jobs" for both the workers and host economies	Above-average local wages often paid to poach and maintain the best workers from domestic firms, wage-adjusted labor productivity is high, many low-wage jobs involving poor working conditions	FDI is associated with high levels of labor exploitation: low wages, high pace of work and poor working conditions
Overall FDI effects in less developed countries	Beneficial	Beneficial only if well targeted and regulated within a long-term development strategy	Negative effects predominate, damaging in the long run

Source: author.

econometric analyses have often arrived at contrasting conclusions about the effects of FDI in host economies (Blomström and Kokko, 2001; UNCTAD, 2001; Dunning and Lundan, 2008; Meyer and Sinani, 2009), including mixed empirical evidence of the benefits of FDI for economic growth (Mencinger, 2003; Curwin and Mahutga, 2014; Bermejo Carbonell and Werner, 2018) and for the behavior and performance of domestic firms in the form of technology spillovers (Görg and Strobl, 2001; Görg and Greenaway, 2004; Iršová and Havránek, 2013).

The mainstream approach to FDI tends ignore the empirical evidence of no or negative FDI effects on economic growth in less developed countries (e.g., Nunnenkamp and Spatz, 2003; Carkovic and Levine, 2005; Sarkar, 2007; Alfaro et al., 2010; Alguacil et al., 2011; Curwin and Mahutga, 2014; Alvarado et al., 2017; Bermejo Carbonell and Werner, 2018), including negative FDI spillovers (e.g., Farole and Winkler, 2014). Not surprisingly, policymakers often assume that FDI contributes to economic growth in host economies (UN, 1992; Harding and Javorcik, 2011; Hallin and Lind, 2012),

FIGURE 1.3 Regulatory changes in national FDI policies, 1991–2022
Note: Data for 1991–1999 were calculated by using a slightly different methodology and are not thus fully compatible with the 2000–2019 data.
Source: author, based on data in UNCTAD (2005; 2013; 2023).

although is not always the case (Mencinger, 2003; Curwin and Mahutga, 2014) as FDI effects strongly depend on the concrete context of different countries and regions (Blomström and Kokko, 2001; Görg and Greenaway, 2004). Indeed, Alfaro et al. (2010: 254) argued as follows.

Although there is a widespread belief among policymakers that FDI generates positive productivity externalities for host countries, the empirical evidence fails to confirm this belief. In the particular case of developing countries, both the micro and macro empirical literatures consistently find either no effect of FDI on the productivity of the host country firms and/or aggregate growth or negative effects.

Similarly, Akyüz (2017: 198) maintained, "there can be no generalization regarding the impact of FDI on capital formation, technological progress, economic growth, and structural change. Indeed there is no conclusive evidence to support the myth that FDI makes a major contribution to growth."

The mainstream perspective recognizes the importance of FDI spillovers to host economies for the long-term economic development in less developed countries (e.g., Narula and Bellak, 2009). However, spillovers are far from being automatic as they depend on a number of factors, such as the existence of linkages between foreign subsidiaries and host country domestic firms, the absorptive capacity of domestic firms, a favorable institutional environment, mode of entry of foreign firms, nature of the targeted industry, nature of TNC operations, and time since the investment (UNCTAD, 2001; Scott-Kennel, 2007; Saliola and Zanfei, 2009; Santangelo, 2009; Dicken, 2015). In addition to overstating reported spillover estimates, a meta-analysis of publications on

FDI spillovers in less developed countries revealed a substantial publication bias in favor of publishing positive and significant spillovers and not publishing the findings of insignificant and negative spillovers (Demena, 2015).

The policy advice of FDI liberalization in less developed countries has been at odds with the past FDI policies of more developed countries that systematically discriminated against FDI through the range of national policy instruments (Chang, 2004; Wade, 1990). In the absence of international regulation of FDI, bilateral investment treaties have been the main instrument governing FDI relationships since 1959 (Seid, 2018 [2002]) with 2,584 bilateral investment treaties (including treaties with investment provisions) in force in 2022 out of 3,265 bilateral investment treaties and treaties with investment provisions signed (UNCTAD, 2023). The main function of bilateral investment treaties has been to protect FDI from being nationalized and expropriated in less developed countries (UNCTAD, 2015). At the same time, trade-related investment measures have been used by more developed countries to limit the regulation of FDI by less developed countries (Dicken, 2015).

The World Bank and other FDI-promoting global institutions failed to promote industrial policies in less developed countries that played an important role in the successful cases of FDI-based development, such as Ireland and Singapore (Thomas, 2011; Morrissey, 2012). The promotion of FDI in less developed countries also tends to ignore the post-WWII experience of countries, such as Japan, South Korea and Taiwan, that achieved rapid economic growth and development without large FDI inflows (e.g., Amsden, 1989; Amsden and Chu, 2003; Paprzycki and Fukao, 2008; Fischer, 2015). Amsden and Chu (2003: 161) argued: "In liberal mainstream theories the heroes of economic development are foreign investors and market forces. But these theories overlook the fact that in the fastest-growing latecomers, high-tech industries tend to be dominated by nationally owned firms, and governments continue vigorously to promote such firms as well as 'new' high-tech market segments."

These geographically varied and uneven experiences with FDI in less developed countries are, however, considered by heterodox perspectives, to which I will now turn.

1.3.2   Heterodox Perspectives

Drawing on the empirical historical evidence and on institutional and evolutionary economics, the heterodox literature argues that on its own, FDI does not automatically lead to successful long-term economic development in less developed countries. It also challenges the emphasis of economic orthodoxy on the decisive role of the free market in promoting development through FDI. Instead, the heterodox literature emphasizes a strong relationship between the strength and quality of state industrial policies and successful economic development that mostly relies on domestic firms (Amsden, 1989; 2001; Amsden and Chu, 2003; Kohli, 2004; Schneider, 2013; Lee et al., 2014; Akyüz, 2017). Countries typified by a weak and ineffective state capacity, industrial policies and policies toward foreign capital and domestic firms (e.g., in Latin America and Africa) have been much less economically successful than countries with a strong and efficient state capacity, industrial policies, policies towards foreign capital and strong support of domestic firms (e.g., in East and Southeast Asia) (Amsden, 1989; 2001; Amsden and Chu, 2003; Kohli, 2004; Morrissey, 2012; Schneider, 2013; Yeung, 2013; 2016; Wade, 2018).

Heterodox economists have for decades been highly critical of the long-term effects of FDI in less developed countries (e.g., Singer, 1950; Baran, 1957). For example, Frank argued in 1967 (2010 [1967]: 43): "with few exceptions, writers from the developed countries have failed to question, much less to analyze, the supposed benefits of this foreign investment to underdeveloped countries." Heterodox scholars have emphasized the negative indirect long-term effects of resource-oriented FDI in less developed countries as it led to the development of foreign-controlled enclaves and the infrastructure that predominantly geared to the needs of foreign capital while being isolated from host economies. By disproportionally benefiting source countries of FDI through their access to primary commodities and the transfer of profits, FDI has ultimately slowed down the development of modern industrial capitalism in less developed countries, while intensifying their foreign exploitation (Baran, 1957; Amin, 1976; Gallagher and Zarsky, 2007; Arias et al., 2014; Narula, 2018).

This criticism of the long-term effects of FDI in less developed countries, particularly in Latin America and Africa, became strongly articulated in the dependency perspective (e.g., Sunkel, 1972; Chase-Dunn, 1975; Fischer, 2015; Taylor, 2016), which acknowledged the short-term positive effects of FDI in less developed countries, such as economic growth and job creation, but maintained that the long-term growth effects of FDI were neutral or negative (Bornschier and Chase-Dunn, 1985; Kentor, 1998; Curwin and Mahutga, 2014). It also pointed out that profit repatriation from less developed countries far exceeded FDI inflows, resulting in a net capital flow from the periphery to the core of the world economy (Amin, 1976; Frank, 2010 [1967]; Sornarajah, 2017; Taylor and Zajontz, 2020). Less developed countries that are more dependent on foreign capital have grown more slowly than those less dependent (Kentor, 1998), which has been supported by the experience of East Asia (Amsden, 1989; 2001; Amsden and Chu, 2003). Nevertheless, the dependency theory has been unable to fully account for "FDI success stories" of once less developed countries, such as Ireland, Hong Kong and Singapore, although Ireland and Singapore used strategic industrial policies to channel FDI into what they considered strategic sectors of their economies (Chang, 2008; Thomas, 2011).

1.4 CONCLUSION

This chapter has considered the contribution of FDI to the development in less developed countries in the context of the sharply increased importance of FDI in the world economy. The brief historical review of FDI in less developed countries has revealed FDI's very uneven distribution and performance in less developed countries. It then reviewed the mainstream and heterodox perspectives on FDI and its development potential in less developed countries.

We may conclude that both the mainstream and heterodox perspectives tend to overlook the empirical evidence that does not necessarily support their one-size-fits-all explanations of FDI effects in less developed countries. Different conclusions of the mainstream and heterodox approaches to FDI in less developed countries (Table 1.2), at least partially, stem from their emphasis on different time horizons of FDI. While the mainstream perspective tends to stress potentially positive short- to medium-term effects of FDI in host economies, heterodox approaches emphasize long-term effects. At the same time, the mainstream and dependency and world-systems perspectives tend to ignore the spatial variation of these effects across different countries and regions in less developed countries. Heterodox scholars recognize the potentially positive effects of FDI in less developed countries. However, they also maintain that different conditions in different countries lead to different FDI outcomes and stress the importance of strong and well-targeted industrial and FDI policies of host country governments for reaping potential FDI benefits, while minimizing its potentially negative effects (e.g., Chang, 2008; Morrissey, 2012).

Despite strong arguments presented by heterodox perspectives and despite the lack of strong empirical evidence that would unequivocally support FDI-centered development strategies in less developed countries advocated by the mainstream perspective, FDI-related public debates and policy recommendations have predominantly been dominated by various perspectives from mainstream economics. Compared to mainstream economics, the insights of heterodox economists have had a limited impact on economic policy in most countries. The only exception is the global value chains (GVCs) approach, which was originally developed from the world-systems perspective (Hopkins and Wallerstein, 1977; 1986) and global commodity chains approach (Gereffi and Korzeniewicz, 1994), and has become increasingly accepted in mainstream analyses of economic development (e.g., Cattaneo et al., 2010; UNCTAD, 2013; AfDB et al., 2014).

Many governments around the world tend to view FDI positively for several reasons. They value the potential immediate (short-run) direct effects of FDI, such as job creation, income generation, infusion of capital, and contribution to a positive trade balance (Dicken, 2015). Governments also tend to assume the long-term indirect positive effects of FDI on economic growth and development (Hallin and Lind, 2012), while often downplaying or ignoring evidence of the negative effects of FDI (Bellak, 2004), such as the transfer of profits abroad through transfer pricing and other mechanisms of rent extraction (Dischinger et al., 2014a) or negative spillovers from FDI in the host economy (Blomström and Kokko, 1998; De Backer and Sleuwaegen, 2003; Görg and Greenaway, 2004; Meyer and Sinani, 2009; Oetzel and Doh, 2009).

The optimistic view of FDI might partially stem from the failure to recognize differences between the effects of FDI in more developed countries and less developed countries. In the eyes of many policymakers, FDI thus potentially represents a relatively easy and quick policy solution to persistent economic problems in less developed countries, such as high unemployment rates and slow growth. FDI might therefore be politically preferable to long-term policies with uncertain outcomes, such as an institutional reform (Fagerberg and Srholec, 2008; Rodríguez-Pose, 2013; Ketterer and Rodríguez-Pose, 2018) or investment in a high-quality education. In turn, this positive perception of FDI has translated into generous state support for FDI in many countries (Meyer, 2004; Smeets, 2008; Harding and Javorcik, 2011; Thomas, 2011; Narula and Driffield, 2012; UNCTAD, 2012).

In the next chapter, which focuses on FDI in less developed (peripheral) regions of more developed countries, I argue that in order to better understand the potential development effects of FDI in peripheral regions, we need to recognize that FDI effects differ between more developed (core) and peripheral regions.

2

Revisiting Foreign Direct Investment in Peripheral Regions

2.1 INTRODUCTION

The previous chapter focused on the development effects of FDI in less developed countries. This chapter continues to focus on the development effects of FDI but shifts its attention to the regional (subnational) scale and to peripheral less developed (henceforth peripheral) regions in more developed countries by evaluating the long-term regional development effects of FDI in peripheral regions and reviewing the main approaches to FDI in peripheral regions that have been developed and applied by economic geographers. Peripheral regions are understood as disadvantaged areas that, compared to more developed core regions, are typified by lower levels of income, a less advanced and less diversified economy, higher unemployment levels, lower levels of innovation, less educated labor and other features identified in Table 2.1. FDI is only one of many transnational business strategies employed by TNCs, such as outsourcing, offshoring, franchising, strategic alliances, cooperative agreements and, more recently, various asset-light strategies related to the growth of the digital economy (e.g., Massini and Miozzo, 2012; Dicken, 2015; UNCTAD, 2017; Casella and Formenti, 2018; Martínez-Noya and Narula, 2018; Alon et al., 2021). Although these strategies are beyond the scope of this chapter, they have allowed TNCs to progressively "fine slice the value chain" (Linares-Navarro et al., 2014), leading to an ever-finer division of labor, more complex location decisions and regional development implications in peripheral regions (Phelps and Wood, 2018a). Given the dramatic changes in the world economy that are affecting FDI flows with significant development implications for peripheral regions (e.g., UNCTAD, 2020; 2023; Zhan, 2021), it is an opportune time to take stock and highlight the continuing importance of research on the regional development effects of FDI by geographers since FDI strongly contributes to uneven development at different geographic scales. A better understanding of the regional development effects of FDI will improve our overall understanding of FDI at different geographic scales.

TABLE 2.1 *FDI in core and peripheral regions*

	Core regions	Peripheral regions
Factors attracting FDI	Large actual or potential markets, higher disposable income Skilled and more educated labor force Innovation capabilities More diversified and technologically advanced economy Competent local suppliers and potential business partners High quality infrastructure Lower transportation costs because of market proximity Better quality institutions (institutional thickness)	Labor surplus Natural resources Lower operating costs based on cheaper factors of production (wages, real estate, land, commercial rents, local taxes) Regional investment incentives lowering start-up sunk costs Often geographic proximity to large core-based markets
Factors deterring FDI	More expensive factors of production (wages, real estate, land, commercial rents, local taxes) Smaller labor surplus, increased labor market competition, potential labor shortages	Less educated labor force and lower labor skills Smaller actual or potential markets, lower disposable incomes Less diversified and technologically less advanced economy Lower quality infrastructure Higher transportation costs Fewer competent local suppliers and potential business partners Low innovation capabilities Weaker and less capable local institutions
Predominant type of FDI	Horizontal (market-seeking)	Vertical (efficiency- and resource-seeking)
FDI linkages	Higher number and intensity of linkages A greater likelihood of developmental linkages More likely positive effects on domestic firms through linkages	Lower number and intensity of linkages, truncation A greater likelihood of dependent and detrimental linkages Less likely positive effects on domestic firms through linkages
FDI spillovers	A greater likelihood of vertical spillovers Higher absorptive capacity of domestic firms	A lower likelihood of vertical spillovers Low absorptive capacity of domestic firms

Source: author.

This chapter identifies different mechanisms of FDI in core and peripheral regions that lead to a greater concentration of horizontal FDI in core regions and vertical FDI in peripheral regions and, consequently, to different regional development outcomes of FDI in core and peripheral regions. It argues three main points. First, FDI has greater potential to benefit core regions than peripheral regions in the long run. Second, despite different conceptual approaches to FDI in economic geography, the empirical research points to similar conclusions about the long-term effects of FDI in peripheral regions. Third, geographers need to maintain a strong interest in examining the effects of FDI in peripheral regions in the overall context of uneven development and a rapidly changing world economy.

The chapter starts with a discussion of the regional development effects of FDI from the perspective of economic geography by focusing on FDI linkages and spillovers in peripheral regions. Second, it evaluates important approaches used to analyze the regional development effects of FDI in peripheral regions that have been developed in economic geography, namely the branch plant economy and truncation, new international division of labor and spatial divisions of labor, new regionalism, and global production networks (GPNs) approaches. Finally, it presents a brief research agenda for the research of FDI in peripheral regions in economic geography, which highlights its continuing importance for the understanding of contemporary uneven development.

2.2 ECONOMIC GEOGRAPHY AND REGIONAL DEVELOPMENT EFFECTS OF FDI

Compared to research on FDI and international activities of TNCs conducted in economics, international business and other disciplines, economic geographers have predominantly focused on the regional development effects of FDI in the context of uneven economic development and spatial divisions of labor. When considering the long-term regional development effects of FDI in peripheral regions, it is important to keep in mind two points. First, FDI is part of the profit-seeking strategies of firms in the capitalist economy and, as such, it is primarily sought for the benefit of investing firms and not for the benefit of host regions. Second, the direct immediate and indirect long-term effects of FDI in host regions can be both positive and negative (Pavlínek, 2004; Spencer, 2008; Akyüz, 2017). This is because the effects of FDI depend on many different factors, such as the size of the investment and its type (e.g., market-, efficiency-, resource-, strategic asset-seeking FDI), the type of industry (e.g., capital-intensive versus labor-intensive), the nature of operations (e.g., manual assembly versus automated production), the mode of entry (e.g., greenfield versus brownfield), the length of investment, the technological gap between foreign and host country firms, the level of development of the host economy, and the capabilities and absorptive capacity of host country firms (Blomström and Kokko, 2001; UNCTAD, 2001; Dunning and Lundan, 2008; Meyer and Sinani, 2009; Farole et al., 2014; Dicken,

2015). The actual outcomes of FDI in concrete regions thus depend on the balance of these various factors. Economic geographers are more likely to recognize and analyze the importance of regional and local conditions for the understanding of different FDI outcomes.

2.2.1 Different Regional Development Outcomes of Horizontal and Vertical FDI

Nevertheless, attempts have been made to identify the general types and features of FDI that are likely to translate into particular regional development outcomes. Already in the early 1970s, Caves (1971) recognized the most important difference between horizontal and vertical FDI. Horizontal FDI involves the production of the same or similar commodity as in the home economy in foreign locations and is therefore typically a market-capture, demand-oriented investment. Vertical FDI is a supply-oriented investment, which involves the location of a particular stage of the production process abroad. Its two basic forms include an efficiency-seeking vertical investment that is seeking to lower production costs and a resource-seeking vertical FDI that is securing access to natural resources, agricultural products or unskilled labor in foreign locations (Milberg and Winkler, 2013; Dunning, 2000). A strategic asset-seeking FDI is a special type of vertical supply oriented FDI that is looking for knowledge-based intangible strategic assets abroad, such as advanced technology, R&D capabilities, managerial know-how and brand assets that could be transferred back to the domestic economy (Kuemmerle, 1999; Pavlínek, 2012; Cui et al., 2014).

Although the regional economic effects of these different types of FDI will depend on the factors listed above, horizontal FDI is more likely to develop stronger and more stable ties with the host economy than vertical FDI (Dicken, 2015; Akyüz, 2017). This is because vertical FDI usually leads to the transnational vertical integration of foreign subsidiaries into home country operations with limited or nonexistent linkages with domestic firms and institutions. Consequently, vertical FDI is also more likely to relocate, should more profitable opportunities emerge elsewhere (e.g., Pavlínek, 2018; 2020). Since linkages with domestic firms and institutions are the main precondition for potential technology transfer from foreign firms to the host economy in the form of spillovers (Blomström and Kokko, 1998; UNCTAD, 2001; Görg and Strobl, 2005; Scott-Kennel, 2007; Santangelo, 2009), horizontal FDI has a greater potential to benefit the host economy in the long run compared to vertical FDI. The concentration of the different types of FDI in different regions is, therefore, likely to lead to different regional development outcomes of FDI.

In this context, it is useful to make the basic distinction between FDI in core regions and peripheral regions (Table 2.1). Core regions have mainly been targeted by horizontal FDI (Milberg and Winkler, 2013), while peripheral regions predominantly by vertical, efficiency-seeking and resource-seeking

FDI (e.g., Yamin and Nixson, 2016). Consequently, more positive effects of FDI have been found in core regions than in peripheral regions (Borensztein et al., 1998; Phelps and Fuller, 2000; Dimitratos et al., 2009; Alfaro et al., 2010; Alvarado et al., 2017).

2.2.2 FDI and Linkages in Host Regions

The existence of linkages with domestic firms and the development of spillovers from foreign to domestic firms have been recognized as potentially the most important long-term regional development effects of FDI in host regions (Javorcik, 2004; Ivarsson and Alvstam, 2005; Blalock and Gertler, 2008; Santangelo, 2009; Narula and Dunning, 2010; Amendolagine et al., 2013; 2019). Economic geographers have identified three basic types of supplier linkages according to their potential impact on domestic firms: developmental, dependent and detrimental (Turok, 1993; Pavlínek, 2018). While developmental linkages are long-term supplier relationships that are based on collaboration and partnership, dependent linkages are short-term and price-based supplier relationships, which are established by foreign subsidiaries in host economies in order to minimize the costs of supplied commodities (Turok, 1993). The cooperation and partnership between firms in developmental linkages encourages the exchange of information, which increases the chances of knowledge and technology transfers from foreign subsidiaries to domestic firms and the chances of their upgrading. In the case of dependent linkages, the exchange of information and knowledge between foreign subsidiaries and domestic firms is limited (UNCTAD, 2001), which undermines the opportunities for the upgrading of domestic firms (UNCTAD, 2001; Gereffi et al., 2005; Pavlínek and Žížalová, 2016).

Horizontal FDI is more likely to generate developmental linkages in host regions, while vertical FDI is more likely to develop dependent linkages. Therefore, developmental linkages are more likely to develop in core regions, while dependent linkages are more likely to develop in peripheral regions. Additionally, the number and intensity of linkages tends to be higher in core regions than in peripheral regions due to the higher number of more capable domestic firms in core regions (Dunning and Lundan, 2008; Meyer and Sinani, 2009). This indicates that FDI is likely to have more positive effects, thanks to the development of linkages, in core regions than in peripheral regions. Detrimental linkages develop in those cases when foreign subsidiaries have negative effects on domestic firms (Hymer, 1972; Bellak, 2004) through, for example, employment and labor market effects (Pavlínek and Žížalová, 2016; Pavlínek, 2018) which are more likely to be associated with vertical than horizontal FDI and, therefore, more likely to develop in peripheral regions than in core regions.

Weak FDI linkages or their absence in peripheral regions have long been recognized. Hirschman (1958) explained that the lack of both backward and forward FDI linkages in peripheral regions was due to the predominant FDI in mining and agriculture, which is supported by empirical evidence (Nunnenkamp and Spatz, 2003; Morris et al., 2011; Morrissey, 2012; Amendolagine et al., 2013). However, limited FDI linkages have also been found in peripheral regions that have managed to attract a sizeable manufacturing investment, such as Latin America, East and Southeast Asia (Amsden, 2001; Schneider, 2013; Dussel Peters, 2016) and in peripheral regions of more developed countries (Stewart, 1976; Phelps, 1993a; Turok, 1993; Lagendijk, 1995b; Rodriguez-Clare, 1996; Carrillo, 2004; Pavlínek, 2018). The rapidly increased global sourcing and follow sourcing by TNCs has further limited the development of linkages (Larsson, 2002; Tavares and Young, 2006; Williams et al., 2008; Hatani, 2009; Pavlínek and Žížalová, 2016; Pavlínek, 2018; Humphrey, 2000). Empirical evidence thus suggests that the integration of domestic firms into foreign-capital-controlled supplier networks in peripheral regions takes place predominantly through dependent linkages, which weakens the potential for long-term positive effects of FDI (Young et al., 1994; Hatani, 2009; Pavlínek, 2018).

2.2.3 FDI Spillovers in Host Regions

The existence of FDI linkages with domestic firms is the precondition for the development of vertical spillovers from foreign subsidiaries to domestic firms (Blomström and Kokko, 1998; UNCTAD, 2001; Görg and Strobl, 2005; Scott-Kennel, 2007; Giroud and Scott-Kennel, 2009; Santangelo, 2009; Pavlínek, 2018), which are potentially the most important long-term benefit of FDI for host regions (Blomström et al., 2000; Blomström and Kokko, 2001; Görg and Strobl, 2001; Dunning and Lundan, 2008; Giroud, 2012). Spillovers are classified as horizontal and vertical. Horizontal spillovers refer to the unintentional effects of foreign firms on domestic firms in the same industry, while vertical spillovers are both the unintentional and intentional effects on local suppliers and customers of foreign subsidiaries via backward and forward linkages (Blalock and Gertler, 2008; Hallın and Lind, 2012). Assuming that foreign firms investing in peripheral regions are more productive than domestic firms because of their firm-specific ownership advantages (Hymer, 1976 [1960]), the operation of foreign subsidiaries in a host economy will encourage domestic firms to become more productive in order to remain competitive (competition effects). Local firms might increase productivity by imitating the better machinery and organization of the production of foreign subsidiaries (demonstration effects). Productivity spillovers might also result from the supplier relationships between foreign subsidiaries and domestic firms in situations in which foreign subsidiaries are more demanding buyers than domestic firms (Pavlínek and Žížalová, 2016), which will force domestic firms to improve their productivity. Know-how and knowledge can also diffuse through worker mobility from foreign subsidiaries to domestic firms (Görg and Strobl, 2005).

Linkages alone do not guarantee that spillovers will develop since they depend on the absorptive capacity of domestic firms (Saliola and Zanfei, 2009; Ascani and Gagliardi, 2020), which is considered to be crucial for their ability to benefit from FDI (Ernst and Kim, 2002; Meyer, 2004; Giroud et al., 2012; Sultana and Turkina, 2020). The absorptive capacity of domestic firms is strongly conditioned by their R&D capabilities (Cohen and Levinthal, 1989; Sturgeon et al., 2010), which are generally higher in core regions than in peripheral regions (Dunning and Lundan, 2008; Meyer and Sinani, 2009; Pavlínek, 2018; 2022a). Consequently, core regions are more likely to benefit from spillovers and hence from positive long-term effects of FDI than peripheral regions.

However, it has been difficult to measure FDI spillovers in host regions. Economists have predominantly used econometric methods to estimate the existence and extent of spillovers in host economies, which, however, do not reveal how spillovers take place (Görg and Strobl, 2001). This is why economic geographers also use targeted interview and survey questions to measure the extent of spillovers and how they take place (e.g., Pavlínek and Žížalová, 2016).

2.3   APPROACHES IN ECONOMIC GEOGRAPHY TO FDI IN PERIPHERAL REGIONS

Geographic research on the effects of FDI in peripheral regions has been conducted in the context of different conceptual approaches. The following section will summarize the understanding of FDI in peripheral regions by the branch plant economy and truncation, new international division of labor and spatial divisions of labor, new regionalism, and GPN approaches (Table 2.2).

2.3.1   Branch Plant Economy and Truncation

In the 1970s and 1980s, the long-term development effects of FDI in peripheral regions of more developed countries were conceptualized as the branch plant economy and truncation. Branch plants are externally owned factories in peripheral regions that tend to specialize in the mass production of simple standardized goods (Firn, 1975; Townroe, 1975; Dicken, 1976; Hood and Young, 1976; Watts, 1981). Unlike locally owned firms, externally owned branch plants benefit from a potentially greater stability and better prospects for development because of their access to financial resources, suppliers and know-how through their parent corporations (Watts, 1981). However, while branch plants inject capital and create jobs in peripheral regions, they suffer from the outflow of profits and a greater propensity to relocate or close during economic crises. They are also usually truncated since they tend to lack higher-level managerial, decision-making, R&D and other strategic nonproduction functions that remain concentrated in parent enterprises located in core regions

TABLE 2.2 *Basic approaches in economic geography to FDI in peripheral regions*

Approach	Period	Basic argument	Application	Geographic focus	Examples of publications
Branch plant economy and truncation	1970s–1980s	FDI and external control are detrimental to long-term regional development of peripheral regions and preempt economically viable indigenous development	Peripheral regions of more developed countries	Western Europe, particularly Britain, Canada	Firm (1975), Townroe (1975), Dicken (1976), Britton (1976; 1980; 1981), Watts (1981), Hayter (1982), Phelps (1993a)
New international division of labor/ spatial divisions of labor	1980s	Development in peripheral regions is linked to their position, function, and integration in the broader national and world economy. FDI in peripheral regions exacerbates regional inequalities and intensifies uneven and dependent development in less developed countries	Peripheral regions of more developed countries, peripheral regions in general	Western Europe, particularly Britain	Massey (1979; 1995 [1984]), Fröbel et al. (1980), Perrons (1981), Lloyd and Shutt (1985), Scott (1987), Henderson (1989)
New regionalism and territorial	1990s	Increased clustering, enhanced innovation and learning, and capable	Peripheral regions of more developed	Western Europe, North America	Dicken et al. (1994), Mair (1993), Amin et al. (1994), Amin

(continued)

TABLE 2.2 (*continued*)

Approach	Period	Basic argument	Application	Geographic focus	Examples of publications
embeddedness of FDI		regional institutions will embed FDI in host peripheral regions and increase its regional development benefits			and Thrift (1994), Malmberg et al. (1996), MacKinnon and Phelps (2001a; 2001b)
Global production networks	2000s–	FDI articulates peripheral regions into GPNs through structural couplings in a disadvantageous position	Peripheral regions in general	East Asia	Coe et al. (2004), Yeung (2009; 2015; 2016), Coe and Yeung (2015), MacKinnon (2012)

Source: author.

(Britton, 1980; 1981; Hayter, 1982). Weak supplier linkages with domestic firms and the dependence of branch plants on technology transfers from parent companies and imports of materials and components from abroad tend to limit indigenous technological development in host economies. Consequently, the branch plant economy and truncation literature considers a high level of foreign control through externally owned branch plants to be detrimental to long-term economic interests of peripheral regions (Hymer, 1972; Firn, 1975; Hood and Young, 1976; Britton, 1980; Hayter, 1982; Schackmann-Fallis, 1989).

The branch plant economy and truncation literature fails to recognize the importance of institutions in enhancing regional development potential of FDI in peripheral regions (e.g., Watts, 1981). Strong local institutions can help to reinforce the transfer of technology from branch plants to domestic firms and increase the local value capture (Perkmann, 2006). For example, in recent decades, peripheral regions in more developed countries have benefited from better-quality regional institutions and their increased focus on attracting FDI into high-value-added activities instead of routine manufacturing and services (Iammarino, 2018).

2.3.2 New International Division of Labor and Spatial Divisions of Labor Approaches

In the late 1970s and 1980s, the political economy approaches became increasingly prominent in economic geography (Peet and Thrift, 1989), including the new international division of labor and spatial divisions of labor approaches. The focus was no longer solely on the effects of FDI in peripheral regions but also on the position and role of peripheral regions in the world economy and the new international division of labor, which was then typified by the FDI-driven industrialization of less developed countries, contemporaneous decline of especially labor-intensive industries in more developed countries, and by intensified uneven development (Fröbel et al., 1980; Perrons, 1981; Scott, 1987). The spatial divisions of labor approach analyzed the regional development effects of the new international division of labor in more developed countries by linking changes at the regional level to increasing levels of internationalization (Massey, 1979; 1995 [1984]; Perrons, 1981; Lloyd and Shutt, 1985).

The pioneering work of Doreen Massey (1979; 1995 [1984]) theoretically explained how peripheral regions with foreign-owned branch plants fit in the overall spatial divisions of labor in the entire economy and how the internal economic geography of Britain reflects the place of Britain in the new international division of labor. Massey emphasized the increased geographical separation of different economic functions, such as R&D, production requiring skilled labor and mass production. She explained how large corporations, which are under constant pressure to decrease the cost of labor, take advantage of spatial inequality by setting up the production of particular commodities in peripheral regions because of low wages, available semiskilled labor, and limited tradition of union resistance (see also Perrons, 1981). FDI capitalizing on this division of labor further reduces the degree of local control in peripheral regions, exacerbates regional inequalities by increasing the transfer of profits and dividends from peripheral regions, and increases the vulnerability of regions to the forces of global competition (Massey, 1979; Perrons, 1981). Massey (1979; 1995 [1984]) explicitly linked the new spatial divisions of labor in Britain to the increased internationalization of the world economy. Underdevelopment in peripheral regions should therefore not be explained by internal characteristics of peripheral regions but by their position and function in the broader national and international economy, which "can only be understood as a single, integrated system" (Fröbel et al., 1980: 15).

Despite building on the branch plant analysis (Perrons, 1981), the spatial divisions of labor approach no longer solely attributed economic difficulties of many branch plant regions to inward FDI and external control because the new international division of labor forced surviving domestic companies to follow similar corporate strategies of rationalization, mergers, acquisitions, relocation and outward FDI. These strategies increasingly affected localities and regions in home economies, often resulting in job losses and factory closures that tended to concentrate in peripheral regions (Fröbel et al., 1980; Perrons, 1981; Lloyd and Shutt, 1985). This further increased the vulnerability of peripheral regions while demonstrating that local firm ownership is no panacea for peripheral regions (Lloyd and Shutt, 1985; Massey, 1995 [1984]). Instead of ownership, the extent of local and regional linkages of branch plants is more strongly affected by different roles these branch plants play in different spatial structures (e.g., a part-process hierarchy and cloning). External ownership itself does not cause problems observed in peripheral regions by branch plant literature, such as the lack of high-value-added activities or the lack of local material linkages, but exacerbates them (Massey, 1995 [1984]). The spatial divisions of labor approach also underlined the need to focus on complex corporate strategies affecting peripheral regions, not only FDI, while also considering the role of political forces and institutions in regional restructuring (Lloyd and Shutt, 1985; Massey, 1995 [1984]).

The new international division of labor/spatial divisions of labor approaches thus highlighted the role of FDI in uneven development at multiple spatial scales and the close relationship between the increased importance of FDI in the world economy and its regional and local economic effects. It is this attention to empirical detail at the local and regional scale of the spatial divisions of labor approach that has been criticized by Marxist economic geographers. They were concerned that it was achieved at the expense of universal abstractions and theory (Harvey, 1987; Smith, 1989) and that it would lead to "a new empiricism" in economic geography (Smith, 1987). The increased attention to the processes taking place at the local and regional scales contributed to the development of new regionalism in economic geography, while, at the same time, the usage of the term "global production networks" by Lloyd and Shutt (1985: 33, 50) signals the importance of the new international division of labor/ spatial divisions of labor approaches for the development of the GPN perspective (Henderson et al., 2002).

2.3.3 New Regionalism and Territorial Embeddedness of FDI

The "institutional turn" in economic geography of the 1990s highlighted the importance of institutions in regional economic development (Amin, 1999; Martin, 2000; Cumbers et al., 2003; Farole et al., 2010; Bathelt and Glückler, 2013). Geographers also recognized that the spatial reorganization of economic activities driven by economic globalization and growing FDI inflows (Figures 1.1 and 1.2) might enhance the beneficial effects of FDI in peripheral regions of more developed countries (Amin et al., 1994; Dicken, 1994). Changes in the organization of manufacturing, such as the development of just-in-time production, increased clustering of manufacturing firms (Mair, 1993; Sturgeon et al., 2008). It was argued that knowledge accumulation within clusters would attract higher-value-added FDI to host regions, while the development of supplier linkages with domestic firms and other foreign firms in these clusters would increase the embeddedness of foreign branch plants in peripheral regions (Dicken et al., 1994). Spillovers from FDI to the local economy, in turn, would create conditions for progressive upgrading in peripheral regions through enhanced learning and innovation supported by dynamic regional institutions and high levels of "institutional thickness" (Amin and Thrift, 1994; Malmberg et al., 1996; Morgan, 1997). Although different types of embeddedness are recognized (Hess, 2004), in terms of FDI, economic geographers mainly focused on the territorial embeddedness of foreign firms in local supply networks in peripheral regions (Dicken et al., 1994; Pavlínek and Smith, 1998; Pavlínek, 2002d). It was argued that "embedded" branch plants combined with dynamic regional institutions would improve the regional competitiveness of peripheral regions and ultimately ease regional development deficiencies related to the branch plant economy and truncation, which would lead to a more balanced, diversified and successful regional economic development (Mair, 1993; Amin and Thrift, 1994). Such optimistic and celebratory claims about the role of FDI in regional development of peripheral regions have been embraced by regional development policy circles in Western Europe and the USA (Lovering, 1999). The new regionalism became a new orthodoxy of regional economic development despite its weak theoretical foundations and inadequate empirical analyses, resulting in weak empirical evidence (Lovering, 1999; MacKinnon et al., 2002) and an "overterritorialized" view of embeddedness (Hess, 2004).

  The claims of the new regionalism about the increased territorial embeddedness of FDI failed to be supported by strong empirical evidence even under the most favorable circumstances, such as in the case of the automotive industry with its dense supply networks and high levels of FDI. New regionalism claimed that automotive branch plants and new investments were gradually transformed into "performance/networked branch plants" that had strong local supplier linkages and spinoffs to host regions based on increased outsourcing, just-in-time production, and increased nonproduction functions related to their greater operating and even strategic autonomy (e.g., Amin et al., 1994; Dawley, 2011). However, the empirical evidence showed that despite the limited functional upgrading and the introduction of new production techniques in assembly plants, domestic firms continued to be excluded from supply networks of foreign-owned branch plants (Phelps, 1996; Pike, 1998; Larsson, 2002). For example, the majority of foreign-owned automotive assembly firms in Western Europe were not locally embedded and had only few direct linkages to the surrounding locality or region (Larsson, 2002). This has also been the case of the rapidly expanding automotive industry in Eastern Europe (Pavlínek and Žížalová, 2016; Pavlínek, 2018). Weak FDI linkages also continued to be the norm in the electronics industry (Turok, 1997) and in other industries (Phelps, 1993a; 1993b; Pike and Tomaney, 1999; Crone, 2002; Crone and Watts, 2003; Phelps et al., 2003).

Waves of closures of flagship foreign investments in Britain since the late 1990s undermined one of the main claims of new regionalism about the increased stability of FDI in peripheral regions due to its increased embeddedness and questioned the continuing FDI-based regional development strategies (Dawley, 2007a; 2007b). Outside of Western Europe and the USA, the application of new regionalism to FDI in peripheral regions has been even more problematic because of few capable domestic firms (Pavlínek and Žížalová, 2016; Pavlínek, 2018), weak institutions and a low quality of governance (Rodríguez-Pose and Di Cataldo, 2015; Ketterer and Rodríguez-Pose, 2018). Empirical evidence provided by economic geographers thus suggests that the limited long-term development effects of FDI in peripheral regions that are identified by the branch plant economy, truncation and spatial divisions of labor approaches mostly continue to persist, despite the significant reorganization of the capitalist economy since 1990.

The new regionalism and territorial embeddedness approach fails to adequately consider the role of extraregional factors in regional development, such as the state and the position of regions in the international division of labor, which represents a departure from the new international division of labor/spatial divisions of labor approaches. However, the embeddedness approach and its critique have strongly influenced thinking in contemporary economic geography by emphasizing the close relationship among FDI, institutions, networks, and embeddedness in regional development. The recognition that the ability to attract FDI and its embedding in peripheral regions strongly depend on the institutional capabilities, institutional environment and the territorial politics of FDI attraction of host regions has been especially important (Phelps et al., 2000; MacKinnon and Phelps, 2001a; 2001b; Fuller and Phelps, 2004; Dawley,

2007a). It has also contributed to the development of the GPN perspective after 2000, to which we now turn.

2.3.4 Global Production Networks and FDI

The GPN perspective emphasizes the importance of the integration of regions into transnational production networks for their successful economic development. It analyzes how and where value is created, enhanced and captured in GPNs, and how it affects the potential of different places and regions for economic development (Henderson et al., 2002; Coe et al., 2004; Coe and Yeung, 2015; 2019). The GPN approach considers the role and multitude relationships of different firm and nonfirm actors in GPNs (Coe et al., 2008; Coe, 2021). Here, however, the focus is on FDI, which is only one of many different ways for TNCs to organize and coordinate GPNs in addition to various forms and strategic mixes of investment and trade (Dicken, 2015). This might explain why the importance of FDI in the contemporary regional economic development is not always fully acknowledged by the GPN perspective (e.g., Coe and Yeung, 2019), especially when compared to the related GVC approach (e.g., Kano et al., 2020; Gereffi et al., 2021; Zhan, 2021), and despite the attempts to bring together GPN research with research on FDI and regional development (MacKinnon, 2012).

Regional development in host regions is conceptualized as the outcome of the strategic coupling between regional assets and the profit-driven needs of TNCs (Coe et al., 2004; Yeung, 2009; Coe and Yeung, 2015). One possible way in which a strategic coupling can form is via FDI (Coe et al., 2004; MacKinnon, 2012; Kleibert, 2014; Pavlínek, 2018; Coe, 2021). Three basic modes of strategic coupling (indigenous, functional and structural) (Table 2.3) therefore also reflect differences in the nature and role of horizontal and vertical FDI in regions occupying different positions in the international and national divisions of labor (Yeung, 2009; 2015; 2016; MacKinnon, 2012; Coe and Yeung, 2015). Core regions are mostly articulated with GPNs through indigenous (organic) couplings. They tend to attract horizontal FDI in higher-value-added manufacturing and services. As the largest source of outward FDI (e.g., Iammarino, 2018), they host a disproportionate share of headquarters and higher-value-added knowledge-intensive activities of TNCs (lead firms), such as R&D and sales, from which TNCs create and capture a significantly greater value than from manufacturing operations (Mudambi, 2008; Rehnberg and Ponte, 2018; Gereffi, 2020). Corporate headquarters wield power and control over the internationally dispersed operations of TNCs in peripheral regions, which further enhances the value capture of core regions through profit repatriations, profit shifting strategies and transfer pricing (Dischinger et al., 2014a; 2014b; Akyüz, 2017).

Peripheral regions are mainly recipients of vertical FDI (Table 2.1) and are articulated with GPNs through structural couplings. Foreign firms establish

TABLE 2.3 *FDI and the modes of strategic coupling in GPNs*

	Indigenous coupling	Functional coupling	Structural coupling
Predominant mode of FDI	Outflows	Mixed	Inflows
Predominant type of inward FDI	Horizontal	Mixed	Vertical
Degree of foreign ownership and control	Low	Medium	High
Power position of firms in GPNs	Control	Partnership	Dependency
Number of indigenous lead firms	High	Medium	Low
Capabilities of domestic firms	High	Mixed	Low
Foreign–domestic firms' supply relations	Partnership	Mixed	Dependency
Embeddedness of foreign firms	High	Medium	Low
Predominant FDI linkages	Developmental	Mixed	Dependent
Value capture	High	Medium	Low
Degree of regional autonomy	High	Medium	Low
Regional position in the division of labor	More developed countries	Emerging economies	Less developed countries

Source: author.

subsidiaries and supplier linkages in peripheral regions mostly for cost-cutting reasons (assembly platforms) or securing access to natural resources (commodity source regions) (Bridge, 2008; Milberg and Winkler, 2013; Coe and Yeung, 2015). Most foreign subsidiaries and subcontracted tasks concentrate on production in the form of standardized export-oriented assembly, mining or routine service functions, while lacking an adequate development of high-value-added strategic nonproduction functions, which are provided by TNC headquarters and R&D centers from the home countries of TNCs (Kleibert, 2016; Pavlínek, 2016; Pavlínek and Ženka, 2016). This results in lower value creation in the FDI host regions than in the source core regions. The value capture is diminished by lower corporate taxes compared to core regions (Pavlínek and Ženka, 2016; Pavlínek, 2020), the transfer of value from foreign subsidiaries into core-based corporate headquarters through profit repatriations (Dischinger et al., 2014a; 2014b) and low wages and weak linkages of foreign subsidiaries with domestic firms (Pavlínek, 2018). Lower value creation and capture translates into smaller long-term economic development effects of FDI in peripheral regions compared with core regions. Additionally, both assembly platforms and commodity source regions are typified by asymmetrical power relations between TNCs and host regions, and are vulnerable to potential decouplings through disinvestment, relocations and factory closures by TNCs (MacKinnon, 2012; Coe and Yeung, 2015). Thus, despite the short-term economic gains from FDI in the form of jobs and economic growth, many host peripheral regions represent an example of the less favorable articulation of regions into GPNs through FDI, what Coe and Hess (2011) called the "dark side" of strategic coupling, which may lock peripheral regions in disadvantageous and dependent positions in GPNs (Akyüz, 2017).

Emerging regions are usually articulated with GPNs through functional couplings (MacKinnon, 2012; Coe and Yeung, 2015; Yeung, 2015). In terms of FDI, these regions differ from peripheral regions in a greater balance between inward and outward FDI, the mixture of horizontal and vertical FDI, and stronger, more capable domestic firms that are able to globalize through investing abroad (Amsden and Chu, 2003; Yeung, 2016; Jo et al., 2023). This provides for greater regional autonomy, less dependency on foreign capital and technology, and greater value creation and capture (Table 2.3).

The formation of strategic couplings based on "FDI is often a highly politicized process (Phelps and Wood, 2006; 2018b; Drahokoupil, 2009; Dawley et al., 2019) that depends on a favorable institutional environment, which is even more important for a potential decoupling from the structural couplings and recoupling into the functional or indigenous strategic couplings (Bair and Werner, 2011a; Horner, 2014; Coe and Yeung, 2015; Yeung, 2015). The decoupling from structural couplings can take place through disinvestment (Clark and Wrigley, 1997; Benito, 2005; Bair and Werner, 2011b; Werner, 2016) or with the help of strategic regional and industrial policies (Yeung, 2015). Given the unfavorable institutional environment in many peripheral regions (Rodríguez-Pose and Di Cataldo, 2015; Ketterer and Rodríguez-Pose, 2018), strategic decoupling and recoupling is difficult to achieve, although successful examples exist (Horner, 2014; Lee et al., 2014; Yeung, 2015).

The role of the state in coupling/decoupling/recoupling efforts is crucial and is reflected in the growing interest of economic geographers to understand the regional development outcomes of various state policies in the context of GPNs (e.g., Smith, 2015; Horner, 2017; Rutherford et al., 2018; Dawley et al., 2019; Werner, 2021). States' bargaining powers with TNCs have decreased mainly due to FDI liberalization, the World Trade Organization's multilateral rules and obligations on investment policies, and bilateral investment treaties (e.g., Phelps, 2008; Akyüz, 2017; Horner, 2017). Consequently, only a few less developed countries, particularly China, have been able to effectively regulate inward FDI after 1990 (Chen, 2018; Schwabe, 2020a).

Overall, GPN analyses focusing on FDI came to similar conclusions about long-term developmental effects of FDI in peripheral regions as the earlier approaches (including the critique of new regionalism) (e.g., Kleibert, 2016; Pavlínek, 2018). Along with heterodox approaches in the international business literature (Andreoni and Chang, 2019; Chang and Andreoni, 2020), the GPN approach has argued that FDI should be part of a broader development strategy, in which peripheral regions systematically develop regional assets that would attract FDI into high-value-added activities (Coe et al., 2004; Coe and Yeung, 2015). In the contemporary economy, it means attracting FDI into strategic nonproduction functions that require a long-term systematic investment into high-quality education, innovation activities and the development of regional institutions that support the growth of the knowledge economy and the upgrading of domestic firms. However, it is unrealistic to expect all peripheral regions to successfully adopt this approach, especially in less developed countries where resources are scarce, high-quality education and skills are limited and technology is less advanced. Moreover, it is reasonable to assume that in the context of peripheral regions, vertical FDI will predominantly continue to search for low-cost manufacturing and service locations, and access to raw materials and select agricultural commodities.

2.4 CONCLUSION

There is little doubt that FDI, along with other transnational strategies of TNCs, will continue to shape the economic development in peripheral regions in the foreseeable future despite the long-term uncertainties related to the global climate crisis, short-term crises such as the COVID-19 pandemic, the transition to the digital economy and the stagnation of GPN trade since the 2008 global financial crisis (Kowalski, 2020; OECD, 2020; World Bank, 2020; UNCTAD, 2020; 2021). There is also little doubt about the geographically uneven nature of these developments at different geographic scales (World Bank, 2020; UNCTAD, 2021).

The conceptual approaches reviewed in this chapter reflect the efforts of economic geographers since the 1970s to understand the effects of FDI in peripheral regions in the context of increasingly complex changes due to rapidly advancing economic globalization. Given the anticipated changes in the world economy in the coming decades, geographers will need to continue these efforts to remain a relevant voice in examining uneven development. Other disciplines, such as economics, international business studies and international political economy, maintain a strong interest in FDI (e.g., Buckley et al., 2017; Zhan, 2021). The unique contribution of geographers revolves around their understanding and analyzing FDI in the context of uneven development, one of the core themes in economic geography (Peck, 2016; Werner, 2016; 2018; Dunford and Liu, 2017; Phelps et al., 2018), and in their regional approach to FDI (Iammarino, 2018). Although the importance of subnational regional analysis has recently been recognized by the international business literature (Hutzschenreuter et al., 2020), it continues to be underdeveloped in both economics and international business compared to geography (Iammarino and McCann, 2018).

There are underrepresented topics in the geographical analyses of FDI in peripheral regions that call for complementing the existing research. In addition to FDI inflows, economic geographers need to pay a greater attention to reinvestment (Phelps and Fuller, 2000; Fuller and Phelps, 2004; Wren and Jones, 2009) and disinvestment (Benito, 2005; Dawley, 2007a), which often have more important regional development effects than new FDI projects (Pavlínek, 2020). Economic geographers should focus more on the developmental effects of the rapidly increasing outward FDI from emerging economies in peripheral regions, especially from China (Taylor and Zajontz, 2020; Lia and Cantwellb, 2021). The service sector now accounts for two-thirds of global FDI stock (UNCTAD, 2017), with financial services alone accounting for more than one third (UNCTAD, 2020). However, despite a growing interest in FDI in services in peripheral regions (e.g., Kleibert, 2016; Gersch, 2019; Murphy, 2019), it continues to be an underrepresented topic, including FDI in financial services (e.g., Coe et al., 2014; Haberly and Wójcik, 2015; 2022; Blažek and Hejnová, 2020). A rapid growth of FDI in the extractive industry in peripheral regions also deserves greater attention (e.g., Phelps et al., 2015; Bridge and Bradshaw, 2017; Narula, 2018), along with FDI in agriculture (UNCTAD, 2009; Santangelo, 2018) and the environmental effects of FDI (Zhang, 2013; Demena and Afesorgbor, 2020).

Projected changes in international production and FDI in the 2020s will have important implications for peripheral regions (Enderwick and Buckley, 2020; UNCTAD, 2020; World Bank, 2020; Zhan, 2021), making FDI research attractive. The increased automation of production will likely decrease the relevance of low labor costs and low-cost locations and lead to increased reshoring and insourcing in higher-tech industries (e.g., the electronics, automotive, machinery industries) and lower-value-added services (e.g., sales and marketing). The increased digitalization of supply chains will likely lead to the development of even more complex GPNs, the expansion of international production in lower-tech industries (e.g., apparel) and higher-value-added services (e.g., finance). Increased automation and digitalization, along with the effects of regional integration trends toward more sustainable local and regional sourcing and the push for a lower dependence on imports of strategic commodities by core regions (e.g., medical supplies, pharmaceuticals, semiconductors), will likely lead to an increased organization of GPNs at the macro-regional scale (e.g., the automotive industry, food processing, agriculture) (UNCTAD, 2020; 2021; Gereffi et al., 2021; Zhan, 2021). The impact of these trends will be uneven across different industries and services, leading to uneven geographic effects and distinct regional development outcomes that will likely intensify the differences between core regions and peripheral regions, providing excellent research opportunities for geographers studying uneven development.

3

Foreign Direct Investment and Supplier Linkages in Integrated Peripheries

3.1 INTRODUCTION

The automotive industry represents an ideal sector to study the effects of FDI in less developed countries and peripheral regions because it has experienced large FDI flows since 1990 and has become one of the most globalized industries (Sturgeon et al., 2008). Between 2003 and 2022, the total value of announced greenfield FDI projects in the automotive industry reached USD1.3 trillion, the highest of all manufacturing sectors (UNCTAD, 2023). Particular groups of less developed countries have been targeted by automotive FDI either because of their large markets (e.g., China, India and Brazil) or the combination of low production costs, geographic proximity to affluent markets and membership in regional trade agreements in what I call integrated peripheries (e.g., Eastern Europe, Spain, Portugal, Turkey, Morocco and Mexico) (Humphrey et al., 2000; Carrillo et al., 2004).

This chapter draws on the GPN perspective (Henderson et al., 2002; Coe et al., 2004; Coe and Yeung, 2015) and Harvey's (1982; 2005b) work on uneven development to conceptualize the growth and regional development effects of automotive FDI in integrated peripheries by analyzing supplier linkages with a particular focus on linkages between foreign subsidiaries and domestic firms. Linkages are considered to be extremely important for stimulating production and job creation, stabilizing investments by embedding investors in host economies, and as a precondition for the transfer of knowledge and technology into host economies (Blomström and Kokko, 1998; UNCTAD, 2001; Giroud and Scott-Kennel, 2009). However, there is a paucity of in-depth firm-level analyses of FDI linkages in integrated peripheries. Empirically, this chapter focuses on Slovakia, which exemplifies the rapid growth of the automotive industry in integrated peripheries since the 1990s, and thus represents an opportunity to study the effects of large automotive FDI on regional economic development through the formation of linkages between foreign subsidiaries and domestic firms.

This chapter uses original qualitative data I collected through a survey of 299 Slovakia-based foreign and domestic automotive firms, and fifty face-to-face interviews with managers of automotive firms in Slovakia. In particular, I will address three research questions. First, how can we conceptualize the growth and regional development effects of FDI in integrated peripheries? Second, how is the nature of automotive FDI in integrated peripheries reflected in the extent (quantity) of supplier linkages between foreign subsidiaries and domestic firms? Third, how can we evaluate the mode of articulation of domestic firms into automotive GPNs and its potential regional development effects in integrated peripheries by measuring the quality of supplier linkages between foreign subsidiaries and domestic firms?

This chapter is innovative for four reasons. First, it advances the spatial concept of integrated peripheries as distinct production areas of the contemporary automotive industry. Second, it builds on Harvey's (2014) spatiotemporal fix and the GPN perspective to conceptualize the growth and regional development effects of the foreign-controlled automotive industry in integrated peripheries. Third, it develops methodology designed to evaluate the quality of supplier linkages between foreign subsidiaries and domestic firms. Fourth, to the best of my knowledge, it represents the first in-depth analysis of supplier linkages in the automotive industry of Slovakia based on original firm-level data. The empirical analysis uncovered weak and dependent linkages between foreign subsidiaries and domestic firms that limit the potential for technology transfer from foreign firms to the Slovak economy, a situation that is typical of peripheral and FDI-dependent regional economic development. As such, underdeveloped linkages constitute a major barrier for the development of a stronger domestic supplier industry and for the weakening of the overwhelming capital and technological dependence of the Slovak automotive industry on foreign capital.

The chapter is organized as follows. I begin with a characterization of the integrated peripheries of the automotive industry and conceptualize their development in contemporary capitalism. Second, I discuss the nature of strategic coupling in integrated peripheries in order to understand their mode of articulation into GPNs. Third, I explain the importance of FDI linkages for regional economic development in integrated peripheries. Fourth, I briefly characterize the Slovak automotive industry and summarize data collection. Fifth, I analyze the quantity of supplier linkages in the Slovak automotive industry. Sixth, I evaluate the quality of linkages between foreign subsidiaries and domestic firms. Finally, I summarize the results in the conclusion.

3.2 THE INTEGRATED PERIPHERIES OF CORE-BASED
MACRO-REGIONAL PRODUCTION NETWORKS

I start by developing the spatial concept of integrated peripheries, which helps us not only understand the ever-changing geography of the global automotive industry but also allows us to highlight the ways in which particular areas of automotive production are articulated in GPNs and the regional development effects of this articulation. Here, although my thinking is influenced by earlier conceptualizations of the international division of labor, such as the "new international division of labor thesis" (Fröbel et al., 1980) and its critique (Schoenberger, 1988; Henderson, 1989), or the "Law on uneven development" (Hymer, 1972), I draw on more recent dynamic notions of international division of labor and uneven development proposed by Harvey (1982) and the GPN perspective.

At a general-system level, the spatial patterns of capitalist economic development are driven by profit-seeking behavior. Capitalist firms can achieve excess profits by employing superior technologies or by investing in more profitable locations. The investment of surplus capital in such superior locations provides a "spatiotemporal fix" for declining profitability in existing locations due to increasing production costs and decreasing growth (Harvey, 1982). In the words of Harvey (2014: 152): "The organisation of new territorial divisions of labour, of new resource complexes and of new regions as dynamic spaces of capital accumulation all provide new opportunities to generate profits and to absorb surpluses of capital and labour." Integrated peripheries thus represent a particular form of the spatiotemporal fix that allows core-based automotive firms to maintain or increase the rate of profit by developing production in lower-cost areas that are geographically adjacent to core regions of production and consumption. However, these spatiotemporal fixes are only a temporary solution to the profitability of individual firms because their excess profits diminish as other firms invest in similar superior locations (Harvey, 1982) and because regional growth does not last since its sources are depleted over time. Consequently, production costs start to rise, and the rate of profit begins to decline, eventually forcing firms to seek new, more profitable locations. However, Harvey does not systematically identify different forms of spatiotemporal fixes that develop based on different sources of economic growth and profit opportunities that make particular regions attractive for capital investment and accumulation. These can include surpluses of low-cost labor, particular labor skills, rapid technological development, rapidly growing markets, high-quality infrastructure and the existence of particular natural resources. Therefore, I need to turn to a meso-level explanation provided by the GPN perspective and its concept of strategic coupling for the understanding of how different spatiotemporal fixes operate and articulate different firms and regions into GPNs.

The GPN perspective has argued that successful regional economic development is attainable through the articulation of peripheral regions and less developed countries into transnational production networks (Henderson et al., 2002; Coe et al., 2004). Despite its primary focus on the subnational region for the understanding of economic development (Coe and Yeung, 2015), the GPN analysis thus recognizes that the patterns of economic development are strongly affected by the processes of global capital accumulation (Harvey, 1982) and by the existing spatial division of labor at different geographic scales (Massey, 1995 [1984]). Regional economic development is conceptualized as the outcome of the strategic coupling between regional assets and the needs of GPNs (Coe et al., 2004; Yeung, 2009; Coe and Yeung, 2015), which means that it is very much dependent on the existence of surplus capital looking for investment opportunities abroad and "spatiotemporal fixes" around the world in order to increase or at least maintain the rate of profit (Harvey, 1982; 2014). The nature and outcome of strategic coupling and regional development are thus affected by the position of that particular place or region in the international division of labor.

It is in this context, I identify the core-based macro-regional organization of GPNs in the automotive industry, while aiming to analyze the regional development effects of this network organization. By focusing on these two spatial scales, I am aiming at a better understanding of the growth and regional development outcomes of the contemporary automotive industry in integrated peripheries than what is offered by traditional national-level analyses (Coe and Yeung, 2015).

An integrated periphery refers to a dynamic area of relatively low-cost (industrial) production that is geographically adjacent to a large market and has been integrated within a core-based macro-regional production network through FDI. In an integrated periphery, production, organization and strategic functions are externally controlled through foreign ownership (Table 3.1). In the world-systems perspective, these integrated peripheries are typically classified as being part of the global semiperiphery but parts of them can also be classified as core (e.g., Spain) or periphery (e.g., Morocco) (Van Hamme and Pion, 2012). Integrated peripheries represent one of the numerous examples of the uneven development dynamics of contemporary capitalism, in which capital is searching for growth and profit opportunities in new geographic areas. Spatiotemporal fix in integrated peripheries is the outcome of the voluntary opening of these new and potentially more profitable territories for penetration by foreign capital (e.g., Mexico after 1965, Spain after 1972, Eastern Europe after 1989) to take advantage of surplus capital from the core areas of the global automotive industry, while offering surplus labor in integrated peripheries (Harvey, 2005b). This spatiotemporal fix is based on the contemporaneous existence of four regional assets in integrated peripheries: low-cost labor, geographic proximity to large markets, membership in regional trade agreements and investment incentives. Spatiotemporal fix in the form of FDI in particular locations and regions of integrated peripheries has thus been made

TABLE 3.1 *Spatial zones in core-based automotive industry macro-regional production networks*

	Core	Semiperiphery	Integrated periphery
Foreign ownership and control	Low to medium	High	Very high
Domestic global assembly firms	Yes	No	No
Number of domestic suppliers in the global top 100	High	Low	None or very low
Structure of automotive FDI	Outflows predominate	Mixed	Inflows predominate
R&D: spending, number of R&D workers, patent applications	High	Medium	Low
Structure of assembled vehicles	High share of expensive vehicles	Mixed	High share of cheap/ small vehicles
Structure of produced components	Higher share of technologically advanced components	Mixed	High share of generic and labor- intensive components
Capabilities of domestic suppliers	High	Mixed	Low
Supplier linkages	Predominantly developmental	Mixed	Predominantly dependent
Labor costs per employee	High	Medium to high	Low
Wage adjusted labor productivity	Low	Low to medium	High
Examples	Germany, USA	Britain, Canada	Eastern Europe, Turkey, Mexico, Morocco

Source: author.

possible not only by the mobility of surplus capital but also by technological and organizational fixes (Yeung, 2009; Coe and Yeung, 2015) in the contemporary automotive industry (e.g., Sturgeon et al., 2008). Although I focus on the automotive industry in this chapter, integrated peripheries also provide the spatiotemporal fix for other globally integrated industries, such as apparel (Pickles and Smith, 2016) and electronics (Starosta, 2010).

Decreases in the cost of production and increased product variety are at the heart of the competitive strategies of vehicle manufacturers attainable through the internationalization of production (Freyssenet and Lung, 2000). Curbing wage costs (7–10 percent of the value of the car) and the price of components (almost 70 percent), although maintaining or not significantly increasing marketing and distribution costs, can be achieved by locating the production of components, assembly of the most cost-sensitive models and the labor-intensive assembly of niche market vehicles to low-cost areas situated in the proximity of large automobile markets. Such areas are woven into transnational automotive production networks through investment by core-based assembly firms and component suppliers. Integrated peripheries therefore include countries that are located close to Western Europe and the USA but have significantly lower production costs, and participate in regional trade agreements that provide tariff-free access to macro-regional markets (Humphrey and Oeter, 2000). These countries are peripheral in the context of automotive industry macro-regional production networks by producing entry-level vehicles, generic and labor-intensive components, and lacking strategic functions such as R&D, strategic decision-making and finance (Layan and Lung, 2004) (Table 3.1).

The first integrated peripheries of the automotive industry were developed in Mexico, Spain and Portugal in the 1980s (Carrillo et al., 2004; Charnock et al., 2016). Turkey followed in the late 1980s and early 1990s (Wasti and Wasti, 2008) and Eastern Europe in the 1990s and 2000s (Pavlínek, 2002d; 2002b). More recently, Serbia and Morocco were integrated on the periphery of the European automotive production system (Benabdejlil et al., 2015; Pavlínek, 2017a) (Table 3.2). The integration of new peripheries and the related spatial shifts in the European and North American automotive industries are the outcome of gradual wage convergence with core areas in older integrated peripheries, and constant efforts of automotive firms to curb wage costs by shifting parts of production to lower-cost countries, while also using lower-cost locations to limit wage increases in the entire production network through inter-plant competition and threats of relocation of production (Phelps and Fuller, 2000; Aláez et al., 2015).

Although this is a varied group of countries, the automotive industry in integrated peripheries shares the following basic features (Table 3.1). (1) predominantly export-oriented production (Table 3.2); (2) a high degree of foreign ownership and control (Contreras et al., 2012; Eurostat, 2016b); (3) significantly lower wages than in the automotive industry core countries (CB, 2016); (4) specialization in the mass production of entry-level vehicles, low-volume production of special models and labor-intensive production of components (Layan, 2000; Pavlínek, 2002d); (5) underdevelopment of automotive R&D and other higher-value-added functions (Layan, 2000; Pavlínek, 2012); (6) more flexible labor practices than in the automotive industry core countries (Pavlínek, 2002d; Aláez et al., 2015); and (7)

TABLE 3.2 *Passenger car production in integrated peripheries, 1990–2015*

	1990 (thousands of units)	1995 (thousands of units)	2000 (thousands of units)	2005 (thousands of units)	2010 (thousands of units)	2015 (thousands of units)	Share of exports in 2015 (%)	Share of global car exports in 2015 (%)	Value of car exports in 2015 (USD billion)
Czechia	188	208	451	594	1,070	1,298	92	2.5	16.9
Hungary	0	51	134	149	209	492	93	1.7	11.2
Poland	266	366	533	540	785	535	99	1.0	6.5
Romania	90	88	77	172	324	387	92	0.5	3.2
Serbia	179	8	11	13	17	82	95	0.2	1.3
Slovakia	0	20	181	218	557	1,039	99	2.1	14.1
Slovenia	74	88	123	138	201	133	99	0.4	2.4
Eastern Europe total	797	829	1,510	1,824	3,162	3,965	95	8.4	55.6
Portugal	60	41	179	189	115	115	96	0.3	2.3
Spain	1,679	2,131	2,366	2,098	1,914	2,219	87	4.9	33.1
Iberia total	1,740	2,172	2,545	2,287	2,028	2,334	87	5.2	35.4
Turkey	168	233	297	454	603	791	73	1.0	6.9
Morocco	0	0	16	8	36	260	98	0.3	1.7
Mexico	720	699	1,279	846	1,386	1,968	82	4.9	32.8
Total	3,424	3,933	5,648	5,419	7,215	9,319	91	19.8	132.4

Sources: OICA (2016) (2000–2015 figures), Ward (2016) (1990–1995 figures), WTEx (2016).

FDI-friendly automotive industry state policies and intense state competition over automotive FDI (Drahokoupil, 2009; Pavlínek, 2016).

The export-oriented automotive industry has grown rapidly in integrated peripheries since the early 1990s (Table 3.2). All high-volume assembly plants in integrated peripheries are foreign-owned, and foreign ownership also dominates the supplier sector, reflecting the rapid internationalization of the supplier industry since the early 1990s (Sturgeon and Lester, 2004). Although the automotive industry in integrated peripheries is based on state-of-the-art factories and technologies, it is almost totally dependent on the import of capital, technologies and operational skills directly related to production from abroad. The majority of parts and components is also imported directly or manufactured in foreign subsidiaries. At the same time, the majority of strategic functions is conducted abroad (Pavlínek, 2016; Pavlínek and Ženka, 2016), which, along with the outflow of profits and the weak linkages of foreign subsidiaries with host economies, is likely to limit the long-term benefits of this growth and contribute to the technological underdevelopment of integrated peripheries (Britton, 1980; Grabher, 1997). In the next section, I draw on the GPN perspective in order to consider the mode of articulation of integrated peripheries in automotive GPNs by focusing on the concept of strategic coupling.

3.3 THE NATURE OF STRATEGIC COUPLING IN INTEGRATED PERIPHERIES

The mode of articulation of regions into GPNs is based on the particular form of time and space contingent strategic coupling, with different forms of coupling leading to different regional development outcomes (Coe et al., 2004; Yeung, 2009; 2016; Coe and Yeung, 2015). Following Coe and Yeung's (2015) classification, I argue that integrated peripheries are articulated into GPNs through structural coupling, which represents the least favorable mode for integrated regions and places. Structural coupling is based on generic regional assets (MacKinnon, 2012), such as surpluses of relatively cheap labor, industrial parks and transportation infrastructure, allowing TNCs to strongly exercise their structural power. The assembly platforms type of structural coupling, which is relevant in the automotive industry, is best illustrated by the FDI-driven export-oriented standardized assembly of goods and services in globally integrated industries and is exemplified by high levels of external dependency and control. This translates into greater value transfer and the greater likelihood of decoupling and cost-driven relocations, especially in the labor-intensive supplier sector. Although significant value creation takes place in foreign subsidiaries, integrated peripheries capture only a low share of the value created because of high shares of low-wage assembly jobs, low shares of nonproduction and strategic functions, the repatriation of profits, and low corporate taxes (Smith et al., 2002; Pavlínek and Ženka, 2016; Pavlínek, 2016). Integrated peripheries thus represent an example of the less favorable articulation of regions into GPNs through FDI.

Spatiotemporal fix in integrated peripheries has been made possible by technological and organizational fixes. The organizational fix is based on the reorganization of the automotive supplier industry since the 1980s, which significantly reduced the number of suppliers and organized the remaining ones into tiers (Humphrey and Memedovic, 2003). The requirements of just-in-time production, along with local content and follow sourcing requirements, led to the increased clustering of especially tier-one suppliers around assembly plants (Sturgeon et al., 2008). However, due to the rapid internationalization of the supplier industry (Sturgeon and Lester, 2004) and global sourcing, the vast majority of these suppliers in integrated peripheries are foreign subsidiaries that tend to assemble components or modules from imported parts or those supplied by other foreign subsidiaries rather than from those supplied by the domestic industry. Consequently, the existence of domestic suppliers and their capabilities are no longer important factors in the location decisions of foreign assembly firms since components that need to be supplied just in time are sourced through follow sourcing and the remaining components can be imported. The technological fix is based on new transportation technologies, logistical systems and the modern transportation infrastructure in integrated peripheries that allow for global sourcing, the just-in-time delivery of preassembled modules and exports of finished vehicles and components (Kaneko and Nojiri, 2008; Coe, 2014).

It is in this context, I will focus on linkages between foreign subsidiaries and host country firms (henceforth domestic firms) in the automotive industry of integrated peripheries. There has been little research on these linkages despite being considered the most important mechanism of technology transfer from core to peripheral regions (Blomström and Kokko, 1998; UNCTAD, 2001; Giroud and Scott-Kennel, 2009; Santangelo, 2009). The quantity *and* quality of linkages thus strongly affect the nature of strategic couplings with automotive GPNs and, consequently, the long-term regional developmental consequences of FDI in integrated peripheries.

3.4   FDI LINKAGES IN INTEGRATED PERIPHERIES

Supplier linkages between foreign subsidiaries and domestic firms represent an important mechanism through which domestic firms become articulated into GPNs. This is especially the case in the automotive industry, which relies on extensive networks of component suppliers. Although the GPN approach recognizes the importance of linkages between foreign and domestic firms (e.g., Coe and Yeung, 2015), to the best of my knowledge, GPN scholars have not developed a systematic approach to evaluate these linkages. Therefore, I will draw on economic geography and international business literature to categorize supplier linkages from the perspective of their regional development potential, and will link these categories to different modes of strategic couplings developed by the GPN approach. This approach will allow me to evaluate the nature of strategic coupling in the automotive industry in integrated peripheries through analyzing supplier linkages between foreign subsidiaries and domestic firms.

FDI linkages are repeated transactions between foreign subsidiaries and domestic firms, including linkages between foreign subsidiaries and various host-country institutions (Hansen et al., 2009). FDI linkages can be classified into three basic categories (Giroud and Scott-Kennel, 2009): vertical (supplier), horizontal (collaborative or relational) and institutional linkages. Vertical linkages can be either backward (i.e., with suppliers, such as foreign subsidiaries buying supplies from domestic firm), or forward (i.e., with customers, such as foreign subsidiaries supplying domestic firms). Horizontal linkages are formed through strategic alliances with other firms. Institutional linkages are linkages with host-country institutions, such as R&D institutes and universities, producing knowledge (Santangelo, 2009). Backward supplier linkages between foreign subsidiaries and domestic firms are considered the most important for the potential upgrading of domestic firms and a crucial precondition for spillovers (Blomström and Kokko, 1998; UNCTAD, 2001; Santangelo, 2009). The formation of such linkages therefore constitutes an important mechanism through which the development potential of FDI in less developed countries and regions can be realized (Giroud and Scott-Kennel, 2009).

Although the number of linkages is important, it is the nature of these linkages that indicates the mode of strategic coupling with GPNs and ultimately determines the long-term developmental effects of FDI in host economies. Turok (1993) categorized linkages into two basic types, "developmental" and "dependent," in order to distinguish between the different developmental potential of different linkages for domestic firms. Developmental linkages are based on long-term collaboration between foreign subsidiaries and domestic firms, which is typical of the international partnership type of functional couplings with GPNs (Coe and Yeung, 2015). Developmental linkages increase the likelihood of technology and knowledge transfer from foreign subsidiaries, which encourages the upgrading of domestic firms, including functional upgrading and the development of higher-value-added functions such as R&D.

In contrast, dependent linkages are typical of the assembly platforms type of structural couplings with GPNs which are characterized by the dependency of firms and regions on external actors (Coe and Yeung, 2015). Dependent linkages are based on shorter-term, price-based and often adversarial relationships between foreign subsidiaries and domestic firms, in which cost-cutting is the main reason for establishing linkages by foreign subsidiaries (Turok, 1993), and the exchange of information and knowledge with domestic firms is limited (UNCTAD, 2001). Domestic firms tend to supply simple standard components, do not engage in product development (Turok, 1993) and are contractually highly dependent on foreign firms in captive production networks which may lock domestic firms into simple, low-value-added activities and undermine the potential of domestic suppliers to benefit from supplier linkages (UNCTAD, 2001; Gereffi et al., 2005; Pavlínek and Ženka, 2011; Pavlínek and Žížalová, 2016).

Developmental linkages thus have a greater positive long-term regional development potential for host economies than dependent linkages by encouraging the functional upgrading and development of domestic firms (Turok, 1993) and by increasing the locational stability of foreign investors in host economies (UNCTAD, 2001). Additionally, I will also consider the possibility of negative effects of foreign subsidiaries on domestic firms (Hymer, 1972; Bellak, 2004) in the assembly platforms type of structural couplings through what I call detrimental linkages relating to employment and labor market effects of FDI such as employee poaching (Pavlínek and Žížalová, 2016).

Firm-level data from less developed host regions typically suggest weak supplier linkages between foreign subsidiaries and domestic firms, indicating a weak potential for spillovers and, therefore, limited development potential of FDI (Phelps, 1993a; Turok, 1993). The potential for local linkages between foreign subsidiaries and domestic firms has further decreased in the contemporary economy mainly because of the increased use of global sourcing by TNCs (Humphrey, 2000; Tavares and Young, 2006; Williams et al., 2008). Furthermore, in the automotive industry, modular production has become a norm in which preassembled modules and the most important components are delivered sequentially just in time from dedicated suppliers located in supplier parks close to car assembly plants. These supplier parks typically have few linkages, if any, to the surrounding region (Larsson, 2002). It should not therefore be surprising that the evidence from integrated peripheries suggests that foreign subsidiaries usually fail to develop supplier linkages with domestic firms (Lagendijk, 1995b; Carrillo, 2004; Pavlínek and Žížalová, 2016). If domestic firms are integrated in captive production networks organized and controlled by foreign TNCs at all, they supply simple, standardized, slow-changing and low-value-added components through dependent linkages and are squeezed by larger and more powerful foreign buyers.

This situation suggests that while FDI in integrated peripheries increased rapidly since the early 1990s (UNCTAD, 2016), FDI's regional development potential has been decreasing because its effects have mainly been short-term, such as job creation, capital formation, trade, and the balance of payment effects, while the limited development of predominantly dependent linkages with domestic firms weakened the potential long-term positive effects of FDI (Young et al., 1994; Hatani, 2009). We might therefore expect a limited development of linkages between foreign subsidiaries and domestic firms and the existence of predominantly dependent linkages in the automotive industry of integrated peripheries. The limited and dependent linkages of domestic firms with foreign subsidiaries would therefore suggest the articulation of integrated peripheries into GPNs through predominantly structural couplings. The validity of these assumptions will be examined in the empirical part of this chapter.

3.5 THE CASE STUDY AREA AND DATA COLLECTION

Slovakia represents a typical example of the integrated periphery of the automotive industry. FDI-driven export-oriented growth started in the 1990s, following an investment by German Volkswagen. But the most rapid development took place in the early 2000s prior to the 2008–2009 economic crisis and was related to Slovakia's entry into the European Union in 2004, the development of an aggressive foreign investment promotion regime by the Slovak state, and a large surplus of cheap labor indicated by the 19.5-percent unemployment rate in 2001 (Pavlínek, 2016). In the early 2000s, Kia and Peugeot Société Anonyme Peugeot Citroën (henceforth PSA) set up assembly operations and Volkswagen was rapidly expanding production in Slovakia. Foreign component suppliers built 128 new factories between 1997 and 2015 (Pavlínek, 2017a). By 2014, foreign capital almost completely controlled the automotive industry in Slovakia, accounting for 98 percent of production value, 97 percent of gross investment in tangible goods, 93 percent of persons employed and 96 percent of value added at factor cost, which represented the highest level of foreign control of the automotive industry in Eastern Europe (Pavlínek, 2017a). Average personnel costs per employee in the automotive industry were 74 percent lower in Slovakia than in Germany in 2014 (86 percent lower in 2001) (Eurostat, 2016b). Wages increased as the surplus of cheap labor diminished especially in western Slovakia, which has been most targeted by automotive FDI (Figure 3.1), but the average gross monthly salary for production workers continued to be very low, at €590 in 2015 (Sario, 2016). The majority of assembled cars are entry-level models or compact cars, although Volkswagen also established the labor-intensive low-volume assembly of luxury models in Slovakia, which is another typical specialization of integrated peripheries (Pavlínek, 2002d). The development of automotive R&D and other higher-value-added functions has been very limited (Pavlínek, 2012; 2016).

I collected the data through a firm-level questionnaire and on-site face-to-face interviews with directors or top managers of automotive firms (Figure 3.1). The goal of the questionnaire and interviews was to collect information about the position, competencies and linkages of foreign subsidiaries and domestic firms in the Slovak automotive industry. The questionnaire was conducted in 2010 and included 299 firms with more than twenty workers in the broadly defined automotive industry, which includes not only firms classified in the automotive industry (NACE 29) but also firms that supply the automotive industry but are classified in different industries, such as rubber, plastic, and iron and steel industries. I received answers from 133 firms (68 foreign subsidiaries and 65 domestic firms), a response rate of 60 percent. The survey data included information about the technological complexity of production, competencies and activities conducted, R&D and supplier linkages.

The interviews were conducted in Slovakia between 2011 and 2015 and involved fifty firms, twenty-two domestic firms and twenty-eight foreign

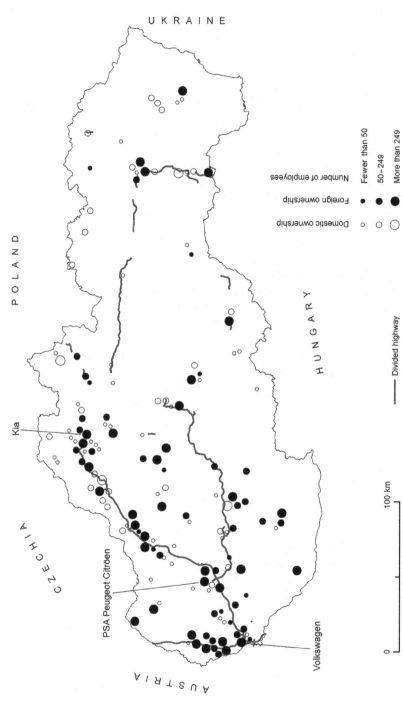

FIGURE 3.1 Spatial distribution of the surveyed and interviewed foreign subsidiaries and domestic automotive firms in Slovakia based on their number of employees

Source: author.

subsidiaries. The interview questions were different from the survey, were tailored differently to foreign and domestic firms and collected more detailed information about individual firms than the survey.

3.6 THE QUANTITY OF SUPPLIER LINKAGES

The quantity of supplier linkages of foreign subsidiaries indicates the form of the spatiotemporal fix in integrated peripheries and the mode of coupling of integrated peripheries into automotive GPNs. The survey and interview data point to weak backward and forward supplier linkages between domestic firms and foreign subsidiaries and high dependence of both on imports of parts and components. Foreign subsidiaries have developed strong forward supplier linkages with assembly firms because of just-in-time delivery and local content requirements but their backward and forward linkages with domestic firms and especially other foreign subsidiaries in Slovakia are weakly developed. Instead, foreign subsidiaries are strongly integrated into transnational production networks and heavily depend on supplies from abroad and on sales of their products abroad, with the exception of tier-one suppliers, which supply assembly operations in Slovakia.

In terms of forward linkages, foreign subsidiaries supply either assembly firms in Slovakia or export their products abroad but do not supply other foreign subsidiaries in Slovakia (Tables 3.3 and 3.4). In terms of backward linkages, foreign subsidiaries buy a very low share of supplies in Slovakia, while being heavily dependent on imports (Table 3.4), with the vast majority buying less than 10 percent and buying mostly various services rather than components, as revealed by the interviews (cf. Contreras et al., 2012). This first suggests that foreign subsidiaries mainly source their supplies from abroad rather than from Slovakia-based firms (both foreign subsidiaries and domestic firms). Second, linkages among foreign suppliers operating in Slovakia are weakly developed. Third, supplier linkages between foreign subsidiaries and domestic firms are also weakly developed.

Domestic firms, as expected, have stronger linkages with other domestic firms than foreign subsidiaries, have weak supply linkages with foreign subsidiaries, and are highly dependent on imports (Table 3.4). These very limited supply linkages between domestic firms and foreign subsidiaries mean that the vast majority of domestic firms cannot benefit from the possibility of direct spillovers from foreign subsidiaries. The actual share of domestic firms not benefiting from spillovers is even higher, since linkages (and dependent linkages in particular) do not automatically translate into spillovers (Saggi, 2002). This suggests a weak long-term potential for the positive firm-level effects of automotive FDI in the Slovak economy.

Interviews with foreign subsidiaries confirmed the survey results (Table 3.5) and identified the underlying reasons for weak supplier linkages of foreign subsidiaries in Slovakia. These include the system of centralized purchasing (79 percent of interviewed subsidiaries), which is a standard practice allowing TNCs to capture

TABLE 3.3 *Structure of procured supplies of surveyed automotive firms in Slovakia*

Share of supplies (%)	From domestic suppliers		From foreign subsidiaries		From abroad	
	No.	%	No.	%	No.	%
0	26	19.5	98	73.7	4	3.0
1–24	51	38.3	22	16.5	24	18.0
25–49	17	12.8	7	5.3	11	8.3
50–74	23	17.3	3	2.3	38	28.6
75–99	14	10.5	3	2.3	48	36.1
100	2	1.5	0	0.0	8	6.0
Total	133	100.0	133	100.0	133	100.0

The meaning of the first line: 19.5 percent of surveyed firms sourced 0 percent of supplies from domestic suppliers, 73.7 percent of surveyed firms sourced 0 percent of supplies from foreign subsidiaries, and 3 percent of surveyed firms sourced 0 percent of supplies from abroad and so on.
Source: author's 2010 company questionnaire.

TABLE 3.4 *Percentage share of surveyed automotive firms in Slovakia by ownership according to what share of their supplies they source from domestic firms, foreign subsidiaries and abroad*

Share of sourced supplies (%)	From domestic suppliers		From foreign subsidiaries		From abroad	
	Foreign subsidiaries (%)	Domestic firms (%)	Foreign subsidiaries (%)	Domestic firms (%)	Foreign subsidiaries (%)	Domestic firms (%)
0	25	14	69	78	0	6
1–24	55	23	22	12	2	33
25–49	8	17	6	4	11	6
50–74	11	23	3	1	25	32
75–99	2	19	0	4	52	22
100	0	3	0	0	11	1
Total	100	100	100	100	100	100

Note: N = 64 for foreign subsidiaries, N = 69 for domestic firms.
The meaning of the first line: 25 percent of foreign subsidiaries and 14 percent of domestic firms source 0 percent of their supplies from domestic suppliers and so on.
Source: author's 2010 company questionnaire.

large economies of scale (Phelps, 1993b), and the fact that some of the sourced components and materials are not available in Slovakia (46 percent). It is also common that buyers dictate to component makers where they have to buy parts

TABLE 3.5 *The share of the total value of supplies sourced by interviewed foreign subsidiaries in Slovakia*

The share of sourced supplies (%)	Total supplies from Slovakia		Supplies from domestic firms	
	No.	%	No.	%
0	9	33.3	17	63.0
0–5	7	25.9	5	18.5
5–10	4	14.8	3	11.1
10–50	7	25.9	2	7.4
Total	27	100.0	27	100.0

Source: author's 2011–2015 interviews.

and materials, which is almost invariably abroad. The low share of supplies bought in Slovakia by foreign subsidiaries could be further explained by two additional factors. The first is the short time since the original investment because the majority of foreign subsidiaries were established in Slovakia in the early 2000s. Supplier linkages might develop over time (UNCTAD, 2001), although the experience from older integrated peripheries, such as Portugal and Mexico, suggests that it is difficult to achieve (Veloso et al., 2000; Carrillo, 2004). Indeed, 63 percent of interviewed foreign subsidiaries argued that the volume and value of supplies from Slovakia slightly increased since the beginning of their production in Slovakia but almost invariably from other foreign subsidiaries and not from domestic firms. The second factor was related to the low competency of domestic suppliers, who were often unable to meet the quality and delivery requirements of foreign subsidiaries. An interview quote from a German supplier illustrates this point: "We were actively looking for domestic suppliers in Slovakia, but we could not find anybody. I don't honestly know why but I think it is because of no previous industrial history here" (interview, June 14, 2011).

Low or nonexistent capabilities of domestic firms in the particular supplier sector thus make it difficult for foreign subsidiaries to establish supplier linkages with domestic firms. A Spanish supplier has reiterated this situation in Slovakia: "If you have no experience in the sector, you are in a difficult position. We use plastic injected items, metallic clamps, items that are common in Western Europe but not here. There is no previous tradition here. We are actively looking for suppliers" (interview, June 20, 2011).

The overall low quantity of supplier linkages suggests that the spatiotemporal fix in the Slovak automotive industry generates excess profits mainly through cost minimization in foreign subsidiaries rather than through accessing and exploiting local capabilities. Low production costs are made possible not only because of low labor costs but also because of organizational and technological fixes, in which local capabilities and linkages with domestic firms are considered unimportant for profit generation by foreign investors. For example, follow sourcing makes it possible for the Slovakia-based car assembly factories of Volkswagen, Kia and PSA not to buy any supplies directly from domestic firms (interviews at Kia, Volkswagen and PSA Slovakia, June 14, 16, 20, 2011), which also saves the costs of establishing and maintaining supplier relationships with domestic suppliers. Modern logistical systems and transportation infrastructure allow for the cost-efficient imports of components from abroad to foreign subsidiaries clustered around assembly plants, exports of components assembled from imported materials in foreign subsidiaries and supplying just in time from custom-built supplier parks (Larsson, 2002; Pavlínek, 2016). The high dependence on imports and very limited linkages among foreign subsidiaries in Slovakia that are primarily integrated in externally organized GPNs (Table 3.4) are all signs of strong dependency on external TNCs, which points toward the assembly platforms type of the structural mode of coupling with GPNs.

   In the next step, I will concentrate on the mode of strategic coupling of domestic firms with automotive GPNs by analyzing the quality of supplier linkages between foreign subsidiaries and domestic firms based on the original data collected by my 2010 firm-level survey and 2011–2015 face-to-face interviews with company directors and managers in Slovakia.

3.7 THE QUALITY OF SUPPLIER LINKAGES

Integrated peripheries represent an example of spatiotemporal fix that allows automotive firms to acquire relative surplus value by locating in superior locations. Excess profits are acquired through significantly lower production costs that are mainly based on lower labor costs compared to the established locations in core regions. The quality of supplier linkages between foreign subsidiaries and domestic firms reflects the nature of spatiotemporal fix in integrated peripheries and the mode of strategic coupling of domestic firms into GPNs. It was evaluated by classifying linkages into developmental, dependent and detrimental, based on three criteria: the main reason for FDI and continuing production in Slovakia, R&D activities in domestic firms and foreign subsidiaries, and the nature of supplied components. Cost-cutting reasons for the investment and continuing production, such as low production costs or investment incentives, the absence of R&D in domestic firms and foreign subsidiaries, and the supply of simple standard components indicate the potential for the development of dependent linkages with domestic firms and their integration into GPNs as assembly platforms. Alternatively, the search for a skilled labor force and innovation capabilities of domestic firms, the existence of R&D activities, and the supply of complex components indicate the potential for developmental linkages and the integration of domestic firms into GPNs through international partnerships.

3.7.1 Reasons for Investment and Continuing Production

The evidence from Slovakia supports my argument that integrated peripheries represent an example of structural coupling of the assembly platform type in GPNs, in which cost-cutting reasons play the prominent role behind their articulation in GPNs. The lower-cost export-oriented production of core-based automotive firms in integrated peripheries helps maintain or improve their overall competitiveness and profitability.

The three most important reasons for investment in Slovakia cited by interviewed foreign subsidiaries are follow sourcing (44 percent of subsidiaries), cheap labor force (28 percent) and investment incentives (21 percent). All three are essentially cost-cutting reasons. Other factors, such as labor skills and manufacturing tradition, play a much less important role than is claimed (Jakubiak et al., 2008; Sario, 2016) because only one of twenty-seven interviewed foreign subsidiaries lists the manufacturing tradition and quality of labor force as one of its reasons for its investment in Slovakia. The three most important advantages of production in Slovakia for foreign firms identified by the interviews include low production costs, especially low labor costs (listed by 42 percent of firms that replied to the question), geographic proximity to the main customers (25 percent) and labor attitudes such as attitudes to work, willingness to learn and labor flexibility (21 percent). Low labor costs continue to be extremely important for foreign subsidiaries since two-thirds of them argued that the low cost of production was by far the most important strategic need of their parent company for the continuing production in Slovakia. As a director of a major French supplier succinctly put it when asked about the most important strategic need of his company in Slovakia, "Labor costs are as low as they can be" (interview, June 23, 2011). However, rapid growth based on large inflows of automotive FDI has absorbed labor surpluses and led to wage increases in Slovakia, which has cut into relative surplus value. In response, some foreign firms have started to look for new superior locations or new spatiotemporal fixes (Harvey, 2014) with lower wages, such as in Romania and Bulgaria, where the average personnel costs in the automotive industry were 50 percent and 73 percent lower than in Slovakia in 2014 (Eurostat, 2016b).

This competition from potentially lower-cost locations increases the relentless cost-cutting pressure in existing locations, which translates into poor labor conditions for workers in integrated peripheries. Wages are low and the pace of work is high, especially in the supplier industry. At the same time, the risk of decoupling and relocation is high, especially in the most labor-intensive production, such as the assembly of cable harnesses (Pavlínek, 2015a). For example, Delphi relocated the production of cable harnesses, which was launched in 2002 and used to employ 2,800 workers in the town of Senica, to Romania, Tunisia and Turkey. The relocation took place in several stages in spite of the low wages paid to Slovak workers (€500 per month gross) and its last phase started just after the ten-year tax holiday expired in 2012 (interview,

June 13, 2011) (Pavlínek, 2017a). However, lower wages elsewhere are not the only threat for decoupling and relocation. Follow sourcing is another one. A British supplier argues as follows.

Yes, we are thinking about relocating to Bosnia and Herzegovina because one of our customers has already relocated four factories there from Germany. Another one is moving to [North] Macedonia. We will have to follow them. Additionally, a monthly wage of a university educated worker is €400 there, which is less than half of what it is here. (Interview, September 18, 2013)

Wages of car assembly workers are generally higher than in the supplier sector and the risk of relocation is lower because of high sunk costs. However, the average net monthly salary of assembly workers was only about €500 at PSA in 2015, with no salary increase in 2013 and 2014. One worker complained in 2015: "[My salary] is not enough to pay for basic needs. I have worked here for nine years and while the pace of work is much higher now than when I started, my salary keeps going down" (NC, 2015). Another assembly worker complained that the number of workers in his unit was reduced from thirty to twenty-four in the last two years while the output and pace of work increased and wages remained the same (NC, 2015). PSA agreed to increase salaries by €70 per month only after six months of negotiations with labor unions, workers' demonstrations and under the threat of an imminent worker strike in June 2015. This indicates high levels of exploitation and only limited local value capture in the form of wages from the car industry operations in integrated peripheries. A six-day strike over wages at Volkswagen Slovakia in 2017 won a 14-percent salary increase over the period 2017–2018 and indicated the growing resistance to working conditions and low wages in assembly factories in Slovakia. Although, while individual factory strikes might be successful in achieving wage increases, low wages compared to core areas of the automotive industry will continue to be the basic precondition for the future development and operation of the automotive industry in integrated peripheries.

The interviews thus suggest that cost-cutting reasons were behind the vast majority of investment decisions by foreign suppliers to enter Slovakia and that they are the basic precondition for the continuing production there. This points toward the potential of establishing predominantly dependent (if any) linkages with domestic firms and their integration into automotive GPNs through the structural mode of strategic coupling as simple assembly platforms.

3.7.2   Firm-Level Research and Development

The location and organization of industrial R&D is strongly related to corporate hierarchy, in which R&D tends to be spatially highly concentrated in core regions. Peripheral regions are generally typified by the low share of R&D activities that predominantly involve the technical support of production and low-level development activities at the plant level (Malecki, 1980; Howells, 1990). We might therefore expect limited automotive R&D in integrated peripheries (Pavlínek, 2012), since these regions are integrated into GPNs as assembly platforms through FDI in routine manufacturing, although depending on the transfer of R&D from core regions (Yeung, 2009; Coe and Yeung, 2015). The potential for learning and knowledge transfer through supplier linkages is greatly enhanced when foreign firms engage in R&D activities in host regions (Giroud, 2012). At the same time, R&D in domestic firms increases their absorptive capacity and, therefore, their capabilities to learn from foreign firms (Cohen and Levinthal, 1989). In this context, firm-level R&D in both foreign subsidiaries and domestic firms would suggest the potential for developmental linkages and points toward international partnerships. Alternatively, the absence of R&D activities indicates the potential for dependent linkages in the assembly platforms type of structural couplings with GPNs.

My research found very limited R&D activities in foreign subsidiaries in Slovakia, which is supported by Eurostat data (Eurostat, 2016b) and also among domestic firms, suggesting their low absorptive capacity and therefore a low ability to benefit from potential linkages. The interviews revealed that despite the advantage of low R&D labor costs, the lack of skilled R&D labor represents the biggest obstacle for establishing sizeable R&D activities. A French supplier that is operating one of the largest automotive R&D centers in Slovakia argues as follows.

The most important reason for the establishment of the R&D center here was to use low labor costs to decrease the R&D costs in France and Germany. However, we are all struggling with technical competencies and knowledge of university graduates. There is lack of technical students, engineers. I have been trying to find fresh graduates that we could train, and I can't find them. (Interview, June 23, 2011)

Eighty-six percent of the surveyed and 82 percent of the interviewed foreign subsidiaries, and 77 percent of the surveyed and 65 percent of the interviewed domestic firms conduct no R&D activities in Slovakia. Those that do typically engage in the technical support of production and talked about *limited R&D, small-scale R&D* with very few workers, usually one or two. Although domestic suppliers have the advantage of lower costs and geographic proximity, they face significant barriers to the development of R&D, such as low competencies and the problems of cultural and relational distance from foreign subsidiaries (Schmitt and Van Biesebroeck, 2013). Both the survey and interview data thus suggest the low contribution of R&D activities of foreign subsidiaries to the potential learning and knowledge transfer to domestic firms, and the low absorptive capacity of domestic firms to benefit from these potential transfers. This points to the dependent rather than developmental nature of the vast majority of linkages in the automotive industry in Slovakia, which underlines its integration into GPNs through the assembly platform type of structural couplings.

3.7.3　The Nature of Components Supplied by Domestic Firms

In order to better understand the nature of linkages between foreign subsidiaries and domestic firms, I classified the surveyed domestic firms based on the nature of their products into standard and niche suppliers. Standard suppliers are typically captive suppliers who supply simple components through dependent supplier linkages to either higher-tier foreign subsidiaries in Slovakia or abroad. Niche-market domestic suppliers do not supply the high-volume car production but typically engage in the low-volume production of niche-market products in the automotive industry. Only 35 percent of the surveyed and 47 percent of the interviewed domestic firms were classified as being involved in standard production, while the remaining ones were classified as niche-market producers. I have also classified the produced components and the nature of production of domestic firms into three categories: simple, more advanced/complex and relatively complex. Among standard domestic suppliers, 87 percent of surveyed firms supplied simple components, 13 percent more advanced/complex components, and none supplied relatively complex components.

The survey data suggest that the majority of domestic automotive industry firms operate at the margins of the high-volume passenger car industry if they are integrated at all, because they do not supply the high-volume production of cars in Slovakia. This suggests the presence of dependent rather than developmental linkages. The weak integration of domestic firms in the high-volume passenger car industry partially explains the weak supplier linkages between domestic firms and foreign subsidiaries, and further reiterates that the Slovak automotive industry is integrated into GPNs predominantly through external actors (foreign subsidiaries), which is typical of the structural mode of coupling into GPNs.

3.7.4　The Classification of Linkages into Dependent, Developmental and Detrimental

I evaluated the quality of supplier linkages between foreign subsidiaries and domestic firms using both the interview and survey data. Backward supplier linkages of foreign subsidiaries with domestic firms and forward supplier linkages of domestic firms with foreign subsidiaries were evaluated separately. First, I analyzed the interview data. For the interviewed foreign subsidiaries, I combined data on the nature of the supplied components and materials by domestic firms; whether their investment was driven primarily by cost savings; the perceived advantages of production in Slovakia; and whether they conduct R&D in Slovakia. Sixty-three percent of the interviewed subsidiaries (seventeen firms) developed no supplier linkages in Slovakia. Each of the remaining ten firms was given one point for investment reasons unrelated to cost-cutting, such as skilled labor or industrial tradition. If a foreign subsidiary listed more than one

TABLE 3.6 *The classification of linkages of the interviewed foreign subsidiaries and domestic firms*

	Foreign subsidiaries		Domestic firms	
	No	%	No	%
No linkages	17	63	13	59
Dependent linkages	10	37	9	41
Developmental linkages	0	0	0	0
Total	27	100	22	100

Note: Foreign subsidiaries refer to the purchase of supplies from domestic firms (backward linkages), domestic firms refer to selling supplies to foreign subsidiaries (forward linkages).
Source: author's 2011–2015 interviews.

reason for investing in Slovakia, points were awarded proportionally. Advantages of production in Slovakia were evaluated the same way. One point was given for buying more advanced parts or components from domestic suppliers, zero points were given for simple components. Finally, firms were given one point if they employed any R&D workers, zero points if they had no R&D workers. The average point value of these four numbers was calculated for each firm. A score higher than 0.5 indicates developmental linkages and a score of 0.5 and less indicates dependent linkages. No firm had a score higher than 0.3. Therefore, all supplier linkages of these ten foreign subsidiaries with domestic firms were ranked as dependent and no interviewed foreign subsidiary has developed developmental linkages with domestic suppliers (Table 3.6).

For the interviewed domestic suppliers, I combined information about the nature of the supplied components, whether the perceived competitive advantage of domestic firms is mainly cost- or technology- and skill-driven, whether domestic firms received any help and learned anything new from foreign subsidiaries, and the existence and extent of their R&D activities. Fifty-nine percent of the interviewed domestic firms (thirteen) had no linkages with foreign subsidiaries. In order to determine the nature of the linkages, the remaining nine firms were given a point each for not making simple products, having other than a low-cost competitive advantage, having R&D workers, being helped before starting to supply components and learning something new from foreign subsidiaries. As in the case of foreign subsidiaries, the average point value was calculated for each firm with a score higher than 0.5, indicating developmental linkages, while a score of 0.5 and less indicated dependent linkages. No firm achieved a higher score than 0.4. Therefore, the linkages of all nine interviewed domestic firms with foreign subsidiaries were ranked as dependent (Table 3.6).

The survey data were not as detailed as the interview data, and I could only use the nature of the supplied components and R&D employment as proxy measures of developmental and dependent linkages. Sixty-four foreign subsidiaries were asked to list five to seven key suppliers and only nine named a domestic firm as one of these key suppliers. All these nine listed domestic suppliers supplied simple components. In terms of R&D, only one foreign subsidiary sourcing from domestic firms employed R&D workers in Slovakia. Two foreign subsidiaries that accounted for 91 percent of R&D workers of all surveyed subsidiaries had no supplier linkages in Slovakia. The remaining sixty-two foreign subsidiaries together employed forty-nine R&D workers, with one accounting for half. These data therefore strongly point toward dependent linkages between foreign subsidiaries and domestic firms in those rare cases when linkages exist.

Surveyed firms were also asked to list their most important customers and supplied components, which allowed me to identify domestic firms that supply foreign subsidiaries in Slovakia. Out of sixty-seven surveyed domestic firms, I identified only seventeen firms that supplied materials and components to foreign subsidiaries in Slovakia, although only four supplied the mass production of cars. Once again, these firms supplied simple components. Only two firms employed any R&D workers. This also suggests the existence of dependent linkages between domestic firms and foreign subsidiaries. Both the interview and survey data thus confirmed the overwhelmingly dependent linkages between domestic firms and foreign subsidiaries in the assembly platform type of structural mode of coupling into GPNs.

Half of interviewed domestic firms experienced negative regional development outcomes of the integration into automotive GPNs in the form of negative direct spillovers (Pavlínek and Žížalová, 2016), which are the outcome of what I call detrimental linkages that are another sign of structural couplings. Detrimental linkages were felt mainly in the labor market, since the competition for especially skilled labor increased, following the investment by foreign firms. More than half of interviewed domestic firms (52 percent) lost workers to foreign subsidiaries and 59 percent argued that it became more difficult for them to hire workers after the investment by foreign firms in Slovakia. Only half of the interviewed domestic firms (ten) answered the question about salaries and half of those were forced to increase salaries because of competition from foreign subsidiaries in order to attract workers or maintain the existing ones. The interviews with domestic firms also suggest that there has been a negligible transfer of knowledge and skills through workers trained in foreign subsidiaries to domestic firms. Only 14 percent of the interviewed domestic firms hired workers who previously worked for foreign subsidiaries and only 5 percent (one firm) agreed that those workers brought with them knowledge that was useful. One manager of a domestic firm argued that: "No, workers formerly working for foreign subsidiaries did not bring anything new to our firm. Foreign subsidiaries concentrate on simple assembly. Workers learn nothing there that could be used in a more complex production. Our firm is small, and workers here need to be more flexible and know more than just a single task" (interview, May 21, 2015).

This quote suggests that instead of transferring skills through FDI, the assembly platform type of structural couplings might lead to the deskilling of the local labor force and negative long-term regional development effects in host regions.

Overall, in those cases where linkages between foreign subsidiaries and domestic firms exist, the majority of them are either dependent or detrimental, while developmental linkages are virtually absent, underscoring the structural mode of strategic coupling of integrated peripheries into GPNs.

3.8 CONCLUSION

In this chapter, I first developed the spatial concept of integrated peripheries of core-based macro-regional production networks and then set out to analyze the regional development effects of the rapid growth of the automotive industry in these integrated peripheries. I conceptualized this growth by drawing on Harvey's (2014) notion of spatiotemporal fix in the context of the dynamics of capitalist uneven development. Faced with rising production costs and declining profitability in Western Europe and the USA, core-based automotive firms have developed automotive production in cheaper and, therefore, more profitable areas in integrated peripheries. At the regional scale, I employed the GPN approach and its concept of strategic coupling in order to conceptualize the mode of articulation of integrated peripheries into transnational production networks and its regional development outcomes. I showed that integrated peripheries were articulated into automotive industry GPNs through structural couplings, the least advantageous and dependent mode of integration into GPNs for countries and regions. The empirical analysis of this mode of integration focused on supplier linkages in Slovakia, which allowed me to examine the implications of the assembly platform type of structural couplings for long-term regional economic development in integrated peripheries because the quality and quantity FDI linkages are crucial for the potential diffusion of technology and knowledge in host regions through FDI. For this purpose, I have developed a methodology to evaluate the quality of supplier linkages between foreign subsidiaries and domestic firms.

The case study of Slovakia revealed only tenuous and predominantly dependent linkages of foreign subsidiaries with domestic firms and weakly developed linkages among foreign subsidiaries, with the exception of backward supplier linkages of assembly firms with their most important foreign-owned suppliers. It shows that Slovakia has been integrated into automotive GPNs mainly through sets of mostly unconnected foreign subsidiaries that operate as assembly platforms vertically integrated into externally organized GPNs and are weakly embedded in the Slovak economy. The nature of this spatiotemporal fix reflects the contemporary spatial organization and operation of the automotive industry, which is based on follow and global sourcing. My analysis, together with other existing evidence, strongly suggests that predominantly dependent (if any) linkages between foreign subsidiaries and domestic firms tend to develop in integrated peripheries (Ellingstad, 1997; Carrillo, 2004; Contreras et al., 2012; Pavlínek and Žížalová, 2016; Castillo and de Vries, 2018), which is typical of the assembly platform type of structural couplings with GPNs. Along with the weak development of higher-value-added functions in foreign subsidiaries (Pavlínek, 2016; Pavlínek and Ženka, 2016), the weak, dependent and also detrimental linkages contribute to limited knowledge transfer from FDI to domestic economies and the truncated nature of automotive FDI in integrated peripheries.

Together with capital, technological, know-how and strategic decision-making dependency, the results of this study thus highlight the dependent nature of the automotive industry development in integrated peripheries based on their structural couplings with GPNs. This suggests that the overwhelming dependency on foreign capital is the underlying structural feature of the automotive industry in integrated peripheries. The similarity of my findings with the conclusions of earlier truncation (Britton, 1980) and branch plant literature (Watts, 1981) indicates that the underlying structural features and effects of industrial FDI in peripheral regions remain little changed despite the changing technological and organizational nature of capitalism. The high degree of dependency on foreign capital, technology and know-how, along with low domestic capabilities and limited value that is captured from the automotive industry in integrated peripheries, thus represent major threats to future successful economic development in these regions. Since spatiotemporal fixes and strategic couplings are space- and time-contingent, the rapidly growing output, exports and, in some cases, GDP will not last in integrated peripheries. More importantly, the overall benefits of the articulation into automotive industry GPNs through structural couplings have been limited, if not negative, for workers in integrated peripheries. These conclusions undermine the optimistic expectations of sustainable regional development outcomes based on the articulation of regions and countries in global value chains (UNCTAD, 2013) and call for more research into how the integration of countries and regions into externally organized GPNs through FDI might contribute to the perpetuation of uneven development, one of the potential *dark sides* of strategic coupling (Coe and Hess, 2011).

With power and control concentrated in the hands of core-based assemblers and global suppliers that relegate the vast majority of domestic suppliers in integrated peripheries to an inferior and unfavorable position (Veloso et al., 2000; Pavlínek and Žížalová, 2016), the quantity and quality of supplier linkages will likely continue to be low in the foreseeable future. This situation will limit the long-term regional development potential of FDI-driven integration into GPNs and cement the peripheral and dependent position of integrated peripheries in the automotive industry's international division of labor for years to come.

4

Restructuring and Internationalization of the European Automotive Industry

4.1 INTRODUCTION

Although the automotive industry is one of the most globalized industries (Dicken, 2015) because of the presence and production of large assemblers and leading (global) suppliers in all major markets, its geographic structure is based on functionally integrated macro-regional production networks and regional or local clusters of production (Frigant and Lung, 2002; Carrillo et al., 2004; Sturgeon et al., 2008). The main advantage of macro-regional integration is the more efficient territorial division of labor through macro-regional specialization, which allows for greater scale economies (Freyssenet and Lung, 2004). Free trade and reduced transportation costs allow firms to better exploit the uneven distribution of factors of production and socially constructed endowments through the more fine-grained territorial division of labor, which leads to greater territorial specialization (Harvey, 2005b).

Despite major shifts in the global geography of the automotive industry (Sturgeon and Van Biesebroeck, 2011; Dicken, 2015), Europe continues to be one of the world's main production regions by accounting for 19 percent of global vehicle production and 22 percent of total passenger car output in 2022 (OICA, 2023). In 2020, the narrowly defined automotive industry (NACE 29) employed 2.6 million workers in Europe directly (excluding Russia, Belarus, Ukraine and Turkey) (Eurostat, 2023c). Including indirect employment, the European Union automotive industry employed almost 13 million workers (ACEA, 2023a). This makes the automotive sector one of the crucial manufacturing industries in the European Union, especially when also considering its positive trade balance (€101.8 billion in 2022) and large spending on research and development (€59.1 billion in 2021) (ACEA, 2023a). Since the 1990s, the geographic distribution of the European automotive industry has been affected by changes in its organization and production strategies (Frigant and Lung, 2002; Sturgeon et al., 2008), the economic and political liberalization in Eastern Europe (Lung, 2004) and its economic integration into the European Union (Frigant and Miollan, 2014). These changes have had significant effects on employment and regional development across Europe and in adjacent automotive industry regions, such as in Turkey and Morocco (Layan and Lung, 2007; Jürgens and Krzywdzinski, 2009a; Benabdejlil et al., 2016; Pavlínek, 2017a).

This chapter seeks to contribute to the analyses of the European automotive industry by examining job creation and job losses by large automotive firms in the European Union plus Norway between 2005 and 2016 and by investigating the investment and location decisions of foreign automotive companies in Eastern Europe. It aims to improve our understanding of the territorial development of the automotive industry through its expansion into peripheral regions adjacent to core areas and their integration into macro-regional production networks. I address five research questions. First, how can we conceptualize the changing geography of the European automotive industry? Second, what was the geography of job creation and job loss in the European Union plus Norway automotive industry between 2005 and 2016? Third, what were the underlying reasons behind the geography of job creation and job loss? Fourth, what kind of firms were driving job creation and job loss in terms of their ownership (domestic or foreign) and nationality? Fifth, what were the most important types of restructuring events resulting in job creation and job loss? I analyze firm-level data on job creation and job loss in the European Union countries plus Norway, which also allows me to evaluate the degree of internationalization of the European automotive industry by examining the role of foreign and domestic firms in these processes. I also draw on ninety-one interviews with foreign automotive industry subsidiaries in Czechia and Slovakia in order to identify the most important reasons behind the investment and location decisions of foreign automotive firms to expand production into Eastern Europe.

In order to conceptualize the geographic expansion and restructuring of the European automotive industry, I continue to draw on Harvey's theory of uneven development and spatiotemporal fix (Harvey, 1982; 2001; 2005b; 2010; 2014), which allows me to further develop the spatial concept of integrated peripheries as a particular form of spatiotemporal fix in the contemporary automotive industry (see Chapter 3). The dynamic and relational view of the uneven development of the European automotive industry helps me understand uneven geographic trends in job creation and job loss. I argue that large national differences in labor costs and corporate taxes along with other cost-cutting reasons played an important role in the geographic restructuring of the European automotive industry between 2005 and 2016. Lower production costs in integrated peripheries created excess profit opportunities for automotive firms, which responded by locating new production to these regions and, in the process, by restructuring their operations in existing automotive industry locations in Western Europe.

I begin with a conceptual discussion of the uneven development of the European automotive industry through the formation of spatiotemporal fixes. I show how this process of territorial expansion integrates peripheral areas into macro-regional production networks while, at the same time, triggering restructuring in existing locations. I also briefly review the development of integrated peripheries in the European automotive industry. Second, I explain the data and methodology employed in the empirical analysis. Third, I analyze the 2005–2016 job creation and job loss in the European Union plus Norway automotive industry and, based on company interviews in Czechia and Slovakia, I investigate the reasons for the investment and location behavior of foreign firms in the Eastern European integrated periphery. Fourth, I examine job creation and job loss in the European Union plus Norway automotive industry by the nationality of the firms, ownership and restructuring events. Finally, I summarize and evaluate the results in the Conclusion.

4.2 SPATIOTEMPORAL FIXES IN THE AUTOMOTIVE INDUSTRY

Although the reasons for the location decisions of automotive firms and the changing geography of the automotive industry are complex and cannot be reduced to one or two factors (Layan, 2006; Pries and Dehnen, 2009), they are ultimately tied to profit-seeking behavior. Despite the pursuit of different profit strategies by automotive firms (Boyer and Freyssenet, 2002), all firms need to keep production costs under control in order to be profitable. Production costs include the costs of factors of production, costs of various material and nonmaterial inputs in production, R&D costs, administrative costs, and transportation and logistics costs. It is easier for firms to squeeze labor costs than the costs of other factors of production. Historically, capitalist firms have controlled labor costs through technological and organizational innovations and the location of production in areas with surplus labor and low wages (Harvey, 1982). One hundred years ago, transportation costs were considered the most important location factor for industries (Weber, 1929). However, as the cost of transport declined by 90 percent during the twentieth century (Glaeser and Kohlhase, 2004) and the mobility of capital increased through deregulation (Freyssenet et al., 2003a), the relative importance of labor costs for the location behavior of firms increased. Large geographic differences in labor costs, labor availability and other labor characteristics, such as labor skills, productivity, motivation, militancy, the degree of unionization, and national labor legislation, affect the location behavior of firms. The average personnel costs per employee in the automotive industry were more than five times higher in Germany than in neighboring Poland and four times higher than in Czechia between 2005 and 2016. Although the average apparent labor productivity was three times higher in Germany than in Poland and two and a half times higher than in Czechia, the average wage-adjusted labor productivity was 41 percent higher in Poland and 64 percent higher in Czechia than in Germany (Eurostat,

2018). During the same period, the average corporate tax rate was 67 percent higher in Germany than in Poland and 54 percent higher than in Czechia (KPMG, 2017). In the absence of trade barriers and with relatively low transportation costs, such differences in labor costs, corporate taxes and other costs, such as land and infrastructure, affect the spatial distribution of production in the long run. In the words of Harvey (2010: 164): "Competition forces individual capitalists and corporations to seek out better places to produce, just as they are forced to seek out superior technologies. As new locations with lower costs become available, so capitalists under the gun of competition have to respond by moving, *if they can*" (emphasis added).

Similarly, Smith (2008 [1984]: 197) argues: "Capital moves to where the rate of profit is highest (or at least high)." In other words, capitalist firms are constantly searching for "spatiotemporal fixes" for their declining profitability that will yield higher profits by locating production to areas with labor surplus and lower wages (Harvey, 2014). Production costs in particular regions can also be lowered by other factors, such as weakly organized labor (Bohle and Greskovits, 2006; Drahokoupil and Myant, 2017), while growth and profit opportunities can be enhanced by the existence of various regional assets, such as particular labor skills, infrastructure, markets, technology, agglomeration economies, natural resources and the institutional environment (Coe et al., 2004; MacKinnon, 2012).

The key point is that excess profit opportunities do not last, as competing firms want to benefit from the same locational advantages by locating their production in the same or similar high-profit areas (Harvey, 1982; Domański and Lung, 2009). The growth, which is based on the influx of profit-seeking capital, depletes labor surplus, which pushes wages up as competition over workers intensifies (Smith, 2008 [1984]), despite strong efforts of firms to minimize wage increases and keep them as low as possible (Freyssenet and Lung, 2000). Ultimately, labor shortages and rising wages decrease the rate of profit and compel some firms to look for new locations with surplus labor and lower wages that can be integrated into macro-regional production networks for future growth and excess profit opportunities. As argued in Chapter 3, spatiotemporal fix is, therefore, only a temporary solution to the problem of profitability and firms are compelled to continue their relentless search for new spatiotemporal fixes in order to increase or at least maintain their rate of profit. This spatial profit-seeking strategy is illustrated in the empirical section of this chapter and supported by other evidence, such as the behavior of the largest tier-one automotive suppliers in Europe who addressed their persistent profitability problems by moving production to lower-cost countries in the late 1990s and 2000s (Jürgens and Krzywdzinski, 2008; Frigant, 2009; Frigant and Layan, 2009). Labor-intensive activities are especially susceptible to variations in labor costs and labor availability and are more likely to seek low-cost locations (Pavlínek, 2015a; 2018). The latest new peripheral areas with excess profit opportunities that saw a significant increase in the influx of surplus capital in the automotive industry include Serbia (average gross salary €368 a month in 2015), Bulgaria (€451), North Macedonia (€521), Moldova (€220) and Morocco (less than €400) (MIEPO, 2017).

The spatial flexibility of capital described by the theory of spatiotemporal fix coexists with the spatial fixity of capital in existing locations that can, to a large extent, be explained by various types of sunk costs (Clark and Wrigley, 1995). High accumulated and exit sunk costs in existing locations and high set-up sunk costs in new locations are important reasons for the continuing commitment of firms to existing locations, even though there might be potentially superior locations elsewhere. Firms that cannot relocate because of high sunk costs therefore employ various in-situ restructuring strategies in order to remain competitive and profitable, such as downsizing, technological change, automation, outsourcing, upgrading, rationalization and corporate reorganization, which may or may not involve labor-shedding (Clark and Wrigley, 1997). Overall, when measured by job creation and job loss, in-situ restructuring plays a much more important role than locational shifts in the restructuring of the European automotive industry, as shown in the empirical section of this chapter.

4.2.1 Geographic Restructuring through Spatiotemporal Fixes in Integrated Peripheries

As firms continue to search for new spatiotemporal fixes, the areas of production expand over time and growth tends to bounce from region to region, which leads to uneven geographical development (Harvey, 1982). The new peripheral automotive production regions that were integrated into core-based macro-regional production networks through "peripheral integration" (Lung, 2000; Pavlínek, 2002d) were originally labeled as "growth-peripheries" (Storper and Walker, 1989; Lagendijk, 1995a), "peripheries of large existing market areas" (Sturgeon and Florida, 2000) and "integrated peripheral markets" (Humphrey et al., 2000), and later conceptualized as "integrated peripheries" (Pavlínek, 2018). As a particular form of the spatiotemporal fix, integrated peripheries are dynamic regions of growth and development within macro-regional production networks that are typified by the features identified in Chapter 3: significantly lower wages than in traditional core regions of the automotive industry; a sizeable labor surplus at the initial stages of growth; geographic proximity to large and lucrative markets that lowers transport costs and is further enhanced by the development of modern transport infrastructure; membership in regional trade agreements or preferential trading arrangements that assure tariff-free access to large and lucrative markets; a high degree of foreign ownership and control through FDI; strongly export-oriented production of standardized cars, niche-market vehicles and generic automotive components; limited development of high-value-added and strategic functions, such as R&D;

FDI-friendly state policies that are actively attracting automotive FDI through low corporate taxes and generous investment incentives; weak labor unions, more liberal labor codes and more flexible labor practices compared to the automotive industry core countries; an underdeveloped domestic automotive industry; and the integration into macro-regional production networks as assembly platforms through predominantly dependent supplier linkages.

However, as Harvey (1982, 2014) reminds us, growth and excess profits in new areas are at least partially gained at the expense of devaluation in less profitable places that are affected by lower growth, which might lead to disinvestment and eventually factory closures or relocations. Growth in new locations has several potential effects on existing locations. First, despite lower levels of investment and higher wages, existing locations may maintain their production and employment for a number of reasons, especially due to high sunk costs (Clark and Wrigley, 1995; 1997) and geographic proximity to suppliers and markets (Frigant and Lung, 2002; South and Kim, 2019). New production capacity in new, more profitable locations, which is developed in order to expand production and meet the growing demand for cars in existing and new markets, contributes to the growth and higher profits of the corporation as a whole. For example, new assembly factories that were built in integrated peripheries to satisfy the growing demand for new cars in Europe (Lagendijk, 1995a; Layan and Lung, 2004) contributed to the growth and profitability of Western European automakers.

Second, investment in new locations may affect existing locations through the more fine-grained division of labor and greater territorial specialization within a particular corporate production network because of the relocation of the generic, labor-intensive and less profitable production, which does not require proximity to other activities, to new lower-cost locations, while the more profitable, less labor-intensive production requiring greater skills and the one requiring proximity to other firms is maintained in existing locations (Frigant and Layan, 2009). The more efficient territorial division of labor through such complementary specialization (Kurz and Wittke, 1998) will likely increase the overall corporate profits. It may also increase wage levels in existing locations because of their increased specialization in higher-value-added activities but often at the expense of job losses as the labor-intensive production is relocated to new places. However, these job losses may be at least partially compensated by new jobs created through upgrading in existing locations (Jürgens and Krzywdzinski, 2008; 2009a). The increased production of luxury cars and a simultaneous decrease in the assembly of small cars in Germany, because of its partial relocation to integrated peripheries after 1990, is an example of this strategy (Krzywdzinski, 2014). By 2010, the share of small and compact cars produced abroad reached 67 percent for German and 72 percent for French automakers, while the assembly of 93 percent of the upper-medium and 96 percent of luxury cars took place in Germany (Danyluk, 2018).

Third, existing locations may be negatively affected by factory closures as the entire production is relocated to new lower-cost locations, although this is the least likely scenario (Dicken, 2015). Lower-tier suppliers engaged in the most labor-intensive production of generic components, which does not require specific labor skills and is the most sensitive to labor costs, such as the assembly of cable harnesses, are most likely to relocate their entire production when wages increase in existing locations (Pavlínek, 2015a). For example, between 2001 and 2006, Valeo, a large French component supplier, closed fifty-nine factories and sold twenty-six, while opening twenty-nine new factories and acquiring an additional thirteen in its effort to regain profitability (Frigant and Layan, 2009).

The closure and relocation of large assembly factories is much less likely because of very high sunk costs. Still, a number of older assembly factories, that have lower sunk costs because they are more depreciated and are more expensive to run than new factories, have been closed in Western Europe since the early 1990s, while new ones were opened in Eastern Europe (Lung, 2004; Jacobs, 2017; Pavlínek, 2017a). Because of domestic political pressures, potential strikes and adverse publicity in their home markets, lead firms are more likely to close assembly factories in foreign locations than in their home countries (Revill, 2008), which makes the foreign-owned factories in older integrated peripheries more vulnerable to plant closure than domestic assembly plants in core regions of Western Europe.

The integration of new peripheries into macro-regional production networks therefore also involves the spatial reorganization of the automotive industry in core areas and older integrated peripheries, such as Belgium and Spain (Bilbao-Ubillos and Camino-Beldarrain, 2008; Lampón et al., 2015), and it leads to increased territorial specialization based on the finer macro-regional division of labor (Frigant and Layan, 2009; Jürgens and Krzywdzinski, 2009a; Pries and Dehnen, 2009). Automotive firms have also used relocation or the threat of relocation to lower-cost regions, along with inter-place competition between factories in core and peripheral regions, to keep wage increases and rising production costs under control in the existing locations (Freyssenet and Lung, 2000; Phelps and Fuller, 2000; Lung, 2004; Layan, 2006).

4.2.2 Technological, Organizational and Institutional Fixes in Integrated Peripheries

The basic features of integrated peripheries suggest that their development and integration into existing automotive production networks depend on various technological, organizational and institutional preconditions or fixes (Harvey, 2010; Jessop, 2013) (Table 4.1). The search for excess profits through location to superior locations is not independent of the search for excess profits through technological change and superior organizational forms (Harvey, 1982; 2005b) as vehicle assembly firms and component suppliers build state-of-the-art factories and experiment with new production and organization strategies in integrated peripheries (Frigant and Lung, 2002; Pavlínek, 2002d; Layan, 2006;

TABLE 4.1 *The basic elements of the spatiotemporal fix and conjoining organizational, technological and institutional fixes in the automotive industry of integrated peripheries*

Spatiotemporal fix	Low labor costs
	Sizeable labor surplus
	Weakly organized labor
	Geographic proximity to large markets
	Membership in regional trade agreements or preferential trading arrangements
Organizational fix	Redefined carmaker/supplier relationships
	Internationalization through global and follow sourcing
	Modularization
	Tiering of the supplier base
	Foreign ownership and control
Technological fix	New transportation and communication technologies
	New logistical systems
	Modern transportation infrastructure
Institutional fix	Local content requirements
	Low corporate taxes
	Liberal FDI policies
	Strong investment incentives
	Intense state competition over FDI
	Weak labor legislation
	Local and regional FDI coalitions

Source: author.

Frigant and Layan, 2009). A technological fix also allows for the integration of new peripheries into macro-regional production networks through new transportation technologies and logistical systems (Kaneko and Nojiri, 2008; Coe, 2014; Danyluk, 2018), which is made possible by the development of modern transportation infrastructure, such as highways, high-speed rail and sea ports. Modern transportation technologies and logistical systems increase the spatial range over which materials, components and finished vehicles move efficiently by taking less time and at lower cost.

These technological changes have been one of the preconditions for organizational fixes in the form of the reorganization from nationally based automotive industries into transnational production networks that depend on efficient global sourcing (Freyssenet and Lung, 2000; Kleinert, 2003), follow sourcing (Frigant, 2007), just-in-time and in-sequence delivery of preassembled modules (Frigant and Layan, 2009), imports of components for assembly in integrated peripheries, and exports of finished vehicles and components from integrated peripheries to markets (Contreras et al., 2012; Pavlínek and Žížalová, 2016; Pavlínek, 2018). Organizational fixes have also involved the redefinition of relationships between assembly firms and their component suppliers (Lagendijk, 1997) with a closely related reduction in the number of suppliers (Freyssenet, 2009) and tiering of the supplier base (Humphrey and Memedovic, 2003; Frigant and Layan, 2009). These organizational fixes significantly increased the internationalization of the automotive industry (Sturgeon and Lester, 2004) and its geographic expansion into new production regions, including integrated peripheries (Humphrey et al., 2000).

An institutional fix creates the necessary preconditions for the free international movement of commodities and capital, including the flow of surplus capital to integrated peripheries in the form of FDI (Pavlínek, 2017a), and the flow of profits and dividends back to the home economies of foreign investors (Pavlínek and Ženka, 2016) (Chapter 6). It operates at multiple geographic scales: at the global scale in the form of the International Monetary Fund and World Trade Organization policies supporting FDI and international trade liberalization; at the macro-regional scale in the form of free-trade agreements, local content requirements and regulations limiting the extent of state support for FDI projects within macro-regional trade blocs such as the European Union (Sadler, 1995; Nicolini et al., 2017); at the national scale in the form of state FDI policies and the willingness of states to compete over FDI with other states (Pavlínek, 2016); and at the regional and local scales in the form of local and regional growth coalitions organized in order to attract and support particular FDI projects (Harvey, 2005b; Phelps and Wood, 2006; Drahokoupil, 2009).

4.2.3 Integrated Peripheries in the European Automotive Industry

Integrated peripheries represent examples of spatiotemporal fixes that developed through the geographic expansion of production into lower-cost areas adjacent to higher-cost regions. The European automotive industry has gradually expanded from its original core areas in Western Europe by integrating peripheral regions into the core-based macro-regional production networks since the 1960s. The automotive industry first expanded into peripheral regions within individual countries, such as expansion from the Paris region along the Seine river and into upper Normandy and Lorraine in France (Oberhauser, 1987), from northern to southern Italy (Hudson and Schamp, 1995b) and from Stuttgart to southern Bavaria, Bremen and Hannover–Braunschweig in Germany (Jones, 1993). The FDI-driven geographic expansion of high-volume production at the international scale started in Belgium with Ford Genk in 1964 and GM Antwerp in 1967, followed by Renault, Audi and Volvo. These greenfield investments in Belgium were driven by typical features of integrated peripheries, including the lowest corporate taxes in Western Europe at the time, relatively low labor costs, investment incentives and membership in the then European Economic Community (Jacobs, 2019). The expansion of integrated peripheries through FDI continued in Spain and Portugal since the 1980s (Ferrão and Vale, 1995; Lagendijk, 1995a; Jacobs, 2019), former East Germany, Czechia, Hungary, Poland, Slovakia and Slovenia since the early 1990s (Pavlínek, 2002d; Lung, 2004; Jacobs, 2017), Turkey and North Africa since the mid-1990s (Layan and Lung, 2007; Benabdejlil et al., 2016) and Southeastern Europe since the early 2000s (Pavlínek, 2017a).

The development of integrated peripheries has been closely tied to European integration (Layan and Lung, 2004) (an institutional fix) with each European Union enlargement and each European Union free-trade association agreement providing opportunities for the integration of new peripheries through tariff-free imports of capital, components and materials and exports of finished vehicles and components back to core areas of the automotive industry and markets in Western Europe. The absence of such institutional fixes was one of the reasons behind the failed attempts of West European automakers to develop the low-cost export-oriented production in Eastern Europe before 1989 (Gatejel, 2017). Almost immediately after the collapse of state socialism, foreign automakers were looking for new markets in Eastern Europe that, however, never lived up to expectations mainly because the region was flooded by millions of used cars from Western Europe (Hudson and Schamp, 1995a). More importantly, foreign firms were also looking for low-cost production sites (Nestorović, 1991; Sadler et al., 1993; Havas, 1997). The influx of automotive FDI in excess of €35 billion between 1990 and 2015 led to growth in output in Eastern Europe from 797,000 cars in 1990 to 4.1 million in 2017 (OICA, 2018), and the output of the supplier industry grew even faster with at least 1,212 supplier factories built by foreign investors between 1997 and 2016 (EY, 2010; ERM, 2017).

At the same time, the output of the automotive industry core regions in Western Europe kept rising until the early 2000s as they continued to attract investment because of skilled labor, well-developed supplier networks, proximity to the large market and corporate headquarters, R&D competencies, and also the strong socioeconomic embeddedness of automakers in home economies and their preferential treatment by home country governments (Lagendijk, 1997; Lung, 2004). The continuing growth of core regions can be further explained by technological and organizational changes in the automotive industry that tended to promote its increased spatial concentration (Frigant and Lung, 2002; Larsson, 2002; Lung and Volpato, 2002), scale economies and also by the general tendency of the spatial concentration and centralization of capital (Smith, 2008 [1984]).

The process of geographic expansion of the automotive industry through the development of new integrated peripheries is illustrated by regional production trends in Europe between 1991 and 2019 (Figure 4.1). The total production of cars, including the integrated periphery in Turkey and Morocco, increased by

24 percent from 14.2 to 17.6 million. While output almost tripled in integrated peripheries (from 2.8 to 8 million cars) and stagnated in Germany (at 4.7 million cars), it declined in the rest of Western Europe (from 6.7 to 4.9 million), which, in addition to Germany, also excludes the older integrated periphery of Spain and Portugal in Figure 4.1.

Although it has been argued that the integration of new peripheries has benefited the European automotive industry as a whole, including its traditional core countries because it increased the competitiveness of their cars (Pries and Dehnen, 2009), empirical evidence suggests the uneven impact of this integration on core countries. With the exception of Germany, and to a lesser extent an increasingly semiperipheral Britain, the traditional European automotive industry core countries suffered steep declines in domestic car production between 1991 and 2017, especially France (–49 percent), Italy (–56 percent), and Sweden (–24 percent), with the deepest declines during the 2008–2009 economic crisis (Figure 4.1). Additionally, several older integrated peripheries suffered declines between 2000 and 2017, such as Belgium (–63 percent), Portugal (–29 percent) and the Netherlands (–28 percent) (OICA, 2018). The declines in France and Italy compared to the continuing growth in Germany can be at least partially attributed to the more extensive offshoring of car assembly by French and Italian automakers, which, in turn, is related to a

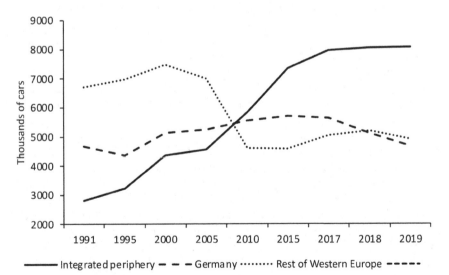

FIGURE 4.1 Car production trends in Europe, including Turkey and Morocco, 1991–2019
Notes: Integrated periphery includes Eastern Europe, Spain, Portugal, Turkey and Morocco.
Source: author, based on data in OICA (2020) (1997–2019 data), USDT (2022) (1991–1995 data) and national statistical offices of individual countries (1991–1995 data).

greater share of small cars in their product portfolio compared to the German automakers. At the same time, the German automakers offshored a greater proportion of the production of components, especially to Eastern Europe, in order to benefit from its lower labor costs (Chiappini, 2012), which resulted in a more efficient intracorporate division of labor (Walker, 1989). Additionally, the high level of production in Germany has been sustained by large exports of mostly premium cars to China, which has not been the case in other Western European core countries (Maiza and Bustillo, 2018).

It is in this context that I will examine the restructuring of the European automotive industry in the rest of this chapter by analyzing job creation and job loss across the European Union plus Norway between 2005 and 2016, and by analyzing investment decisions of foreign automotive firms in the integrated periphery in Czechia and Slovakia since the early 1990s.

4.3   DATA AND METHODOLOGY

The automotive industry restructuring database has been constructed and analyzed for the European Union countries plus Norway for the 2005–2016 period. It involved the manual extraction of individual restructuring events in the automotive industry from the European Restructuring Monitor (ERM) (ERM, 2017), resulting in the creation or loss of at least 100 jobs or 10 percent or more of the labor force in firms or factories employing at least 250 workers. The ERM database is based on the screening of national media sources in daily newspapers, business press and online. Its basic advantage is that it provides firm-level data about job creation and job loss and reasons behind these dynamics that are not otherwise available. The nationality of firms creating or cutting jobs can be determined, which allows for the analysis of the role of foreign and domestic firms in the restructuring of the automotive industry.

The ERM database has five important limitations. First, it is not strictly representative since it relies only on selected media titles. Second, it does not include small and also many medium-sized enterprises that continue to play an important role in the supplier industry (Frigant, 2013), despite the increased domination of the automotive industry by large firms (Humphrey and Memedovic, 2003; Sturgeon and Lester, 2004). Third, the level of media coverage of restructuring events differs from country to country, which may lead to the overrepresentation of restructuring events in some countries and underrepresentation in others. Fourth, the ERM database covers job loss more accurately than job creation because companies are less likely to report job creation and its media coverage tends to be lower. Fifth, it does not cover non-European Union countries in Europe, such as Serbia, North Macedonia, Bosnia and Herzegovina, and Moldova, that saw significant FDI-driven job creation in the automotive industry during the study period. We have to keep these limitations in mind when interpreting the data. Since our goal is to understand the overall trends in restructuring and geographic shifts in the European automotive industry, and the analysis of restructuring events of large firms should reveal basic trends in job creation and job loss at the national level, the advantages of the ERM database outweigh its disadvantages.

The extracted dataset was carefully checked for mistakes, such as double entries in the original ERM database or the announced restructuring events that never materialized. The average values have been used in the cases of ranges of announced job creation or job loss. Restructuring events were classified by their announcement year even though some were planned over the course of several years. The parent company of the firm owner was determined and the descriptive information of each restructuring event was used to classify the reasons for the job creation or job loss. Overall, a total of 2,124 restructuring events were extracted from the ERM database in the European Union plus Norway automotive industry for the 2005–2016 period (Table 4.2).

TABLE 4.2 *Job creation and job loss in the European Union plus Norway automotive industry by country, 2005–2016*

	No. of cases	Jobs created	Jobs lost	Net gain/loss
Poland	309	74,771	21,889	52,882
Germany	238	50,926	145,536	−94,610
Czechia	228	72,598	28,751	43,847
France	212	21,908	83,140	−61,232
Britain	161	19,796	42,028	−22,232
Romania	141	77,844	10,657	67,187
Slovakia	141	51,673	6,368	45,305
Sweden	119	8,803	31,773	−22,970
Hungary	118	29,048	12,594	16,454
Italy	75	5,390	18,658	−13,268
Spain	73	8,386	22,193	−13,807
Slovenia	71	6,675	9,257	−2,582
Belgium	51	3,197	17,912	−14,715
Austria	50	7,105	6,659	446
Bulgaria	33	15,440	0	15,440
Portugal	32	3,786	9,606	−5,820
Finland	18	1,250	2,560	−1,310
Netherlands	17	1,850	3,820	−1,970
Lithuania	10	940	855	85
Ireland	7	140	1,212	−1,072

(continued)

TABLE 4.2 (*continued*)

	No. of cases	Jobs created	Jobs lost	Net gain/loss
Norway	6	170	878	−708
Estonia	5	112	1,215	−1,103
Denmark	4	0	940	−940
Latvia	2	420	0	420
Greece	1	0	200	−200
Luxembourg	1	0	79	−79
Malta	1	170	0	170
Total	2,124	462,398	478,780	−16,382

Note: No automotive industry restructuring events were recorded for Croatia during its 2012–2016 coverage in the ERM database.
Source: calculated by author from data in ERM (2017).

The second unique dataset is based on ninety-one interviews with managers of foreign automotive subsidiaries in Czechia and Slovakia conducted by the author and members of his research team (Schoenberger, 1991) that collected information about the reasons for investment, location choice, perceived national competitive advantages in the automotive industry, strategic needs of parent companies in foreign locations, relocations and reasons for the continuing production in these countries. Sixty-four interviews were conducted in Czechia between 2009 and 2013 and twenty-seven in Slovakia between 2011 and 2015.

4.4   JOB CREATION AND JOB LOSS IN THE EUROPEAN AUTOMOTIVE INDUSTRY, 2005–2016

I will start the empirical analysis with mapping and testing the relationship between job creation/loss on one side and wages and corporate taxes on the other side. The European Union plus Norway automotive industry was dynamic during 2005–2016 with 462,398 jobs created and 478,780 jobs lost for a net loss of 16,382 jobs (Table 4.2). However, if we also consider job creation in countries not included in the ERM database, the total balance for Europe (excluding Russia, Belarus and Ukraine) was slightly positive. Foreign firms created more than 18,000 jobs in Serbia alone (SIEPA, 2014) and several thousand jobs were also created in North Macedonia, Bosnia and Herzegovina, and Moldova (Bolduc, 2017a; MIEPO, 2017). Western Europe recorded a net loss of 254,317 jobs, while Eastern Europe recorded a net gain of 237,935 jobs (Figure 4.2). The data thus suggest a partial spatial shift in production from Western to Eastern Europe, which started in the early 1990s (Sadler et al., 1993).

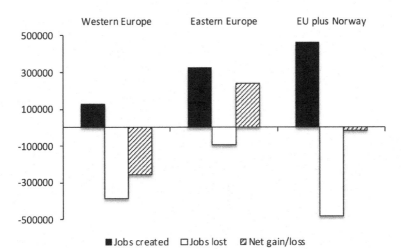

FIGURE 4.2 Job creation and job loss in the European automotive industry, 2005–2016
Note: EU stands for the European Union.
Source: calculated by author from data in ERM (2017).

However, the bulk of change was concentrated into one third of the analyzed countries. Poland, Germany, Czechia, France, Britain, Romania, Slovakia, Sweden and Hungary recorded more than 100 restructuring events each (78 percent of the total) and accounted for 88 percent of all created jobs (407,367) and 80 percent of jobs lost (382,736). Overall, job creation was more concentrated in Eastern Europe with 71 percent of all jobs created, while job loss was more concentrated in Western Europe with 81 percent of jobs lost. Romania, Poland, Czechia and Slovakia recorded the largest job creation (276,886 jobs), while Germany, France, Britain and Sweden together lost 302,477 jobs (Table 4.2, Figure 4.3).

The Pearson correlation coefficient revealed highly significant negative statistical correlation at the 95 percent confidence interval between the national level ERM data on 2005–2016 job creation and average personnel costs in the automotive industry (Eurostat 2018) (Figure 4.4).[1] The negative correlation is also highly significant between the average corporate tax rate for the 2005–2016 period (KPMG, 2017) and job creation.[2] Similarly, the net job creation/loss negatively correlates (highly significant) with both personnel

---

[1] P (two-tailed) = 0.0007, r = –0.6323, N = 25. Luxembourg, Cyprus, Malta and Croatia had to be removed from the analysis for the lack of data, but none is a major automotive producer. I have controlled for the size of the automotive industry in different countries.

[2] P (two-tailed) = 0.0007, r = –0.6327, N = 25.

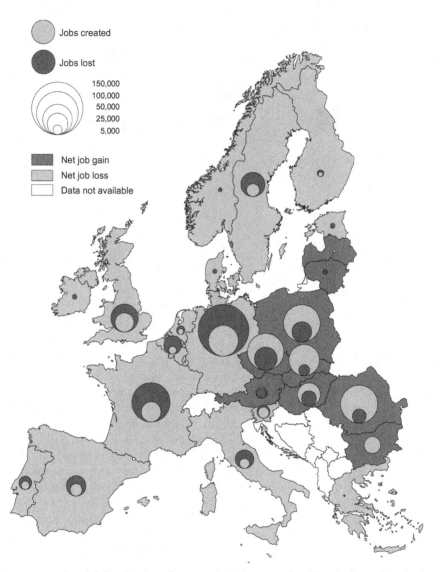

FIGURE 4.3 Spatial distribution of automotive jobs created and lost by large firms in the European Union plus Norway, 2005–2016
Source: author, based on data in ERM (2017).

costs[3] and corporate taxes.[4] The correlation between job losses and average personnel costs is statistically significant only after the removal of one outlier

---

[3] P (two-tailed) = 0.0008, r = −0.6273, N = 25.
[4] P (two-tailed) = 0.0024, r = −0.5797, N = 25.

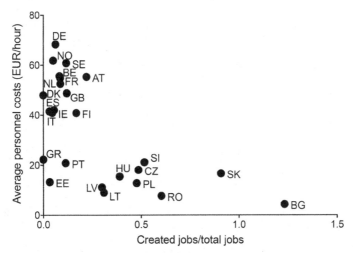

FIGURE 4.4 The relationship between 2005–2015 average personnel costs in the automotive industry and 2005–2016 jobs created in the automotive industry
Note: Country codes in this figure and in Figure 4.5 are based on the ISO 3166-1 standard.
Source: author, based on data from ERM (2017) and Eurostat (2018).

(Slovenia) (Figure 4.5).[5] The correlation between job losses and average corporate tax rates is significant only after the removal of two outliers (Slovenia and Ireland).[6] Although the Pearson correlation coefficient revealed that national differences in labor costs and corporate taxes were related to job creation and job losses in the European Union plus Norway automotive industry between 2005 and 2016, it also suggested that labor costs and corporate taxes were more important for job creation in new locations than for job loss in existing locations. This highlights the importance of other factors in corporate decisions to cut or keep jobs in existing locations.

[5] P (two-tailed) = 0.0168, r = −0.4831, N = 24. Slovenia has relatively low average personnel costs compared to Western Europe but suffered by far the highest job losses relative to the size of its automotive industry in the European Union plus Norway mainly due to the bankruptcy of Prevent Global (−3,907 jobs) and large employment fluctuations in Renault Slovenia.

[6] P (two-tailed) = 0.0228, r = −0.4726, N = 23. Slovenia is again an outlier because of its highest relative job losses combined with relatively low average corporate taxes. Ireland is an outlier because of its extremely low average corporate tax rate at 12.5 percent combined with the fourth-highest job losses relative to its size of the automotive industry in the European Union plus Norway. Ireland accounted only for 0.12 percent of the European Union automotive industry employment and Slovenia for 0.52 percent in 2015.

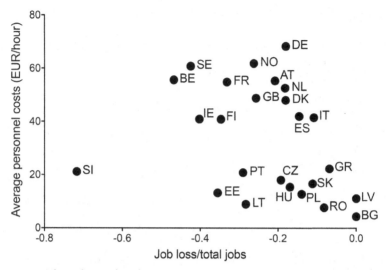

FIGURE 4.5 The relationship between 2005–2015 average personnel costs in the automotive industry and 2005–2016 jobs lost in the automotive industry
Source: author, based on data from ERM (2017) and Eurostat (2018).

4.4.1   The Formation of Spatiotemporal Fixes in Integrated Peripheries

The interviews support the results of the correlation analysis by identifying low labor costs as one of the most important reasons for investment by automotive TNCs in Eastern Europe since the early 1990s. More importantly, the interviews capture other factors behind the investment decisions of foreign firms (Laulajainen and Stafford, 1995) that are not revealed by the ERM data but are equally important for the understanding of the formation and nature of the spatiotemporal fix in Eastern Europe. The interviews show that the decisions to invest are generally in line with the logic conceptualized by the theory of spatiotemporal fix and take place through several interconnected steps at different geographic scales with the changing of relative importance of different location factors at each step. First, a corporate decision is made to invest in Eastern Europe, typically with a goal of establishing a low-cost production site within the European Union. This has been the case for large assembly factories (Pavlínek, 2002d; 2017a), smaller-scale investments, such as export-oriented cross-border and market-capture investments (Pavlínek, 1998), but not for follow sourcing (Frigant, 2007), in which suppliers follow an assembly firm or other suppliers into a specific country. After the decision to invest in Eastern Europe is made, a specific country is selected and, finally, a specific location is chosen in the selected country.

The interviewed firms usually listed more than one reason for investing in Czechia and Slovakia, suggesting a number of factors being considered. Overall, however, cost-cutting reasons, namely low labor costs, follow sourcing and

TABLE 4.3 *Reasons for investment by foreign-owned automotive firms in Czechia and Slovakia*

Reasons for investment	Czechia		Slovakia		Total	
	No.	% of firms	No.	% of firms	No.	% of firms
Low labor costs	43	67	12	41	55	60
Follow sourcing	21	33	13	45	34	37
Acquisition of existing firm	17	27	3	10	20	22
Investment incentives	10	16	8	28	18	20
Skilled labor	10	16	2	7	12	13
Proximity of Germany	10	16	0	0	10	11
Proximity and transportation accessibility of Western European markets	7	11	2	7	9	10
Industrial tradition	7	11	1	3	8	9
Market capture	4	6	2	7	6	7
Access to local know-how and technology	4	6	0	0	4	4

Notes: The number of interviewed firms: Czechia sixty-four, Slovakia twenty-seven. "% of firms" refers to the percentage of interviewed firms. Each firm could list more than one reason for investing. *Source:* author's interviews.

investment incentives, were cited more frequently than other reasons, highlighting their greater importance in investment decisions (Table 4.3). The cost-cutting nature of follow sourcing was revealed during an interview with a car assembly firm in Czechia.

Our company has strongly exploited and supported follow sourcing because we were looking for lower production costs. We have invested in Central Europe where labor costs are lower and we have strongly encouraged our key suppliers to build their factories here too for two fundamental reasons: first, to lower transportation and logistical costs and, second, by starting production here, they produce with lower labor costs too. And this has been the main reason why many firms have moved production from Germany to Central Europe with the goal of lowering production costs. (An interview with an assembly firm, August 8, 2011).

Additionally, follow sourcing decreases set-up sunk costs for assembly firms because it lowers their entry costs into new regions as these are shared with their most important suppliers (Lung, 2004). At the same time, the importance of follow sourcing highlights the role of organizational fixes in the formation of spatiotemporal fixes in the automotive industry in integrated peripheries. The reduction in the number of suppliers and their organizational restructuring into distinct supplier tiers has led to the spatial restructuring of the supplier base with assembly firms requiring their most important module and tier-one suppliers to be located close to assembly plants in order to minimize logistical and transportation costs (Frigant and Lung, 2002; Pavlínek and Janák, 2007). Table 4.3 also underlines the importance of investment incentives in the location decisions of foreign firms. As a form of institutional fix, investment incentives lower set-up sunk costs for investing firms and are therefore another cost-cutting measure. As one supplier argued: "There were several reasons for our investment here. But if I speak openly, I think that investment incentives were really the most important one and the final impulse that made it possible for this factory to be built here. Simply put, it was a financial reason" (interview, November 16, 2010).

Other factors, such as labor skills, industrial tradition and the proximity and transportation accessibility of Western European markets, have also played an important role in the selection of a particular country for investment, although they have been cited less frequently than cost-cutting reasons. The importance of cost-cutting reasons in investment decisions, especially low labor costs, was reiterated by the evaluation of the competitive advantages of Czechia and Slovakia by the interviewed automotive firms, with low labor costs topping the list (listed by 84 percent of the interviewed firms in Czechia and 85 percent in Slovakia), followed by proximity to the Western European market (66 percent of the interviewed firms in Czechia and 30 percent in Slovakia) and proximity to assembly plants and other customers (23 percent in Czechia and 48 percent in Slovakia). However, it also highlighted the importance of labor skills (59 percent of the interviewed firms in Czechia and 44 percent in Slovakia) and industrial tradition (38 percent in Czechia and 19 percent in Slovakia) for investing firms. Similarly, low labor costs (listed by 91 percent of the interviewed firms in Czechia and 93 percent in Slovakia), skilled labor and industrial tradition (56 percent in Czechia and 33 percent in Slovakia) and market proximity (33 percent both in Czechia and Slovakia) were listed as the most important strategic needs of parent TNCs for production in foreign locations.

The interview data further suggest that a specific location choice in a selected country is influenced by technological fixes that help investing firms minimize transportation and logistical costs. Foreign subsidiaries attempt to cut these costs by locating close to their customers and through an easy access to high-quality infrastructure, especially highways (Table 4.4), which is supported by previous research (Klier and McMillen, 2015). The theory of spatiotemporal fix highlights the existence of labor surplus as one of the preconditions for the formation of spatiotemporal fixes and the interviews showed that labor surplus plays an important role in site selection. The availability of cheap land and buildings combined with investment incentives are also significant in location choice as additional ways to lower set-up sunk costs by investing firms.

As in the case of country selection, labor skills and industrial tradition were cited less frequently than cost-cutting reasons among the important factors in the selection of a particular locality. This may indicate two things. First, given the relatively high level of education and labor skills in Czechia and Slovakia, automotive firms are confident that they can train local labor to meet their needs. Second, they are also confident they can find skilled labor in local labor markets

TABLE 4.4 *Reasons for the location choice of foreign-owned automotive firms in Czechia and Slovakia*

Reasons for location choice	Czechia		Slovakia		Total	
	No.	% of firms	No.	% of firms	No.	% of firms
Proximity of customers (other firms)	22	34	8	30	30	33
Transportation accessibility and infrastructure	19	30	9	33	28	31
Existing location (acquisition or JV)	22	34	5	19	27	30
Availability of labor	18	28	7	26	25	27
Proximity of Germany or Austria	18	28	1	4	19	21
Availability of (inexpensive) land or building(s)	10	16	8	30	18	20
Investment incentives	8	13	4	15	12	13
Industrial tradition	8	13	3	11	11	12
Low labor costs	5	8	5	19	10	11
Qualified labor	7	11	2	7	9	10
Help from local politicians	4	6	2	7	6	7
Proximity of the capital city	4	6	1	4	5	5
Low transportation costs	2	3	0	0	2	2

Notes: The number of interviewed firms: Czechia sixty-four, Slovakia twenty-seven. "% of firms" refers to the percentage of interviewed firms. Each firm could list more than one reason for the location choice. *Source:* author's interviews.

even if it would mean poaching existing workers from local companies, which has become commonplace (Pavlínek and Žížalová, 2016; Pavlínek, 2018). At the same time, the interviewed managers, both in Czechia and Slovakia, almost universally complained about the disappearance of labor surplus and growing labor shortages due to the rapid growth of the automotive industry, which prompted some of them to relocate parts of production to lower-cost countries with surplus labor, such as Bosnia and Herzegovina.

I would expect to find similar interview results in Poland and Hungary, as these countries are comparable with Czechia and Slovakia in wage levels, distance from markets, the institutional environment, labor skills, and in the post-1990 development of the automotive industry. The findings might be more different in Southeastern Europe because of significantly lower labor costs than in Czechia and Slovakia, larger distances from markets in Western Europe, weaker industrial tradition and lower manufacturing skills. Overall, the ERM data, correlation analysis and interviews conducted in Czechia and Slovakia point to the even greater importance of low wages for cost-driven automotive industry investments in Southeastern Europe than in Czechia and Slovakia.

The interviews thus highlight the importance of cost-cutting reasons in the formation of the spatiotemporal fix in the Eastern European integrated periphery as conceptualized by the theory of spatiotemporal fix and supported by the correlation analysis. At the same time, they provide evidence of the importance of organizational, technological and institutional fixes for the formation of the spatiotemporal fix, especially follow sourcing (organizational fix), modern transportation infrastructure (technological fix) and investment incentives (institutional fix). Low labor costs alone would be insufficient for the growth of integrated peripheries without the presence of these contributing factors, as argued in the conceptual section of this chapter.

4.5   JOB CREATION AND JOB LOSS BY THE NATIONALITY OF FIRMS, FIRM OWNERSHIP AND RESTRUCTURING EVENTS

4.5.1   Job Creation and Job Loss by the Nationality of Firms

Firms from the contemporary automotive industry core countries accounted for the vast majority of jobs created in the European Union plus Norway between 2005 and 2016. German firms were by far the most active in job creation by creating 37 percent of the European Union plus Norway total and, together with French firms, accounted for 51 percent (Table 4.5). Firms from the top six countries worldwide (Germany, France, Japan, the USA, South Korea and Italy) accounted for 81 percent. At the same time, Eastern European firms created only 4 percent of the total, with almost half created by Polish firms and an additional one fourth by Czech firms. In Eastern Europe, domestic firms accounted for only 5 percent of all automotive jobs created. This demonstrates the marginal role of domestic Eastern European firms in automotive industry development and underlines the dominant role of foreign capital behind the growth in integrated peripheries. Only Czech firms recorded any job creation abroad (in Slovakia), which shows that Eastern European firms have not internationalized their production.

Firms from five countries (Germany, the USA, France, Britain and Japan) accounted for 80 percent of total job losses, which means that firms from Germany, the USA, France and Japan were responsible for both the majority of jobs created (71 percent) and lost (74 percent). German firms were also most active in job losses by accounting for 37 percent of the total. In Western Europe, German firms accounted for 38 percent of the total job losses and together with French firms for 57 percent. Both large German and French automotive firms were predominantly shedding jobs in their home economies (84 percent in the case of German firms and 88 percent in the case of French firms), while creating the majority of new jobs abroad (72 percent in the case of German firms and 71 percent in the case of French firms). Their job creation was geographically highly concentrated in the integrated periphery of Eastern Europe, which accounted for 93 percent of all jobs created abroad by German firms and 92

TABLE 4.5 *Job creation and job loss by the nationality of the firm and by country, 2005–2016*

Nationality of the firm		Germany	France	Italy	Britain	Belgium	Spain	Portugal	Sweden	Rest of Western Europe	Bulgaria	Czechia	Hungary	Poland	Romania	Slovakia	Slovenia	Baltic states	Total	Net gain/loss
Germany	Jobs created	47591	380	0	1290	400	700	2786	2050	1185	1950	32861	10940	19599	31695	15389	1748	300	170864	−5331
	Jobs lost	123896	5318	323	4470	1228	6319	856	2473	2855	0	12259	3563	4445	3870	190	4080	50	176195	
France	Jobs created	0	18928	0	130	0	2450	1000	0	140	560	6140	637	5260	16938	10700	2120	120	65123	−12753
	Jobs lost	510	64340	746	4440	412	1573	1030	388	130	0	683	512	0	1542	250	1320	0	77876	
Italy	Jobs created	0	100	5240	950	0	600	0	0	130	0	2055	0	4960	1075	1788	115	0	16883	−3281
	Jobs lost	1440	784	14151	337	0	1215	0	120	0	0	200	157	1760	0	0	0	0	20164	
Japan	Jobs created	0	1666	0	5540	550	1786	0	0	450	4800	5999	5050	13085	6985	2100	0	300	48311	27780
	Jobs lost	1043	886	303	3776	333	2095	1733	350	1255	0	1252	2604	2350	0	2301	0	250	20531	
USA	Jobs created	2875	250	0	2560	407	2700	0	555	170	3000	5222	1625	12755	9105	4787	0	0	46011	−34931
	Jobs lost	14808	7100	2348	11822	10676	4958	4035	11194	1928	0	5243	1511	2317	1244	1364	394	0	80942	
India	Jobs created	0	0	0	7275	0	0	0	0	0	0	600	1990	0	0	200	0	0	10065	6562
	Jobs lost	0	0	0	1600	0	0	0	176	0	0	1727	0	0	0	0	0	0	3503	
Canada	Jobs created	0	0	0	0	0	0	0	0	4800	250	0	1250	90	0	210	0	0	6600	1002
	Jobs lost	664	0	0	408	607	900	0	310	2000	0	0	709	0	0	0	0	0	5598	
South Korea	Jobs created	120	0	0	0	0	0	0	0	79	0	10984	4050	1781	0	9734	0	0	26669	26636
	Jobs lost	100	27	260	0	167	0	0	0	0	0	0	0	0	0	0	0	0	633	
Britain	Jobs created	200	0	150	1921	0	0	0	0	0	0	0	590	600	1700	250	100	0	5511	−22041
	Jobs lost	825	2003	173	13701	160	2917	1952	898	288	0	1850	800	378	724	835	48	0	27552	
Rest of world	Jobs created	140	584	0	130	1840	150	0	6198	3940	4880	8737	2916	16641	10346	6515	2592	752	66561	−1152
	Jobs lost	2250	2682	354	1474	4329	2216	0	15864	7813	0	7264	2738	10639	3277	1428	3415	1770	67513	
Total	Jobs created	50926	21908	5390	19796	3197	8386	3786	8803	10685	15440	72598	29048	74771	77844	51673	6675	1472	462398	−16382
	Jobs lost	145536	83140	18658	42028	17912	22193	9606	31773	16348	0	28751	12594	21889	10657	6368	9257	2070	478780	
	Net gain/loss	−94610	−61232	−13268	−22232	−14715	−13807	−5820	−22970	−5663	15440	43847	16454	52882	67187	45305	−2582	−598	−16382	

Note: Rest of Western Europe includes Austria, Denmark, Finland, Greece, Ireland, Luxembourg, Malta, the Netherlands and Norway. Baltic states include Estonia, Latvia and Lithuania. Under "nationality of the firm" only countries whose firms created more than 4,000 jobs in the European Union and Norway between 2005 and 2016 are shown. All other investing firms from an additional seventeen countries are grouped under "rest of world."
Source: calculated by the author based on data in ERM (2017).

TABLE 4.6 *Job creation by foreign and domestic firms in the European Union plus Norway automotive industry by country, 2005–2016*

Country	Total jobs	Domestic firms	Foreign firms	Share of foreign firms (%)	Share of domestic firms (%)
Austria	7,105	1,120	5,985	84.2	15.8
Belgium	3,197	0	3,197	100.0	0.0
Britain	19,796	1,921	17,875	90.3	9.7
Bulgaria	15,440	480	14,960	96.9	3.1
Czechia	72,598	3,725	68,873	94.9	5.1
Estonia	112	0	112	100.0	0.0
Finland	1,250	1,250	0	0.0	100.0
France	21,908	18,928	2,980	13.6	86.4
Germany	50,926	47,591	3,335	6.5	93.5
Hungary	29,048	955	28,093	96.7	3.3
Ireland	140	0	140	100.0	0.0
Italy	5,390	5,240	150	2.8	97.2
Latvia	420	0	420	100.0	0.0
Lithuania	940	170	770	81.9	18.1
Malta	170	0	170	100.0	0.0
Netherlands	1,850	1,400	450	24.3	75.7
Norway	170	0	170	100.0	0.0
Poland	74,771	8,200	66,571	89.0	11.0
Portugal	3,786	0	3,786	100.0	0.0
Romania	77,844	500	77,344	99.4	0.6
Slovakia	51,673	665	51,008	98.7	1.3
Slovenia	6,675	1,942	4,733	70.9	29.1
Spain	8,386	150	8,236	98.2	1.8
Sweden	8,803	2,141	6,662	75.7	24.3
Total	462,398	96,378	366,020	79.2	20.8

Note: No automotive jobs were created in Denmark, Greece and Luxembourg.
Source: calculated by author from data in ERM (2017).

percent by French firms. It supports the theoretical argument about the spatiotemporal fixes being sought by core-based surplus capital in integrated peripheries, which leads to restructuring in existing locations. It also further supports the argument that production costs along with corporate taxes were the important driving forces behind the job creation and job losses between 2005 and 2016.

4.5.2 Job Creation and Job Loss by Domestic and Foreign Firms

Firm-level data make it possible to determine the geographic variation in the role of domestic and foreign-owned firms in job creation and job loss. Overall, foreign firms were more active in job creation outside their domestic economies by accounting for 79 percent (366,020) of all created jobs (Table 4.6). This indicates the high degree of internationalization of the European automotive industry. However, an important difference existed between Eastern and Western Europe. In Eastern Europe, 95 percent of the jobs were created by foreign firms and only 5 percent by domestic firms. The dependence on job creation by foreign firms among major producing countries of Eastern Europe was the highest in Romania and Slovakia and lowest in Slovenia and Poland (Table 4.6). National differences in job creation by foreign and domestic firms closely correspond with the degree of foreign control in the automotive industry, which is extremely high in Eastern Europe (Table 4.7). This high dependence on foreign capital is one of the underlying structural features of integrated peripheries. At the same time, the 5 percent share of domestic firms on the job creation in Eastern Europe shows their marginal role in the FDI-driven growth of the automotive industry.

The situation in Western Europe was different with 60 percent of the new jobs created by domestic firms and 40 percent by foreign firms. However, compared to the universally high dependence on foreign firms for job creation in Eastern Europe, there are significant differences among Western European countries. On one hand, the dependence on job creation by foreign firms was extremely high in the older integrated peripheries of Portugal, Belgium and Spain, and also in Britain (Table 4.6), which corresponds with the fact that these four countries have the highest degree of their automotive industries under the control of foreign capital in Western Europe (Table 5.7 in Chapter 5). On the other hand, the lowest shares of automotive jobs created by foreign firms were in Italy, Germany and France, which also have the lowest degrees of control of their automotive industries by foreign firms, which clearly sets these countries apart from the rest (Tables 4.6 and 5.7). These three countries constitute the traditional core area of the European automotive production system with a long history of strong domestic automotive industry.

The vast majority of jobs (86 percent) created by foreign firms were created in Eastern Europe with Romania, Czechia, Poland, Slovakia and Hungary accounting for 80 percent of the European Union plus Norway total, which supports the theoretical argument of the spatiotemporal fix being sought by surplus capital in the integrated periphery. Between 2005 and 2016, these five countries had new foreign assembly plants either built (Czechia, Hungary and Slovakia) or expanded (Poland, Romania) and also saw a major expansion in the supplier industry because of follow sourcing and export-oriented production by foreign firms (Pavlínek, 2017a). The concentration of growth into these five countries shows the uneven development in the integrated periphery as some countries were able to attract much larger volumes of surplus capital than others based on the particular combinations of institutional, technological and organizational fixes.

German automotive firms were the most active in creating jobs abroad by creating 123,273 jobs in the European Union plus Norway outside of Germany, which was 34 percent of all jobs created by foreign firms. German, Japanese (48,113), French (46,195) American (46,011) and South Korean (26,669) firms accounted for 79 percent of all automotive industry jobs created by foreign firms outside their home economy in the European Union plus Norway between 2005 and 2016. This indicates that TNCs from these five automotive industry core countries were the main driving force behind the restructuring of the European automotive industry during this period.

Compared to jobs created by foreign firms being concentrated in Eastern Europe, 83 percent of the jobs created by domestic firms were created in Western Europe and only 17 percent in Eastern Europe. The majority of jobs created by domestic firms in Western Europe were created in Germany (60 percent of the Western European total and 49 percent of the European Union plus Norway total) and France (24 percent and 20 percent). Domestic firms played a much less important role in job creation in the rest of Western Europe. In the old integrated peripheries of Western Europe, no job creation was recorded by large domestic firms in Belgium and Portugal, and only 150 jobs were created in Spain, which was only 2 percent of Spain's total. In Eastern Europe, large domestic firms failed to create more than 5,000 jobs in all countries with the exception of Poland (8,200 jobs), which accounted for 49 percent of all jobs created by domestic firms in Eastern Europe (Table 4.6). This situation underscores the weak position of domestic firms in the automotive industry in both older and newer integrated peripheries.

In contrast to job creation, domestic firms accounted for higher job losses (55 percent – 261,302) than foreign firms (45 percent – 217,478). Job losses by domestic firms were concentrated in Germany (47 percent of the total) and France (25 percent). Overall, foreign firms created net 148,542 jobs abroad (outside their home economy) in the European Union plus Norway, while domestic firms had a net loss of 164,924 jobs in their home economies. This is clear evidence of the increased internationalization of the European automotive industry. At the same time, it suggests the weakening role of domestic firms in the fiercely competitive supplier industry, which is increasingly dominated by large TNCs and follow sourcing. In order to survive, large Western European suppliers have been forced to internationalize production by setting up factories in the integrated periphery. From these factories, they supply newly built foreign assembly plants in Eastern Europe through follow sourcing or export standardized components that do not have to be supplied just in time to Western Europe. This partial shift in production to Eastern Europe has often involved cuts in the automotive employment in Western European countries, such as Germany and France. Domestic firms in Western Europe that were unable to internationalize found it difficult to compete with rapidly growing imports of cheaper components from newly built foreign factories in the integrated periphery in Eastern Europe, Turkey and North Africa, and were often forced to cut employment or declare bankruptcy, as we will see in the next section.

Despite the overall net gain of 237,935 jobs in Eastern Europe, domestic firms recorded a net loss of 6,276 jobs between 2005 and 2016. This suggests that large domestic firms in Eastern Europe failed to benefit from the massive job creation by foreign firms and the strong growth of the automotive industry. Existing firms were often unable to meet quality, quantity and delivery demands of foreign firms and were excluded from newly formed production networks that were set up and are controlled by foreign firms (Pavlínek and Janák, 2007). At the same time, new domestic firms found it difficult to get established, because of high entry barriers, and to succeed, because of the fierce competition in the automotive industry. This means that between 2005 and 2016, the benefits of large FDI in the automotive industry did not significantly spread from foreign to domestic firms in the form of spillovers in integrated peripheries (Pavlínek and Žížalová, 2016; Pavlínek, 2018), confounding the basic premise of expected positive effects of FDI on host country economies stressed by the economic theory (Blomström and Kokko, 2001; Dunning and Lundan, 2008). Overall, large domestic firms were losing ground both in Western and Eastern Europe at the expense of foreign firms, which has also been a long-term trend in other automotive industry regions, such as the USA (Klier and Rubenstein, 2010), Canada (Rutherford and Holmes, 2008), South Africa (Barnes and Kaplinsky, 2000), Brazil and India (Humphrey, 2000), and one of the signs of the increasing corporate concentration and internationalization of the automotive industry.

4.5.3 Job Creation and Job Loss Classified by Restructuring Events

The information provided in the ERM database for each restructuring event allows for their classification and comparison among different countries and macro-regions. In terms of job creation, I have differentiated between new investments in new and existing locations in the form of new factories and the expansion of production in existing locations. Between 2005 and 2016, in-situ expansions were responsible for 59 percent of all newly created jobs, followed by 39 percent of new jobs created in 460 newly built factories. The remaining 2 percent of jobs were created in service units, such as R&D, technical and logistics centers. In terms of job losses, I have classified restructuring events into in-situ rationalizations, plant closures and plant relocations. The frequency of these events and their job impacts followed the expected distribution identified in literature with in-situ restructurings being the most frequent and plant relocations being the least frequent (Dicken, 2015). In-situ restructurings accounted for 71 percent of total job losses, plant closures for 21 percent, plant

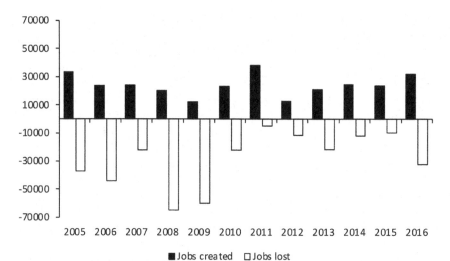

FIGURE 4.6 Job creation and job loss through in-situ restructuring in the European Union plus Norway by year, 2005–2016
Source: calculated by author from data in ERM (2017).

relocations for 5 percent and partial relocations for 2 percent (Table 4.7). In-situ job creation and job loss tends to follow business cycles as firms tend to expand production and create jobs during periods of economic prosperity and rationalize production and cut jobs at the same locations during periods of economic stagnation or decline (Figure 4.6).

The main difference between Western and Eastern Europe was in the construction of new factories. Out of 460 new factories built in the European Union plus Norway between 2005 and 2016, 438 (95 percent) were built in Eastern Europe as surplus foreign capital was exploiting the spatiotemporal fix there. Foreign firms also rapidly expanded production in factories they built in Eastern Europe between 1990 and 2004 (Jacobs, 2017; Pavlínek, 2017a). In Western Europe, the vast majority of new jobs were added in existing factories through the expansion of production rather than building new factories and the vast majority of job loss took place through restructuring in existing locations (Table 4.7). At the same time, out of 222 factory closures, 181 (86 percent) took place in Western Europe, which was also more affected by relocations, partial relocations and job cuts in existing locations than Eastern Europe. Britain, France, Germany, Spain and Italy accounted for 63 percent of all closures and relocations and 62 percent of jobs lost through closures and relocations (Figure 4.7). This is evidence of restructuring in existing locations as production partially shifted from Western to Eastern Europe, which supports the theoretical argument about the close relationship between new spatiotemporal fixes and restructurings and devaluations in existing locations

TABLE 4.7 *Summary of main restructuring events in the European Union plus Norway automotive industry, 2005–2016*

	Western Europe		Eastern Europe		Total	
	No.	Jobs	No.	Jobs	No.	Jobs
New factory	22	9,569	438	169,238	460	178,807
Expansion of production	240	121,163	364	152,868	604	274,031
Rationalization, job cutting	529	-276,652	170	-65,050	699	-341,702
Plant closure	181	-86,395	41	-15,920	222	-102,315
Plant relocation	50	-14,667	18	-8,516	68	-23,183
Partial relocation	35	-9,480	4	-2,100	39	-11,580
New R&D or technical center	2	355	9	4,425	11	4,780
Expansion of R&D center	7	1,790	7	1,760	14	3,550
New logistics center	0	0	5	550	5	550
New shared services center	0	0	1	180	1	180
New administration unit	0	0	1	500	1	500
Total	1,066	-254,317	1,058	237,935	2,124	-16,382

Source: calculated by author from data in ERM (2017).

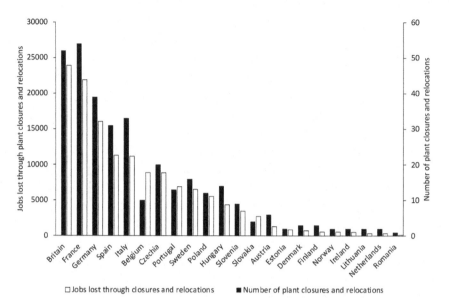

FIGURE 4.7 The number of plant closures and relocations (including partial relocations) and resulting job losses in the European Union plus Norway by country, 2005–2016
Source: calculated by author from data in ERM (2017).

(Harvey, 1982). It also shows the strong location inertia and commitment of firms to existing locations. The large number of in-situ restructurings, resulting in large numbers of job losses and job creations, compared to relocations, suggest that relocations tend to take place only after an unsuccessful in-situ restructuring and might be the last option for a company to regain profitability before declaring bankruptcy.

The increased production in Eastern Europe also required increased technical, R&D, logistics and administrative support (Table 4.7). However, the increase in the number of these jobs was disproportionally low compared to jobs in production as the majority of higher-value-added jobs remained in Western Europe or in parent economies of non-European firms (Pavlínek and Ženka, 2011; 2016; Pavlínek, 2012). The vast majority of new factories (410) were built in just five Eastern European countries that have assembly plants (Poland, Czechia, Slovakia, Romania and Hungary) (Figure 4.8), underlying, once again, the importance of follow sourcing and the export-oriented low-cost manufacturing of components in the contemporary automotive industry and also uneven development of the automotive industry in integrated peripheries.

However, the number of plant closures and relocations was also relatively high in Czechia (twenty), Hungary (fourteen) and Poland (twelve), which is evidence of the temporary nature of the spatiotemporal fix and of the constant

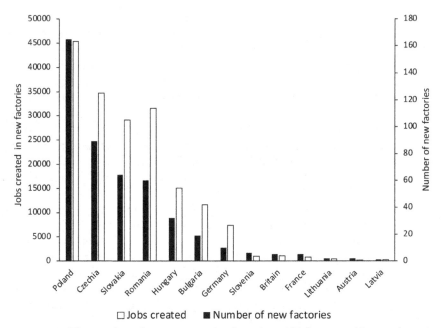

FIGURE 4.8 The number of new automotive factories and jobs created in new factories in the European Union plus Norway by country, 2005–2016
Source: calculated by author from data in ERM (2017).

search of automotive firms for cheaper and more profitable locations in lower-cost countries, such as Romania, which experienced only one factory closure (in 2009) and no relocations. The average 2005–2016 personnel costs in the automotive industry in Romania were 53 percent lower than in Czechia, 49 percent lower than in Hungary and 38 percent lower than in Poland (Eurostat, 2018), which made Romania the most important target country for labor-cost-driven relocations in Eastern Europe, as revealed by the ERM data (Table 4.2) and the interviews. At the time of the interview, 24 percent of the interviewed foreign subsidiaries in Czechia and 26 percent in Slovakia already relocated parts of their production abroad, while 16 percent in Czechia and 21 percent in Slovakia were considering future relocations. These figures tend to underestimate the extent of relocations since foreign subsidiaries that already relocated their entire production were not interviewed. Foreign subsidiaries engaged in labor-intensive and low-value-added production were the most likely to experience and consider relocations to lower-cost countries, such as Romania, Bulgaria, Ukraine and China, which is in line with previous studies on manufacturing relocation (Pennings and Sleuwaegen, 2000; South and Kim, 2019), including the automotive industry (Lampón et al., 2015; Pavlínek, 2015a). These subsidiaries tended to compare their labor costs with those in lower-cost countries, rather than with Western Europe, and frequently argued that labor costs were no longer low in Czechia and Slovakia. Although the gap in manufacturing labor costs between Eastern Europe and Western Europe narrowed between 1996 and 2016 because of FDI-driven growth in Eastern Europe that pushed wages up, it continues to be large. In 1996, the hourly costs in manufacturing in Czechia were 90 percent and in Slovakia 92 percent lower than in Germany. In 2016, the hourly manufacturing costs were still 75 percent lower in Czechia and 73 percent lower in Slovakia than in Germany (CB, 2018), while the average personnel costs in the automotive industry were 74 percent lower in both Czechia and Slovakia than in Germany (Eurostat, 2018). The importance of this continuing wage gap was acknowledged as one of the reasons for not considering relocation by 48 percent of the interviewed firms that were not planning relocation or partial relocation at the time of the interview both in Czechia and Slovakia.[7] Sunk costs (61 percent of the interviewed firms in Czechia and 38 percent in Slovakia), supplier relations (35 percent in Czechia and 48 percent in Slovakia) and skilled labor (39 percent in Czechia and 10 percent in Slovakia) were also frequently cited reasons behind the continuing production in Czechia and Slovakia and the lack of plans to relocate production abroad. These results show that labor costs are only one of the factors firms consider when deciding whether to relocate and that other factors, such as sunk costs, supplier relations, labor skills and proximity to the market are equally or even more important. The interviews also emphasized that the role of labor costs in relocation decisions depends on the nature of production and is especially important for the labor-intensive and simple-assembly type of manufacturing operations.

4.6 CONCLUSION

This chapter has demonstrated the dynamic nature of the automotive industry, which is in a constant state of flux as automotive firms strive to improve or maintain their competitiveness and profitability not only through ongoing technological and organizational innovations in existing locations, but also through the location of production in superior locations from which they can derive excess profits. I have conceptualized the crucial importance of spatial strategies for the profit-seeking behavior of automotive firms through Harvey's theory of spatiotemporal fix. I have explained how the formation of spatiotemporal fixes leads to the geographical expansion of the automotive industry into new areas, which I have called integrated peripheries, and, at the same time, restructuring in existing locations. I have also shown that the development of spatiotemporal fixes in integrated peripheries is conditioned by various organizational, technological and institutional fixes.

---

[7] The number of interviewed firms that were not planning relocation or partial relocation at the time of the interview was forty-six in Czechia and twenty-one in Slovakia.

In the context of the European automotive industry, the empirical evidence presented here highlights the latest development of the spatiotemporal fix in the Eastern European integrated periphery. In line with the theoretical argument, I have argued that this spatiotemporal fix has been driven by the search for low-cost locations compared to exiting locations in Western Europe, both the traditional core countries and older integrated peripheries. The theoretically explained importance of low wages and low corporate taxes for the development of this spatiotemporal fix (Harvey, 1982) was supported by the correlation analysis and by company interviews in Czechia and Slovakia, which also highlighted the importance of other cost-cutting reasons, along with organizational, institutional and technological factors (Layan, 2006; Pries and Dehnen, 2009) as important preconditions for the spatiotemporal fix to develop. Lower production costs in Eastern Europe compared to Western Europe created excess profit opportunities in Eastern Europe, which affected the geography of job creation and loss in the European automotive industry.

The firm-level analysis of large restructuring events in the European Union plus Norway automotive industry provided evidence of the increased internationalization of the European automotive industry through the increased role of foreign TNCs in both job creation and job loss. The geographic change in the European automotive industry was driven by the investment/disinvestment activities of automotive TNCs, mainly based in the global automotive industry core countries as TNCs from France, Germany, Italy, Japan, South Korea and the USA accounted for four-fifths of all created and lost jobs in the European Union plus Norway, and also for four-fifths of all created and lost jobs outside their home economies between 2005 and 2016. Four-fifths of all newly created jobs in the European Union plus Norway were created by foreign firms, which also accounted for almost half of all job losses. The fact that large domestic firms accounted for only one fifth of created jobs, but more than half of jobs lost, shows that large domestic firms, both in Western and Eastern Europe, were losing ground at the expense of foreign firms. This finding supports existing research pointing to the significantly enhanced role of large global suppliers and the weakening role of domestic firms in the fiercely competitive automotive industry (Barnes and Kaplinsky, 2000; Humphrey, 2000; Pavlínek, 2018). However, as I have shown, the automotive industry in integrated peripheries and other peripheral regions is under the control of foreign capital and is more significantly affected by this development than the automotive industry in core regions. In the European automotive industry, this situation is reflected in the overall weak performance of domestic firms compared to foreign firms in job creation in both old (Belgium, Portugal, Spain) and new (Eastern Europe) integrated peripheries. The empirical evidence presented in this chapter thus also demonstrates that large domestic firms in Eastern Europe failed to significantly benefit from the spatiotemporal fix and the massive job creation by foreign firms between 2005 and 2016. Instead, the position of domestic firms continued to weaken during the study period.

The high degree of concentration of job creation into several countries in Eastern Europe illustrates how spatiotemporal fixes operate; excess profit opportunities enjoyed by first-movers attract competing firms to the same or similar locations in order to benefit from the same locational advantages that have been enhanced by institutional fixes in the form of large investment incentives, organizational fixes in the form of follow sourcing and technological fixes in the form of modern infrastructure. At the same time, the analyzed data also underscore the vulnerability of integrated peripheries since spatiotemporal fixes are only temporary. This is not only supported by significant job losses in older integrated peripheries of Belgium, Spain and Portugal but also in several countries of new Eastern European integrated periphery, especially Czechia and Poland. This is another evidence of automotive firms constantly searching for more profitable locations within the European Union and adjacent regions with lower wages, lower taxes and greater labor surplus that also have other preconditions for the development of the automotive industry in the form of necessary technological, organizational and institutional fixes. This spatial profit-seeking behavior is especially prominent in labor-intensive manufacturing operations. The empirical analysis also demonstrated that the ongoing spatiotemporal fix in the Eastern European integrated periphery results in geographic restructuring in existing locations in Western Europe, which is reflected in in-situ restructurings, job losses, factory closures and relocations. The largest number of jobs created and lost were through in-situ restructuring in Western Europe, which shows the continuing attractiveness of traditional automotive industry regions and strong commitment of automotive companies to existing locations.

The expansion of the automotive industry into new integrated peripheries and the related restructuring in existing automotive industry locations is not unique to Europe. Similar processes have taken place in North America at the continental scale through the peripheral integration of Mexico (Layan, 2000; Sturgeon et al., 2010) and the southern USA (Klier and Rubenstein, 2010), and the related deindustrialization and restructuring in the traditional core of the North American automotive industry centered on Detroit and southeastern Michigan (Klier and Rubenstein, 2008; Sturgeon et al., 2008). As the relentless search of automotive firms for excess profit opportunities through spatiotemporal fixes continues in Europe, we are likely to see further shifts in production from the existing locations in Western Europe into integrated peripheries and the related restructuring in Western Europe. These processes will result in the increased territorial specialization and finer division of labor within the European automotive industry. However, the traditional automotive industry regions of Western Europe will continue to function as the core area of the European automotive industry, accounting not only for the vast majority of high-value-added functions, but also for the majority of jobs and European production. Due to the persistent gap in labor costs, corporate taxes and generous investment incentives compared to core regions, the Eastern

European integrated periphery will continue to attract mostly lower-value-added and labor-intensive production of standardized cars and generic components, despite the gradual upgrading of its automotive industry (Pavlínek et al., 2009; Pavlínek and Ženka, 2011). Regional and local development effects of these changes will be significant in both the existing locations through job losses and in new locations through job creation and will thus contribute to the ongoing uneven development in Europe.

5

The Core–Periphery Structure of the European Automotive Industry

5.1 INTRODUCTION

The geographic structure of the European automotive industry has been described in the form of hierarchical core–periphery relationships based on the position of countries and regions in the spatial division of labor (Layan and Lung, 2004; Frigant and Layan, 2009; Lampón et al., 2016). In addition to the core and periphery, it usually includes an "intermediate" or "pericentral" spatial zone (Jones, 1993; Bordenave and Lung, 1996; Lung, 2004), which is often labeled as the semiperiphery (Hopkins and Wallerstein, 1977; Arrighi and Drangel, 1986; Martin, 1990; Hudson and Schamp, 1995b; Mordue and Sweeney, 2020). Core–semiperiphery–periphery structures are networks of relations (Borgatti and Everett, 1999) that link integrated production processes structured in GVCs and GPNs (Hopkins and Wallerstein, 1977; Arrighi and Drangel, 1986). Core and peripheral areas are integrated in spatial systems at different geographic scales through authority–dependency relationships, in which cores dominate peripheries (Friedmann, 1967), often through external control in the case of the automotive industry (Jacobs, 2017; 2019; Pavlínek, 2017a).

In the European automotive industry, core regions have been distinguished by large and affluent markets, the presence of strategic functions, especially R&D, management (decision-making) and marketing, and complex activities based on highly skilled labor, such as the assembly of high-end models and components requiring complex knowledge. Peripheral regions have been distinguished by smaller and less affluent markets, export-oriented assembly of inexpensive mass-market models and simple components, weak presence of strategic functions (Bordenave and Lung, 1996; Lung, 2004), risky low-volume export-oriented production of special models, and by experimenting with new organizational innovations (Hudson and Schamp, 1995b; Layan, 2006). As shown in Chapter 3, additional indicators that help distinguish the core, semiperiphery and periphery of the contemporary core-based automotive industry transnational macro-regional production networks include the degree of foreign ownership and control, the structure of automotive FDI, the presence of domestic global assembly firms, the number of domestic suppliers in the global top 100, the capabilities of domestic suppliers, labor costs and wage-adjusted labor productivity (Table 3.1 in Chapter 3).

There have been disagreements about the relative position of individual countries in the core–periphery structure of the European automotive industry. For example, some authors consider Eastern Europe to be part of the periphery of the European automotive industry (Lung, 2004; Pavlínek, 2018; 2020), while others have argued that the most advanced Eastern European countries, such as Poland and Czechia, have become part of the semiperiphery (e.g., Layan and Lung, 2007; Domański et al., 2014). There are similar ambiguities about the relative positions of other countries, such as Spain (Layan, 2000; Layan and Lung, 2007; Lampón et al., 2016; Frigant and Zumpe, 2017). These differences stem from different criteria and time periods used to evaluate the relative positions of countries in the European automotive industry.

These studies, however, usually fail to provide empirical evidence that would support the existence of this spatial hierarchy in the European automotive industry (for an exception, see, e.g., Jones, 1993), determine the position of individual European countries in this hierarchy and in the transnational division of labor, and allow for the analysis of changes in the position of individual countries in this hierarchy over time. This chapter aims to fill this gap theoretically by drawing on Friedmann's core–periphery model and Harvey's theory of the spatiotemporal fix and uneven development in the context of GVC and GPN perspectives in order to explain the geographic expansion of the automotive industry production networks into peripheral areas. In particular, it builds on the GVC and GPN perspectives and spatial divisions of labor in spatial systems to evaluate the relative position of countries in transnationally organized production networks and the integrated spatial system of the European automotive industry. It also addresses this gap by developing a methodology that allows for empirical evaluation of the position of countries in the European production network in the automotive industry and its changes over time. It is based on mutual trade flows with automotive industry products among individual countries (Mahutga, 2014), the power distribution and control through the degree of foreign ownership and control over production (Pavlínek, 2018) and the innovation activity in the automotive industry. The specific goal of this chapter is to investigate the position of individual countries in the European automotive industry production system based on what I call automotive industry power, to empirically determine their position in the core, semiperiphery and periphery, and to analyze the changes in their position during the 2003–2017 period, which was selected because of data availability. Despite the spatial restructuring of the European automotive industry since 1990 (e.g., Lung, 2004; Brincks et al., 2016; Pavlínek, 2020), the empirical analysis has revealed a stable core–semiperiphery–periphery structure during the 2003–2017 period.

The chapter is organized as follows. First, I start with a conceptual explanation of the division of labor in transnational production networks in the automotive industry. Second, I propose a methodology for delimiting the core, semiperiphery and periphery of the European automotive industry, which is based on the combination of trade-based positional power, ownership power and innovation power of European countries. Third, I present the results of the empirical analysis for the 2003–2017 period. Fourth, I summarize the main findings in the conclusion.

5.2 GLOBAL VALUE CHAINS, GLOBAL PRODUCTION NETWORKS AND THE DYNAMIC GEOGRAPHY OF TRANSNATIONAL PRODUCTION NETWORKS

The dependency and world-systems approaches have employed the concepts of the core and periphery in order to conceptualize development and economic relations since the beginning of states and the system of states (Wallerstein, 1974; Chase-Dunn and Hall, 1991; 1997; Chew and Lauderdale, 2010). The world-systems perspective has also introduced the concept of commodity chains (Hopkins and Wallerstein, 1977; 1986; Arrighi and Drangel, 1986), which was popularized by Gereffi and Korzeniewicz (1994) and evolved into the global commodity chains and, later, the GVC approaches (e.g., Gereffi, 2018; Kano et al., 2020). The global commodity chains and GVC approaches broke away from the world-systems perspective by shifting focus away from states to industries. They emphasized three fundamental features of transnationally organized industries in order to explain how industries and places evolve over time: the geography of value chains, including the geographic distribution of value-adding activities; the power distribution among firms and other actors in the chain with emphasis on the power and role of lead firms, particularly transnational corporations; and the role of institutions in influencing and structuring the operation of industries in different regions and at multiple geographic scales, with a particular emphasis on the role of the state and regional development strategies (e.g., Sturgeon et al., 2008; Gereffi, 2018). The global commodity chains and GVC approaches have also emphasized the importance of the integration of peripheries into the commodity or value chains of larger transnationally integrated systems and how it affects their chances for successful economic development (Gereffi, 2018).

The GPN approach shares with the GVC approach the focus on the integration of places, regions and countries via trade and FDI into transnationally organized production networks and how it affects their potential for development. It is particularly concerned with how and where the processes of value creation, enhancement and capture take place in GPNs and how their uneven distribution affects economic development (Coe et al., 2004; Coe and Yeung, 2015; 2019). The GPN approach recognizes different modes of articulation or strategic couplings (namely indigenous, functional and structural) of regions into transnational production networks, which reflect different regional assets of regions in the core, periphery and semiperiphery of the world economy that are being sought by TNCs. It also recognizes the unfavorable position of peripheral regions integrated in GPNs via structural couplings that might ultimately reiterate their peripheral status in the international division of labor (Yeung, 2009; 2015; 2016; Coe and Yeung, 2015; MacKinnon, 2012) (Table 5.1).

Both GPN and GVC approaches have argued, however, that the relative position of host country firms and regions in the international division of labor can be improved through upgrading (e.g., Rodríguez-De La Fuente and Lampón, 2020), which is defined as the movement of countries, regions, firms and workers from low- to high-value-added activities (Gereffi, 2005). The notion of industrial upgrading has evolved from that of a one-directional process (e.g., Gereffi, 1999) to a more nuanced understanding of different upgrading and downgrading trajectories (Coe and Yeung, 2015; Blažek, 2016), which recognizes both the potentially positive and potentially negative long-term effects of integration of firms and regions into GPNs.

Approaches related to divisions of labor in spatial systems distinguish the core, semiperiphery and periphery by different functions that receive different economic rewards (Hopkins and Wallerstein, 1977). Consequently, relative positions of countries in spatial systems have implications for their value creation and capture in particular economic activities that, in turn, influence their long-term effects for economic development (see Chapter 6). It has long been recognized in both economic geography and economics that higher-value-added, knowledge-intensive and decision-making activities and control functions tend to concentrate in core regions, while lower-value-added routine production functions tend to concentrate in peripheral regions (e.g., Hymer, 1972; Dicken, 2015).

The core-like processes in the automotive industry include: (1) dominant trade relations with noncore countries, which is reflected in the high aggregate positional power of resident firms in the automotive industry; (2) ownership and control power in the form of direct ownership and control by core-based TNCs over production facilities and processes in noncore countries, resulting in the dominance effect and the transfer of value from the periphery to the core; and (3) a high rate of innovation in the automotive industry. The peripheral processes include: (1) dependent trade relations with core countries, which is reflected in the low aggregate positional power of resident firms in the automotive industry; (2) a high degree of foreign control of the automotive industry via the core by core-based TNCs, resulting in a net transfer of value to the core; and (3) a low rate of innovation in the automotive industry compared to the core. Semiperipheral regions are zones with a mixture of core and

TABLE 5.1 *Contemporary approaches to the automotive industry in economic geography*

	Global value chains	Global production networks	Spatial divisions of labor
Focus	Transnational organization and control over the automotive industry, governance	Transnational organization of production networks, different modes of strategic couplings of regions and places into these networks	Territorial division of tasks between core and peripheral regions
Main vehicle of development	Different forms of upgrading, the ultimate goal is shifting from lower-value-added activities to higher-value-added activities in the value chain	Strategic coupling between extra-regional actors (TNCs) and regional assets, value creation, enhancement and capture	Regional specialization and competitiveness based on the uneven distribution of factors of production (e.g., regional innovation systems in core regions, FDI in peripheral regions)
Driving actors of development	TNCs, various institutions, especially the state	TNCs, states, local firms, regional and local institutions, labor	TNCs, states (e.g., via facilitating FDI in peripheral regions), regional institutions
Examples of publications	Sturgeon et al. (2008); Sturgeon and Van Biesebroeck (2011); Contreras et al. (2012); Rodríguez-De La Fuente and Lampón (2020)	Coe et al. (2004); Coe and Yeung (2015); Pavlínek (2018); Pavlínek and Ženka (2016)	Brincks et al. (2018); Mordue and Sweeney (2020); Pavlínek (2020); Trippl et al. (2021)

Source: author.

peripheral processes, in which neither core nor peripheral processes dominate. They are positioned in-between the core and periphery by housing both peripheral processes in relation to the core and core-like processes in relation to the periphery in the core–periphery structure (Hopkins and Wallerstein, 1977).

The dominant position of core areas is the outcome of their earlier innovations that allowed core-based institutions, such as TNCs, to penetrate and control the periphery (Friedmann, 1967). The innovation tends to gradually and selectively spread from the core to the periphery, although core regions continue to have higher rates of innovation because of more favorable conditions for innovative activities. These include the already existing highly localized concentrations of knowledge and innovation, strong institutional support and favorable governmental policies, high corporate and public spending on innovation, educated and skilled labor, diversified economy, high-quality technological infrastructure and agglomerations of firms in related industries (Tödtling and Trippl, 2005; Isaksen and Trippl, 2017). The control of peripheries by core-based institutions leads to a net transfer of value from peripheries to the core that economically strengthens the core and weakens the periphery in the long run (Friedmann, 1967; Dischinger et al., 2014a; Pavlínek and Ženka, 2016). It is in this context that I investigate the core–periphery structure of the European automotive industry.

5.2.1 The Integration of New Peripheries into Transnational Production Networks

Transnational production networks in the automotive industry are integrated through investment and trade flows with automotive industry commodities: raw materials, parts, components, preassembled modules, semi-finished and finished vehicles, flows of capital in the form of FDI, dividends and the transfer of profits, flows of labor and personnel, and flows of information, know-how and knowledge that allow for a fine-grained division of labor and increased regional specialization. The spatial dynamism of transnational production networks in the contemporary automotive industry is based on the investment strategies of core-based firms that are constantly looking for investment opportunities in peripheral areas in order to improve or maintain the rate of profit by lowering production costs, which are the total cost of production and delivering finished products to the market (Pavlínek, 2018; 2020).

The transnational integration in the automotive industry has been extensively analyzed generally (e.g., Carrillo et al., 2004) and in the context of the European automotive industry since the early 1990s (e.g., Jones, 1993; Freyssenet et al., 2003b). Chapters 3 and 4 of this book conceptualize the geographic expansion of automotive industry production networks into new geographic areas and the contemporaneous restructuring in the existing production regions by drawing on Harvey's theory of uneven development and spatiotemporal fix (Harvey, 1982; 2005b), which emphasizes the investment strategies of core-based automotive firms in peripheral lower-production-cost regions. Although core-based automotive firms use various strategies to ensure profitability (Boyer and Freyssenet, 2002), they always strive to minimize production costs by controlling the cost of factors of production. Firms can more easily control labor costs than the costs of other factors of production (Dicken, 2015) through technological and organization innovations and through the location of production into areas with labor surplus and low labor costs (Harvey, 1982). A sharp decrease in transportation costs by more than 90 percent in the twentieth century (Glaeser and Kohlhase, 2004), because of new transportation technologies (Levinson, 2006) and logistical systems (Kaneko and Nojiri, 2008; Danyluk, 2018), along with the lowering of trade barriers and deregulation of FDI, made it easier for firms to establish production in low-cost areas at the international scale. The potential for higher profits in such areas has been further enhanced by government policies of investment incentives, low corporate taxes and financing the construction of modern infrastructure that lower set-up sunk costs for investing firms and, therefore, lower their investment risk (Clark and Wrigley, 1995; Jacobs, 2019; Pavlínek, 2016; 2020).

Chapters 3 and 4 of this book demonstrate how both assembly firms and component suppliers are attracted to lower-cost peripheral locations by the potential of a higher rate of profit. However, along with Harvey (1982), I have argued that spatiotemporal fixes in the form of the establishment of production in new low-cost areas are only a temporary solution to declining profitability. As more and more firms are exploiting a spatiotemporal fix by establishing production in the same or similar peripheral regions, an increased demand for labor exhausts labor surplus, leading to rising wages that undermine the rate of profit and future growth. Rising production costs and declining profits eventually force firms that are most dependent on low labor costs to look for new production areas with labor surplus and lower wages, which often leads to relocations of the most labor-intensive activities, such as the assembly of cable harnesses, from the existing integrated peripheral regions to previously unintegrated peripheries (e.g., Aláez-Aller and Barneto-Carmona, 2008; Lampón et al., 2015; 2016; Pavlínek, 2015a). These new peripheral areas thus become competitive in attracting new investments of core-based firms especially in labor-intensive and routine production compared to the more expensive core or existing integrated peripheries (e.g., Frigant and Layan, 2009). The influx of profit-seeking investment capital into areas with a potential for a higher rate of profit results in economic growth in new low-cost peripheral regions. The outcome of this spatial investment behavior is the geographic expansion of production into new areas that are integrated into a transnational production network through capital, commodity, trade and technology linkages (hence the *integrated* peripheries), along with the economic growth bouncing from region to region (Harvey, 1982).

These processes can be demonstrated in the European automotive industry, where, as argued in Chapter 4 of this book, the geographic expansion of the automotive industry into peripheral regions and the development of transnational production networks have been strongly related to state development policies (Ward, 1982; Oberhauser, 1987; Pavlínek, 2016), regional integration, the establishment and expansion of the common market in the European Union and regional free-trade agreements with non-European Union countries (Hudson and Schamp, 1995b; Layan and Lung, 2004; Jacobs, 2019). Since the early 1960s, carmakers have actively lobbied for the geographic expansion of European regional integration that would give them opportunities to establish production in low-cost areas (Layan, 2000; Freyssenet and Lung, 2004). This has led to the geographic expansion of the automotive industry from its established centers into new areas since the 1960s, as documented in Chapter 4 of this book.

5.2.2 Restructuring in Core Areas

The growth of production in newly integrated peripheries impacts the existing locations within a transnational production network. The automotive industry in core areas continues to be favored by several crucial factors that make it attractive for additional investment, including large internal and external scale economies, high accumulated and exit sunk costs, an accessibility to large markets, low transportation costs, high-quality labor force, the proximity of R&D facilities, highly developed infrastructure and high-quality institutions (Bordenave and Lung, 1996; Clark and Wrigley, 1997; Carrincazeaux et al., 2001; Frigant and Lung, 2002). Core areas might benefit from the expansion of production in integrated peripheries because the finer division of labor and increased regional specialization within the transnational production network increase the specialization of core regions in capital-intensive production, skill-intensive, high-value-added activities and strategic functions. At the same time, the high-volume assembly of small cars with weaker engines and labor-intensive production of generic components can be gradually relocated to the integrated periphery because of lower production costs and labor surplus (Jones, 1993; Pavlínek, 2002d; 2020; Layan, 2006; Frigant and Layan, 2009; Jürgens and Krzywdzinski, 2009a). German automotive firms led by Volkswagen have been particularly successful in such complementary specialization by setting uplow-cost production of small cars and/or low-volume production of special models in Spain since the late 1980s (Jacobs, 2019), and Portugal (Ferrão and Vale, 1995) and Eastern Europe (Pavlínek, 2002d) since the early 1990s. It resulted in the more efficient territorial division of labor in automotive GPNs and, consequently, in improved competitiveness and higher corporate profits (Chiappini, 2012).

At the same time, existing core locations and older integrated peripheries, such as Belgium and Spain, may experience declining production and job loss due to the expansion of production in new integrated peripheries, especially in labor-intensive, low-value-added and less profitable production of generic components that does not require proximity to other firms. In extreme cases, this restructuring may lead to factory closures and relocations of production, especially of automotive components (Frigant and Layan, 2009; Lampón et al., 2015; Jacobs, 2019; Pavlínek, 2020). As we can see in Chapter 4 of this book, in Western Europe, between 2005 and 2016, large restructuring events, resulting in the creation or loss of at least 100 jobs or 10 percent or more of the labor force in automotive industry firms or factories employing at least 250 workers, led to 181 factory closures, 50 relocations and 35 partial relocations. Additionally, 529 firms experienced rationalization and job cuts, leading to 387,000 job losses altogether. At the same time, 133,000 jobs were created, resulting in the overall loss of 254,000 jobs. Some labor-intensive activities that for various reasons cannot be relocated continue to persist in core areas. In those cases, labor surplus can be imported from abroad and immigrant labor has been used for the expansion of existing plants in Western Europe for decades (Ward, 1982).

Overall, therefore, the integration of peripheral regions into transnational automotive industry GPNs triggers restructuring in core regions, semiperipheries and older integrated peripheries that results in a finer division of labor and greater regional specialization. As we can see, this continuous process of change has underlined the dynamic geography of the European automotive industry since the early 1960s. Based on the conceptual discussion, I will next explain a methodology that I will use to delimit the spatial hierarchy of the European automotive industry, before presenting empirical results of the analysis.

5.3   DELIMITING THE CORE, PERIPHERY AND SEMIPERIPHERY OF THE EUROPEAN AUTOMOTIVE INDUSTRY

The national economies of European Union member countries are the basic unit of analysis for two reasons. First, the methodology has specifically been developed to evaluate the relative positions of individual countries in the transnational macro-regional (European) production system. Second, the necessary automotive industry data for the conducted analysis are only available for national economies from Eurostat since 2003. These data are unavailable for subnational units.

The starting point of my analysis is Mahutga's (2014) measurement of the positional power of countries in GPNs as the aggregate positional power of country firms in a particular industry based on bilateral national trade data. I apply this approach in the automotive industry of European Union countries by using data extracted from Eurostat's ComExt database for the

2003–2017 period. However, following Friedmann (1967), I argue that trade relations alone and trade-based measures, such as the value and volume of exports, are insufficient for determining the relative position of countries in transnational production systems. We also need to consider the decision-making power and the strength of innovation activities in the automotive industry. Therefore, I normalize the positional power of countries in the automotive industry by the indices of the degree of foreign control and innovation into an aggregate index, which I call the automotive industry power. I then use a cluster analysis of automotive industry power to determine the relative position of European Union countries in the European automotive industry production network between 2003 and 2017.

5.3.1 Positional Power

The positional power of countries estimates the average network position of firms in its territory (Mahutga, 2014). It focuses on power asymmetries within GVCs/GPNs and considers the uneven economic power position of individual countries in transnational production networks based on international trade. The positional power of countries is calculated from national trade data in a particular industry. In the case of the automotive industry, we can measure country's j's producer driven power (P_j^P) as follows.

$$P_j^P = \sum_{i=1}^{n} \log(X_{ji}/Y_{i.} + 1)$$

where X_{ji} is the value of automotive industry exports from country j to country i, Y_i is the total value of imports of the receiving country i and log is the base 10 logarithm. Country j has a high producer-driven power when it captures a large share of markets in many other countries through its exports, that is, these other countries depend on imports from country j. It has a low producer-driven power when it has a small number of such trade partners (countries).

Since the producer driven power is only based on exports, it ignores the buyer-driven power of large assembly firms and global tier-one suppliers in GPNs. It also underestimates the positional power of countries whose automotive industry is geared to large domestic markets rather than exports. Therefore, I have also calculated the buyer-driven power (P_j^B) of country j as follows (Mahutga, 2014).

$$P_j^B = \sum_{i=1}^{n} \log(Y_{ij}/X_{i.} + 1)$$

where Y_{ij} is the value of automotive industry imports imported by country j from country i, X_i is the total value of exports of the exporting country i and log is the base 10 logarithm. Country j has a high buyer-driven power when it has many trade partners (countries) from which it imports a high share of these countries' total automotive industry exports, that is, these other countries depend on exports to country j. It has a low buyer-driven power when it has a small number of such trade partners.

The trade data were calculated for the product categories 870120–871690 of the HS6 product specification from the Eurostat ComExt database (Eurostat, 2020a). The positional power of a particular country in the automotive industry was then calculated as the average of its producer-driven and buyer-driven power for each year between 2003 and 2017 (Table 5.2). Since positional power does not measure the size of the automotive industry, countries with a larger output can have a smaller positional power than countries with a smaller output and vice versa.

5.3.2   Ownership and Control Power

Spatial systems based on the core–periphery structure are integrated through authority–dependency relationships, in which core areas dominate peripheral areas (Friedmann, 1967). Therefore, if we want to evaluate the power position of countries in such structures, we need to include a measure of power and control other than the one based on trade relations. We need to consider the uneven distribution of decision-making power among automotive industry firms, that is, who controls the industry and has the power to decide about the production and the distribution of its rewards. In other words, who controls who will produce what, where, for what price and how the benefits of production (e.g., profits) will be distributed within the GPN? These dominance and control relationships are very important proxies of the core and periphery position of countries (e.g., Friedmann, 1967; Lung, 2004; Fischer, 2015).

Generally, core countries are those that control production in other countries through resident TNCs that directly own production facilities abroad in the case of the automotive industry. Indirectly, TNCs control production abroad also through setting the terms of trade with automotive products and through dominating captive local suppliers in peripheral regions (e.g., Pavlínek and Žížalová, 2016; Pavlínek, 2018). The decision-making power about the entire TNC and its GPN tends to be highly concentrated in the TNC headquarters in their home countries (e.g., Pries and Wäcken, 2020).

Peripheral countries are those whose industry is predominantly controlled from abroad typically through the direct ownership of production facilities in the automotive industry by foreign TNCs. This capital dependency has strong implications for the strategic decision-making, technological, know-how and managerial dependency. Firm-level empirical evidence from the Eastern European automotive industry shows that the most important strategic decisions about foreign-owned factories are made by parent companies abroad in their TNC headquarters (Pavlínek, 2016; Pavlínek and Ženka, 2016).

TABLE 5.2 *Positional power of countries in the European automotive industry, 2000–2018*

	2000	2001	2002	2003	2004	2005	2006	2007	2008	2009	2010	2011	2012	2013	2014	2015	2016	2017	2018
Austria	0.358	0.355	0.349	0.360	0.352	0.304	0.300	0.291	0.307	0.314	0.327	0.312	0.314	0.301	0.279	0.298	0.307	0.297	0.279
Belgium	0.836	0.823	0.891	0.844	0.825	0.762	0.709	0.744	0.878	0.828	0.830	0.789	0.855	0.859	0.845	0.868	0.883	0.847	0.822
Britain	0.962	0.892	0.906	0.836	0.825	0.838	0.857	0.820	0.776	0.805	0.809	0.787	0.798	0.808	0.778	0.791	0.748	0.659	0.630
Bulgaria	0.014	0.011	0.013	0.015	0.014	0.017	0.022	0.137	0.119	0.063	0.053	0.052	0.050	0.067	0.058	0.064	0.076	0.083	0.074
Croatia	0.027	0.024	0.021	0.025	0.025	0.024	0.022	0.020	0.022	0.020	0.018	0.019	0.017	0.021	0.025	0.032	0.032	0.031	0.036
Czechia	0.148	0.145	0.142	0.131	0.220	0.269	0.296	0.309	0.321	0.391	0.413	0.411	0.415	0.413	0.458	0.444	0.438	0.467	0.469
Denmark	0.112	0.115	0.147	0.134	0.135	0.128	0.129	0.118	0.130	0.136	0.128	0.117	0.111	0.104	0.098	0.103	0.101	0.090	0.088
Estonia	0.045	0.049	0.055	0.065	0.121	0.146	0.162	0.152	0.120	0.097	0.093	0.112	0.136	0.158	0.124	0.098	0.102	0.100	0.106
Finland	0.232	0.214	0.201	0.194	0.180	0.178	0.152	0.136	0.140	0.138	0.127	0.126	0.124	0.118	0.125	0.119	0.118	0.119	0.120
France	1.204	1.123	1.134	1.105	1.141	1.108	1.002	0.948	0.959	1.036	1.077	1.036	1.018	0.987	0.912	0.870	0.870	0.902	0.933
Germany	2.568	2.568	2.655	2.735	2.838	2.841	2.805	2.704	2.706	2.777	2.838	2.835	2.841	2.812	2.861	2.904	2.899	2.862	2.716
Greece	0.050	0.046	0.044	0.050	0.054	0.049	0.048	0.058	0.056	0.055	0.036	0.022	0.020	0.022	0.024	0.023	0.030	0.033	0.037
Hungary	0.074	0.071	0.082	0.073	0.137	0.192	0.220	0.220	0.203	0.170	0.179	0.190	0.200	0.208	0.232	0.237	0.239	0.250	0.247
Ireland	0.036	0.032	0.031	0.026	0.029	0.030	0.031	0.030	0.025	0.013	0.015	0.014	0.016	0.018	0.022	0.026	0.026	0.025	0.026
Italy	0.705	0.690	0.658	0.678	0.686	0.661	0.662	0.681	0.698	0.631	0.616	0.589	0.550	0.535	0.524	0.538	0.555	0.546	0.551
Latvia	0.153	0.156	0.154	0.163	0.131	0.127	0.162	0.173	0.141	0.112	0.117	0.153	0.158	0.144	0.131	0.131	0.135	0.134	0.129
Lithuania	0.027	0.028	0.027	0.024	0.200	0.164	0.196	0.222	0.214	0.125	0.171	0.188	0.173	0.183	0.168	0.175	0.175	0.186	0.182
Luxembourg	0.013	0.014	0.012	0.018	0.018	0.017	0.018	0.020	0.023	0.023	0.021	0.019	0.021	0.021	0.021	0.018	0.019	0.023	0.023
Netherlands	0.374	0.331	0.334	0.332	0.325	0.308	0.315	0.343	0.359	0.326	0.362	0.395	0.370	0.370	0.349	0.361	0.355	0.433	0.442

(continued)

TABLE 5.2 (*continued*)

	2000	2001	2002	2003	2004	2005	2006	2007	2008	2009	2010	2011	2012	2013	2014	2015	2016	2017	2018
Poland	NA	NA	NA	NA	0.238	0.252	0.284	0.298	0.362	0.394	0.398	0.380	0.402	0.426	0.420	0.438	0.436	0.478	0.499
Portugal	0.083	0.076	0.072	0.067	0.070	0.073	0.075	0.072	0.077	0.082	0.088	0.079	0.071	0.073	0.075	0.075	0.074	0.093	0.116
Romania	0.017	0.025	0.019	0.024	0.034	0.045	0.057	0.298	0.317	0.222	0.157	0.170	0.180	0.170	0.179	0.181	0.172	0.160	0.188
Slovakia	NA	NA	NA	NA	0.096	0.100	0.121	0.172	0.201	0.200	0.193	0.215	0.250	0.258	0.245	0.266	0.260	0.253	0.275
Slovenia	0.118	0.100	0.089	0.085	0.125	0.147	0.163	0.197	0.185	0.200	0.190	0.185	0.181	0.179	0.162	0.178	0.179	0.172	0.174
Spain	0.650	0.645	0.640	0.910	0.687	0.678	0.668	0.657	0.605	0.580	0.605	0.604	0.530	0.603	0.632	0.658	0.672	0.649	0.641
Sweden	0.436	0.388	0.364	0.404	0.418	0.399	0.429	0.413	0.397	0.347	0.409	0.430	0.409	0.408	0.390	0.384	0.383	0.366	0.359

Source: calculated by author from data available at Eurostat (2020a).

Semiperipheral countries are positioned in-between; they control production in foreign (mostly peripheral) countries through TNCs based in semiperipheral countries and, at the same time, a significant share of their domestic industry is controlled through direct ownership from abroad, mostly from core countries. In Chapter 4 of this book, in terms of foreign ownership and control, I consider semiperipheral countries of the automotive industry as those that lack high-volume domestic assembly firms but have domestic "global suppliers" that invest in foreign countries (e.g., Britain, Canada, Sweden) (see also Mordue and Sweeney, 2020).

The positional power of countries has been therefore normalized by the index of foreign control (Pavlínek, 2018), which calculates the relative importance of foreign-owned firms in the automotive industry in a given country. The index of foreign control has been calculated for each country and year between 2003 and 2017 as the average value of the share of foreign-controlled enterprises of five indicators in the manufacture of motor vehicles, trailers and semi-trailers (NACE 29 (2008–2017) and NACE 34 (2003–2007)) (Eurostat, 2020c): production value, value added at factor cost, gross investment in tangible goods, number of persons employed, and turnover or gross premiums written. A low degree of foreign control indicates a core position, while a high degree of foreign control indicates a periphery position in transnational production networks. The index of foreign control can vary between 0 and 1, with 1 indicating a total foreign control of the automotive industry and 0 indicating zero foreign control. The positional power of each country for each year was normalized by dividing it by the index of foreign control, which strengthened the relative position of countries with the low degree of foreign control of its automotive industry (e.g., Germany), while weakening it for countries with the high degree of foreign control (e.g., Slovakia).

5.3.3 Innovation Power

As discussed in the conceptual section of this chapter, the core areas of spatial systems are the prime zones of innovation activities while peripheral regions are typified by lower innovation activity (Friedmann, 1967; Lung, 2004; Tödtling and Trippl, 2005; Isaksen and Trippl, 2017). In order to estimate the intensity of innovation activities in the automotive industry as a whole, the index of innovation was calculated from the share of total R&D personnel and researchers of persons employed and the share of business expenditure on R&D of the total value of production in the automotive industry (NACE 29 (2008–2017) and NACE 34 (2003–2007)) (Eurostat, 2020d). Both measures were normalized for each country and year using the following method. A country with the highest value was set to 1 and the values of all other countries were calculated in proportion to the strongest country. Therefore, the values for all countries and both variables fall between 0 and 1. In the next step, I calculated the average of these two normalized measures for each country and a particular year, which I call the index of innovation. The index of innovation thus measures the relative importance of innovation activities in the automotive industry of a given country. Next, I used the index of innovation to further normalize the positional power to arrive at the automotive industry power through multiplying the index of foreign control normalized positional power by the index of innovation, which lowers the index of foreign control normalized positional power by a greater degree for countries with a weak index of innovation than for countries with a strong index of innovation (Table 5.3).

5.3.4 Data Limitations

The 2003–2017 study period was selected because the data for the index of foreign control and innovation index is unavailable prior to 2003. The automotive industry product categories 870120–871690 of the HS6 product specification from the Eurostat ComExt database, which were used for the trade data, are not 100 percent compatible with the automotive industry product specification NACE Rev. 2 (NACE 29), which was used for the index of foreign control and the index of innovation for the 2008–2017 period.[1] No trade data is available for Malta and Cyprus. Luxembourg, Greece and Croatia also had to be removed from the analysis due to data unavailability for the index of foreign control and the index of innovation. Luxembourg had the lowest average 2003–2017 positional power of all European Union countries and Greece and Croatia were positioned just above the second-lowest-ranked Ireland but below Bulgaria, which suggests periphery positions for these three countries. Since none of them is an important automotive producer, their removal should not affect the overall analysis. Because trade data are unavailable for Poland and Slovakia for 2003, I used their 2004 trade data for 2003. The data for the index of foreign control and innovation index are based on NACE 34 for the 2003–2007 period and NACE 29 for the 2008–2017 period.[2] The 2003–2007 data for the index of foreign control and the index of innovation are unavailable for Ireland. I have used the average values of the 2008–2012 data for these two indicators to

---

[1] In particular, the ComExt database includes the manufacture of agricultural tractors, tractors used in construction or mining, off-road dumping trucks, and trailers and semi-trailers specially designed for use in agriculture, which are excluded from NACE 29 (Eurostat, 2008; 2020a).

[2] NACE 34, used until 2008, refers to the NACE Rev. 1.1 classification of the automotive industry and NACE 29, introduced in January 2009, refers to its NACE Rev. 2 classification. These two classifications are not fully compatible because compared to NACE 34, NACE 29 includes the manufacture of electrical ignition or starting equipment for internal combustion engines, electrical sound-signaling burglar alarms for motor vehicles and the manufacture of car seats. Compared to NACE 34, NACE 29 excludes the manufacture of pistons, piston rings, carburetors and such for all internal combustion engines, diesel engines etc., the manufacture of inlet and exhaust valves of internal combustion engines, and the repair and maintenance of containers (Eurostat, 2020b).

TABLE 5.3 *Values of automotive industry power in the European automotive industry by country, 2003–2017*

	2003	2004	2005	2006	2007	2008	2009	2010	2011	2012	2013	2014	2015	2016	2017
Austria	0.255	0.234	0.172	0.195	0.279	0.284	0.263	0.279	0.267	0.250	0.236	0.222	0.251	0.249	0.236
Belgium	0.078	0.115	0.099	0.091	0.106	0.145	0.138	0.139	0.150	0.186	0.198	0.188	0.229	0.228	0.226
Britain	0.302	0.358	0.396	0.464	0.547	0.490	0.489	0.490	0.580	0.554	0.546	0.561	0.641	0.578	0.492
Bulgaria	0.000	0.000	0.000	0.000	0.000	0.000	0.000	0.000	0.000	0.000	0.000	0.000	0.005	0.005	0.004
Czechia	0.031	0.060	0.076	0.080	0.093	0.066	0.062	0.062	0.065	0.069	0.070	0.073	0.070	0.062	0.071
Denmark	0.032	0.046	0.042	0.045	0.017	0.049	0.104	0.073	0.103	0.098	0.118	0.052	0.054	0.063	0.053
Estonia	0.027	0.030	0.033	0.048	0.060	0.016	0.014	0.011	0.016	0.019	0.012	0.012	0.012	0.023	0.013
Finland	0.168	0.193	0.158	0.170	0.162	0.140	0.148	0.136	0.117	0.095	0.095	0.095	0.144	0.149	0.130
France	2.391	3.152	2.315	2.099	1.614	2.762	2.955	2.510	2.560	1.991	1.694	1.700	1.689	1.582	1.386
Germany	13.427	17.059	16.541	17.344	17.971	18.230	15.717	16.916	19.924	17.091	15.592	16.150	18.448	16.857	18.536
Hungary	0.006	0.009	0.014	0.016	0.028	0.026	0.021	0.023	0.027	0.029	0.030	0.031	0.032	0.032	0.036
Ireland	0.007	0.005	0.005	0.005	0.005	0.006	0.002	0.002	0.005	0.006	0.004	0.004	0.003	0.006	0.008

(continued)

TABLE 5.3 (*continued*)

	2003	2004	2005	2006	2007	2008	2009	2010	2011	2012	2013	2014	2015	2016	2017
Italy	0.943	1.207	1.146	1.261	1.563	1.614	1.439	1.438	1.514	1.344	1.502	1.458	1.454	1.484	1.255
Latvia	0.008	0.012	0.010	0.016	0.032	0.021	0.023	0.020	0.011	0.012	0.018	0.015	0.023	0.019	0.016
Lithuania	0.001	0.060	0.004	0.008	0.061	0.043	0.038	0.045	0.066	0.050	0.063	0.041	0.043	0.031	0.028
Netherlands	0.151	0.215	0.180	0.178	0.199	0.156	0.152	0.176	0.299	0.275	0.316	0.313	0.295	0.269	0.322
Poland	0.009	0.015	0.018	0.020	0.020	0.025	0.018	0.013	0.021	0.033	0.047	0.051	0.058	0.061	0.075
Portugal	0.006	0.006	0.003	0.014	0.027	0.041	0.027	0.024	0.022	0.014	0.014	0.018	0.018	0.016	0.018
Romania	0.007	0.008	0.011	0.010	0.064	0.042	0.019	0.013	0.013	0.012	0.009	0.017	0.020	0.018	0.016
Slovakia	0.003	0.003	0.004	0.004	0.005	0.005	0.005	0.006	0.006	0.007	0.012	0.018	0.017	0.021	0.021
Slovenia	0.013	0.018	0.020	0.032	0.043	0.103	0.080	0.087	0.128	0.130	0.096	0.077	0.075	0.078	0.050
Spain	0.130	0.149	0.136	0.140	0.149	0.140	0.192	0.167	0.165	0.136	0.137	0.178	0.150	0.162	0.149
Sweden	0.714	0.808	0.767	0.724	0.792	0.851	0.738	0.684	0.708	0.729	0.676	0.591	0.548	0.560	0.527

Source: calculated by author from data available at Eurostat (2020a; 2020c; 2020d).

normalize the positional power of Ireland for the 2003–2007 period. In cases when one or two data values of the individual components used for the calculation of the index of foreign control for a particular country was not available for a particular year, I used the data for the closest available year as these values do not change dramatically from year to year. Belgium, Germany, Austria, Sweden and Britain provide the data of the share of total R&D personnel and researchers of persons employed only every other year. I have calculated the data for missing years as an average value of the previous and following years. Denmark, France and Britain did not provide the 2003–2006 data for R&D expenditures and I have used the 2007 values for these years instead.

5.3.5 Delimiting Spatial Categories

The K-means cluster analysis was applied on the descendent order of the natural logarithm of average automotive industry power values in order to delimit five clusters for the 2003–2017, 2003–2007, 2008–2012 and 2013–2017 periods. Five-year automotive industry power averages were used in order to minimize the effect of data limitations on annual fluctuations in automotive industry power. Five delimited clusters correspond with the spatial categories as follows: a higher-order core, lower-order core, semiperiphery, periphery and lower-order periphery (Table 5.4).

Drawing on the cluster analysis, I have evaluated changes in the position of countries during 2003–2017 as follows. First, I have used the clusters based on the 2003–2017 automotive industry power averages to determine positions of individual countries during the entire 2003–2017 period. Second, I have compared the 2003–2017 position of each country with its 2003–2007, 2008–2012 and 2013–2017 positions. If a country was classified in the same cluster during all three five-year periods as during the entire 2003–2017 period, I considered its relative position to be stable. If not, I considered its relative position to be unstable.

5.4 RESULTS

5.4.1 Core Countries

5.4.1.1 Stable Core
The cluster analysis based on the natural logarithm of the average 2003–2017 automotive industry power values classified five countries in the core of the European automotive industry: Germany, France, Italy, Sweden and Britain (Table 5.4, Figures 5.1 and 5.2). Germany, France and Italy were delimited in the stable core, with Germany being classified in a separate cluster corresponding with its higher-order core position. France and Italy represented a much weaker

TABLE 5.4 Classification of countries into spatial zones in the European automotive industry system delimited by cluster analysis based on the natural logarithm of average values of automotive industry power during 2003–2007, 2008–2012, 2013–2017 and 2003–2017

	2003–2017				2003–2007				2008–2012				2013–2017			
#	Country	Cluster	Distance	Zone	Country	Cluster	Distance	Zone	Country	Cluster	Distance	Zone	Country	Cluster	Distance	Zone
1	Germany	1	0.000	C	Germany	1	0.000	HC	Germany	1	0.000	HC	Germany	1	0.000	HC
2	France	2	0.331	LC	France	2	0.583	LC	France	2	0.845	LC	France	2	0.059	LC
3	Italy	2	0.135	LC	Italy	2	0.054	LC	Italy	2	0.292	LC	Italy	2	0.059	LC
4	Sweden	2	0.162	LC	Sweden	2	0.529	LC	Sweden	2	0.391	LC	Sweden	3	0.778	SP
5	Britain	2	0.305	LC	Britain	3	0.802	SP	Britain	2	0.746	LC	Britain	3	0.748	SP
6	Austria	3	0.296	SP	Austria	3	0.005	SP	Austria	3	0.698	SP	Netherlands	3	0.127	SP
7	Netherlands	3	0.275	SP	Netherlands	3	0.202	SP	Netherlands	3	0.458	SP	Austria	3	0.110	SP
8	Belgium	3	0.096	SP	Finland	3	0.639	SP	Spain	3	0.179	SP	Belgium	3	0.222	SP
9	Spain	3	0.089	SP	Spain	3	0.275	SP	Belgium	3	0.124	SP	Spain	3	0.543	SP
10	Finland	3	0.054	SP	Belgium	3	0.085	SP	Finland	3	0.050	SP	Finland	3	0.779	SP
11	Slovenia	3	0.255	SP	Czechia	4	0.020	P	Slovenia	3	0.234	SP	Slovenia	4	0.856	P
12	Czechia	3	0.265	SP	Estonia	4	0.970	P	Denmark	3	0.448	SP	Czechia	4	0.774	P
13	Denmark	3	0.290	SP	Denmark	4	0.352	P	Czechia	3	0.726	SP	Denmark	4	0.759	P
14	Lithuania	4	0.341	P	Lithuania	4	0.446	P	Lithuania	4	0.735	P	Poland	4	0.604	P
15	Poland	4	0.261	P	Slovenia	4	0.047	P	Portugal	4	0.096	P	Lithuania	4	0.255	P
16	Hungary	4	0.130	P	Romania	4	0.577	P	Hungary	4	0.084	P	Hungary	4	0.006	P
17	Estonia	4	0.117	P	Poland	4	0.508	P	Poland	4	0.050	P	Latvia	4	0.565	P
18	Romania	4	0.021	P	Latvia	5	0.455	LP	Romania	4	0.163	P	Slovakia	4	0.583	P
19	Portugal	4	0.003	P	Hungary	5	0.604	LP	Latvia	4	0.292	P	Portugal	4	0.644	P
20	Latvia	4	0.019	P	Portugal	4	0.252	P	Estonia	4	0.411	P	Romania	4	0.687	P
21	Slovakia	4	0.286	P	Ireland	4	0.433	LP	Slovakia	5	0.162	LP	Estonia	4	0.776	P
22	Ireland	4	0.568	P	Slovakia	4	0.149	LP	Ireland	5	0.162	LP	Ireland	5	0.314	LP
23	Bulgaria	5	0.000	LP	Bulgaria	5			Bulgaria	5			Bulgaria	5	0.314	LP

Notes: HC = higher-order core, LC = lower-order core, SP = semiperiphery, P = periphery, LP = lower-order periphery.
Source: author.

lower-order stable core. The stable core countries consistently kept their automotive industry power rank positions during 2003–2017 (Table 5.5).

Germany dominated trade relations with all European countries during the entire period (i.e., had the highest value of the positional power every year) (Tables 5.2 and 5.6), had the lowest index of foreign control (Table 5.7) and the second-highest average level of the innovation index (Table 5.8). Germany's dominant position of the higher-order core is reflected by its automotive

TABLE 5.5 *Change in the relative position of European Union countries between 2003–2007 and 2013–2017 according to automotive industry power*

	Rank 2003–2017	Rank 2003–2007	Rank 2013–2017	Difference between 2003–2007 and 2013–2017
Germany	1	1	1	0
France	2	2	2	0
Italy	3	3	3	0
Sweden	4	4	4	0
Britain	5	5	5	0
Austria	6	6	7	−1
Netherlands	7	7	6	1
Belgium	8	10	8	2
Spain	9	9	9	0
Finland	10	8	10	−2
Slovenia	11	15	11	4
Czechia	12	11	12	−1
Denmark	13	13	13	0
Lithuania	14	14	15	−1
Poland	15	17	14	3
Hungary	16	19	16	3
Estonia	17	12	21	−9
Romania	18	16	20	−4
Portugal	19	20	19	1
Latvia	20	18	17	1
Slovakia	21	22	18	4
Ireland	22	21	22	−1
Bulgaria	23	23	23	0

Source: calculated by author from data available at Eurostat (2020a; 2020c; 2020d).

TABLE 5.6 *Change in the relative trade position of European Union countries between 2003–2007 and 2013–2017 according to positional power*

	Rank 2003–2017	Rank 2003–2007	Rank 2013–2017	Difference between 2003–2007 and 2013–2017
Germany	1	1	1	0
France	2	2	2	0
Belgium	3	4	3	1
Britain	4	3	4	−1
Spain	5	5	5	0
Italy	6	6	6	0
Sweden	7	7	9	−2
Poland	8	10	8	2
Czechia	9	11	7	4
Netherlands	10	8	10	−2
Austria	11	9	11	−2
Slovakia	12	19	12	7
Hungary	13	12	13	−1
Lithuania	14	14	14	0
Slovenia	15	16	15	1
Romania	16	20	16	4
Latvia	17	15	17	−2
Finland	18	13	18	−5
Estonia	19	17	19	−2
Denmark	20	18	20	−2
Portugal	21	21	21	0
Bulgaria	22	22	22	0
Ireland	23	23	23	0

Source: calculated by author from data available at Eurostat (2020a).

industry power being on average 8.4 times higher than that of France and 12.5 times higher than that of Italy (Table 5.3, Figure 5.1).

The lower-order core position of France is based on its second-strongest positional power, the third-lowest degree of foreign control and the fifth-strongest innovation index. The relative position of France weakened between 2003 and 2017 due to the relative decline of the French automotive industry since the second half of the 2000s (Pardi, 2020). France's relative position also worsened in automotive innovation due to the partial relocation of automotive R&D abroad. Renault Technology Romania was opened in 2007 and it has employed 2,300 engineers at three sites in Romania who, in addition to providing technical support for Renault's factories in Eastern Europe, Turkey and North Africa, develop and test vehicles on the Mo platform, which was previously done in France (Benadbdejlil et al., 2017). Similarly, the Kwid had been the first Renault model that was completely designed abroad (in India) instead of the corporate R&D center in France (Midler et al., 2017). Consequently, despite the fact that French automakers continue to conduct the most important automotive R&D in France, the R&D's share of total business expenditures and employment has declined in France.

Italy's automotive industry power has been the weakest of the three stable core countries because of Italy's weaker average positional power compared not only to France but also Belgium, Britain and Spain. Its car production halved after 2000 (Calabrese, 2020), weakening its positional power (Table 5.2). At the same time, Italy's index of foreign control and index of innovation are similar to those of France. The second-lowest index of foreign control therefore differentiates Italy from unstable core countries and is the basis of its stable lower-order core position (Table 5.7).

5.4.1.2 *Unstable Core*
Sweden and Britain represent the unstable core since Sweden was delimited as the semiperiphery during 2013–2017, while Britain was delimited as the semiperiphery during 2003–2007 and 2013–2017, indicating their borderline core–semiperiphery position. Sweden's core position was mainly based on the consistently highest index of innovation, with the exception of 2007 and 2008. Sweden's weakening automotive industry power position after 2008 was related to its worsening positional power ranking and to the increased index of foreign control related to the collapse of Saab and takeover of Volvo cars by Ford and then Geely. The core position of Britain is based on its strong positional power and strong innovation combined with a high degree of foreign control. Britain was the fourth-largest vehicle producer in the European Union until 2018, with its export-oriented production geared toward European Union markets. The declining output since 2017 suggests that Brexit might negatively affect Britain's relative position in the European automotive industry in the long run (e.g., Coffey and Thornley, 2020).

5.4.2 Semiperipheral Countries

The semiperiphery is an intermediate spatial zone that is geographically concentrated in Western Europe and is mainly distinguished by a high degree of foreign control, weaker positional power than Germany and France and variable strength of innovation activities (Tables 5.1–5.5, Figures 5.1 and 5.2).

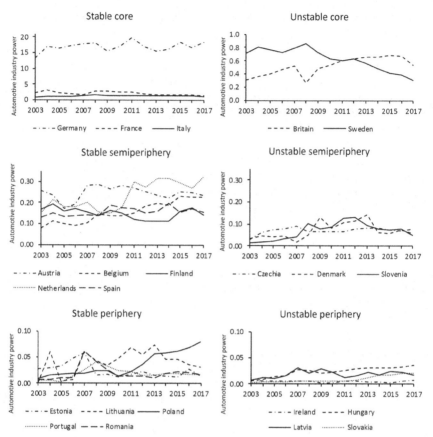

FIGURE 5.1 Automotive industry power of selected European Union countries, 2003–2017
Source: author, based on data in Table 5.3.

5.4.2.1   *Stable Semiperiphery*

The cluster analysis delimited Austria, the Netherlands, Spain, Belgium and Finland in the stable semiperiphery. Spain is the second-largest vehicle producer in Europe. It represents an example of an older integrated periphery which developed based on FDI-driven growth (Jacobs, 2019) and advanced into the semiperiphery. Spain's weaker-than-expected fifth average positional power is due to its specialization in the production of smaller low- to medium-value-added vehicles (Aláez et al., 2015). Spain's relatively low automotive industry power also reflects its high dependence on foreign capital (Aláez et al., 2015; Jacobs, 2019) and a lower relative importance of R&D given the overall size of its automotive industry.

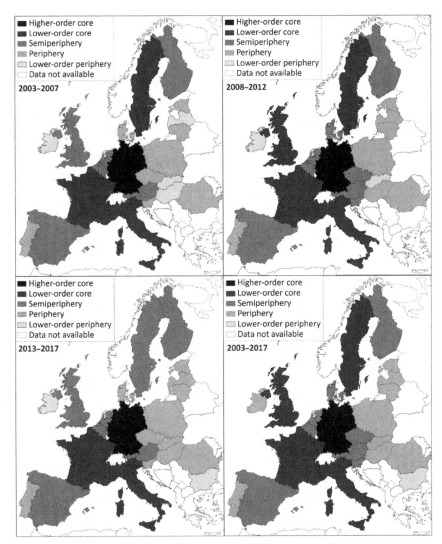

FIGURE 5.2 The core, semiperiphery and periphery of the European automotive industry delimited by cluster analysis based on the natural logarithm of average values of automotive industry power during 2003–2007, 2008–2012, 2013–2017 and 2003–2017
Source: author.

Belgium represents the second example of an old integrated periphery that advanced into the semiperiphery. Belgium's positional power was the third-strongest in the European Union after Germany and France mainly due to the specialization of the two remaining assembly plants (Audi Brussels and Volvo

Car Gent) in the export-oriented high-value-added production of luxury SUVs and electric vehicles (Jacobs, 2019). Despite the improvements in the comparative positions of Belgium in the index of foreign control, as a number of foreign-owned factories closed (Jacobs, 2019), and in innovation capacity, its automotive industry power continues to be undermined by a high degree of foreign control and a weak innovation index, which is at the level of Spain.

Austria had the highest average automotive industry power in the stable semiperiphery despite its weak positional power compared to other semiperipheral countries with larger automotive industries. Its position was mainly based on a strong innovation capacity (Trippl et al., 2021) with the

TABLE 5.7 *Index of foreign control in the European automotive industry by country, 2003–2017*

	Average 2003–2017 (%)	Average 2003–2007 (%)	Average 2013–2017 (%)	Rank 2003–2017	Rank 2003–2007	Rank 2013–2017	Change in rank between 2003–2007 and 2013–2017
Germany	14.6	14.1	14.8	1	1	1	0
Italy	20.3	20.8	19.6	2	2	2	0
France	22.8	23.1	23.5	3	3	3	0
Finland	28.4	26.5	29.7	4	4	4	0
Denmark	33.5	34.9	33.5	5	5	5	0
Slovenia	53.7	45.3	63.3	6	6	6	0
Sweden	56.9	52.3	66.1	7	7	8	-1
Estonia	64.5	59.8	66.2	8	9	9	0
Netherlands	68.0	71.0	64.8	9	13	7	6
Lithuania	68.8	56.5	80.9	10	8	14	-6
Ireland	72.6[a]	65.7[b]	79.4	11	10	13	-3
Austria	77.3	72.8	79.4	12	15	12	3
Latvia	78.1	65.8	85.3	13	11	16	-5
Spain	78.4	71.1	86.1	14	14	18	-4
Portugal	79.3	80.4	79.3	15	17	11	6
Britain	80.0	76.7	82.9	16	16	15	1
Belgium	81.0	81.9	79.2	17	20	10	10
Romania	82.8	67.3	91.6	18	12	20	-8
Poland	83.6	80.8	85.6	19	18	17	1
Bulgaria	85.0	81.5	87.8	20	19	19	0
Czechia	91.8	91.2	92.0	21	21	21	0
Hungary	93.1	92.1	94.6	22	22	22	0
Slovakia	95.6	93.1	96.4	23	23	23	0

Notes: [a] 2008–2017 average, [b] 2008–2012 average.
Source: calculated by author from data available at Eurostat (2020c).

TABLE 5.8 *Index of innovation in the European automotive industry by country, 2003–2017*

	Average 2003–2017 (%)	Average 2003–2007 (%)	Average 2013–2017 (%)	Rank 2003–2017	Rank 2003–2007	Rank 2013–2017	Change in rank between 2003–2007 and 2013–2017
Sweden	97.6	97.9	98.9	1	1	1	0
Germany	88.4	85.2	87.6	2	2	2	0
Austria	62.0	54.2	64.0	3	3	3	0
Britain	50.8	38.5	62.0	4	7	4	3
France	47.7	48.1	41.8	5	4	7	−3
Italy	46.6	38.6	52.7	6	6	6	0
Netherlands	44.0	39.9	53.3	7	5	5	0
Finland	28.3	26.8	29.8	8	8	8	0
Slovenia	21.3	8.2	26.4	9	17	9	8
Portugal	18.8	13.4	17.1	10	14	14	0
Spain	18.7	14.4	20.8	11	13	11	2
Czechia	18.4	25.3	14.3	12	9	16	−7
Denmark	18.1	9.8	22.2	13	16	10	6
Ireland	16.0[a]	15.8[b]	16.2	14	11	15	−4
Lithuania	15.3	8.0	18.8	15	19	13	6
Belgium	14.9	10.3	19.6	16	15	12	3
Estonia	12.5	19.1	8.8	17	10	20	−10
Hungary	11.1	8.0	13.0	18	18	17	1
Romania	10.5	15.0	8.5	19	12	21	−9
Latvia	10.0	6.8	11.5	20	20	18	2
Poland	7.1	5.1	11.3	21	21	19	2
Slovakia	4.2	3.2	6.7	22	22	22	0
Bulgaria	1.1	0.0	3.2	23	23	23	0

Notes: [a] 2008-2017 average, [b] 2008-2012 average.
Source: calculated by author from data available at Eurostat (2020d), Statistics Sweden (2020).

third-highest average value of the index of innovation (after Sweden and Germany). The Netherlands' average automotive industry power was only slightly lower than that of Austria but the Netherlands' positional power grew faster after the 2008–2009 economic crisis. Its automotive industry power is also based on the sixth-highest index of innovation and a below-average index of foreign control for semiperipheral countries despite a weak positional power. Finally, Finland had a weak positional power combined with a very low degree of foreign control (the largest automotive firm in Finland is a domestic-owned contract manufacturer Valmet) and the eighth-strongest innovation index in the European Union.

5.4.2.2   Unstable Semiperiphery

The unstable semiperiphery was composed of Denmark, Czechia and Slovenia. However, these three countries were classified as peripheral during 2003–2007 and 2013–2017, highlighting their borderline periphery–semiperiphery position (Table 5.4, Figures 5.1 and 5.2). The automotive industry power of these countries increased during 2003–2012 but decreased after 2012 (Denmark and Slovenia) or stagnated (Czechia) and was significantly lower than the automotive industry power of the stable semiperiphery. Czechia has by far the largest automotive industry of these three countries with 1.4 million vehicles assembled in 2017 (Slovenia 189,000, Denmark zero). Denmark has a low positional power but the fifth-lowest index of foreign control and its innovation index is higher than any Eastern European country except for Slovenia. Slovenia had the sixth-lowest index of foreign control and recorded the largest improvement in rank by innovation index in the European Union between 2003 and 2017. This improvement was caused by a sixfold increase in the share of Slovenia's business expenditure on R&D of the total value of production between the 2003–2007 and 2008–2012 averages, which might be related to changes in statistical accounting from NACE 34 to NACE 29.

Czechia had a strong and increasing positional power based on its rapidly growing automotive industry during the study period, which was undermined by the high degree of foreign control and worsening innovation index. Czechia used to have a relatively significant domestic automotive R&D before 1990. After 1990, the domestic sector decreased R&D spending and employment as it was taken over by foreign firms and the surviving domestic firms rationalized their R&D activities. At the same time, the growth in R&D spending and employment by foreign firms was slower than the growth of production (Pavlínek, 2004; 2012).

5.4.3   Peripheral Countries

The cluster analysis delimited two clusters that are classified as the periphery and lower-order periphery. With the exception of Portugal and Ireland, the automotive industry periphery is located in Eastern Europe and is typified by the highest degree of foreign control, the lowest innovation index and mostly low positional power. Due to the rapid growth of the FDI-driven export-oriented automotive industry (e.g., Pavlínek, 2017a), all Eastern European countries, with the exception of the Baltic countries, improved their positional power. However, the relative ranking of the most rapidly growing Eastern European countries worsened in innovation activities as the increase in production and trade was much faster than the increases in R&D expenditures and employment

(Pavlínek, 2012). The index of foreign control increased in all Eastern European countries but most in those with the largest and fastest-growing automotive industries. Eastern Europe thus recorded the highest degree of foreign control in the automotive industry, which underscores its peripheral position.

5.4.3.1 Stable Periphery

The stable periphery included Poland, Portugal, Romania, Estonia and Lithuania. Poland's automotive industry power was rapidly growing after 2010, reaching the levels of Czechia in 2016 and 2017, and its relative position in innovation activities also improved, suggesting progression towards the semiperiphery. Romania experienced the second-largest improvement in the positional power ranking of all European Union countries, as the large influx of FDI led to the rapid development of low-cost production and the largest automotive industry job creation by large and medium-sized firms in the European Union between 2005 and 2016 (Pavlínek, 2020). At the same time, Romania suffered the second-largest decrease in innovation index ranking and the largest drop in the index of foreign control ranking. This is despite the already-discussed significant growth of R&D expenditures and employment at Renault Technology Romania, which, however, did not keep pace with the rapid FDI-driven growth of the automotive industry in Romania as a whole (Pavlínek, 2020). Consequently, the relative importance of R&D activities in the automotive industry as a whole decreased. This development reiterated Romania's peripheral position as its overall automotive industry power-based relative position worsened during the study period. Portugal has a weak positional power but a stronger position of its domestic sector than Eastern European countries and an above-average index of innovation among peripheral countries. Estonia and Lithuania have small automotive industries with a significantly lower index of foreign control compared to the rest of Eastern Europe, which is the main reason behind their stable periphery position.

5.4.3.2 Unstable Periphery

Although the cluster analysis delimited Ireland, Hungary, Latvia and Slovakia as the periphery during 2003–2017, it delimited them in the lower-order periphery during one or two of the 2003–2007, 2008–2012 and 2013–2017 periods. Despite having large automotive industries, Slovakia was delimited as the lower-order periphery during 2003–2007 and 2008–2012, while Hungary was delimited as the lower-order periphery during 2003–2007. This is because Slovakia had the highest and Hungary the second-highest index of foreign control and Slovakia had the second-lowest index of innovation. The improvement in the relative automotive industry power position of both countries was therefore driven by large increases in the export-oriented production that strengthened their positional power. Indeed, Slovakia recorded the largest rank position improvements in both positional power and automotive industry power during the study period. Ireland and Latvia have small automotive industries, with Ireland recording the lowest average positional power during 2003–2017.

5.5 CONCLUSION

The goal of this chapter has been to analyze the core–semiperiphery–periphery spatial structure of the European automotive industry during the 2003–2017 period and determine the position of individual countries in these spatial zones. I have explained the different roles of these spatial zones in the integrated transnational automotive industry production system and, based on Harvey's theory of spatiotemporal fix, the geographic expansion of the European automotive industry through the integration of new peripheries into transnational GVCs and GPNs. As we can see in Chapter 4, this integration is driven by the investment of predominantly core-based automotive TNCs that are continuously searching for new low-cost production sites with a potential for a higher rate of profit. I have also shown how this expansion and integration of new peripheries affects the existing automotive industry locations in the core and semiperipheral regions.

The combination of theoretical and conceptual insights of the GVC, GPN and spatial divisions of labor approaches has allowed for the identification of critical indicators for determining the relative position of countries in transnational production networks of the automotive industry. The GVC approach, along with the spatial divisions of labor approach, highlights the importance of transnational control in the automotive industry and its relationship to the core–periphery position of countries. The GPN approach, along with the spatial divisions of labor approach, reveals the importance of specialized regional assets, such as R&D and innovation assets, in reflecting the core–periphery position. The GPN and GVC approaches, with their emphasis on the transnational network organization of the automotive industry, have been instrumental for estimating the trade-based network position of firms of individual countries in the European automotive industry.

Drawing on this conceptual explanation of the spatial structure of transnational automotive industry production networks, this chapter has introduced a methodology for determining the automotive industry power of countries in order to evaluate their relative positions in the core, semiperiphery and periphery of the European automotive industry during the 2003–2017 period. The analysis revealed mostly stable relative positions of countries in this spatial hierarchy, although several countries were classified in less stable borderline positions. The stable core is dominated by Germany and also includes France and Italy. Sweden and Britain represent the unstable core countries on the borderline between the core and semiperiphery due to a significantly larger foreign control of their automotive industries, which also applies to the semiperiphery. The stable semiperiphery is located in Western

Europe. The most distinguishable features of the periphery, which is mostly located in Eastern Europe, include a very high degree of foreign control and weak innovation capabilities, despite a large automotive industry in several peripheral countries. The results presented here are broadly in line with several previous studies (e.g., Jones, 1993; Bordenave and Lung, 1996; Mordue and Sweeney, 2020) but they differ from studies that distinguish the core and periphery of the European automotive industry mainly on the basis of geography (e.g., Brincks et al., 2016). It would be interesting to extend this methodology to the subnational regional level in order to determine the relative position of regions within the core–periphery structure of the European automotive industry, because it would show a more complex spatial pattern due to the high degree of spatial concentration and clustering of the contemporary automotive industry in particular regions (e.g., Sturgeon et al., 2008). On one hand, it would reveal semiperipheral and peripheral regions of the automotive industry in core countries, while on the other hand it would identify the semiperipheral regions in peripheral countries. Unfortunately, the statistical data for this subnational analysis using the same methodology is currently unavailable.

The most likely changes in the foreseeable future will include the consolidation of positions of countries that were classified in unstable positions. Sweden and Britain have been trending from the unstable core towards the semiperiphery. Denmark, Czechia and Slovenia were classified in the semiperiphery only during the 2008–2012 period, which was affected by the global economic crisis, and are likely to consolidate their positions in the periphery rather than the stable semiperiphery in the foreseeable future. Slovakia and Hungary are likely to stabilize their periphery positions due the continuing growth of their automotive industries. The automotive industry in the periphery was the most dynamic during the study period as theorized in the conceptual explanation. Can we therefore expect the potential transitions of the most advanced peripheral countries into the semiperiphery in the long run, as happened in the cases of previous integrated peripheries of Western Europe, such as Belgium and Spain? Although Domański et al. (2014) argue that it has already happened based on the structure of production, exports and product quality, the conceptual approach, methodology and empirical analysis presented in this chapter only partially support this conclusion. Still, the narrowing gap in automotive industry power between the most advanced and rapidly growing peripheral countries, such as Poland, and the stable semiperiphery suggests that it is a plausible scenario. However, a large modern automotive industry may not be sufficient to advance a country into the semiperiphery of automotive transnational production networks unless it has a reasonably strong domestic sector, including firms that are able to globalize, and have sizeable innovation activities (see also Lampón et al., 2016; Mordue and Sweeney, 2020). The rapid growth of the automotive industry in the stable periphery has been slowing down and is unlikely to continue in the future because of the increasingly exhausted sources of labor surplus and, consequently, rising wages. Since the Eastern European automotive industry is overwhelmingly under foreign ownership and control, the only remaining ways to improve its relative position is through the strengthening of innovation activities and shifting to a higher-value-added production, which takes time. Given the spatial organization of the automotive R&D (Frigant, 2007; Sturgeon et al., 2008; Pavlínek, 2012), the Eastern European periphery is likely to continue to trail behind Western Europe in innovation activities despite some selective recent growth. Additionally, despite some exceptions, the relative position of domestic firms in Eastern Europe has continued to weaken as they have been unable to strongly benefit from the FDI-driven growth of the automotive industry (Pavlínek, 2020). For these reasons, we should not expect a shift of east European countries into the stable semiperiphery any time soon.

   A policy advice to countries wishing to improve their relative position in transnational automotive industry production networks and increase the relative rewards accrued from the automotive industry is twofold. They should support the development of automotive R&D and other high-value-added activities through strategic industrial policies as well as nurture domestic automotive firms so they can grow and eventually globalize by investing abroad. In the coming decades, the European automotive industry will be affected by the transition to the production of electric vehicles, automation, robotics and digitalization (Industry 4.0), autonomous driving and new forms of car ownership. All these changes will potentially have significant impacts on the structure, employment and geography of production. Although the precise effects are currently unknown, this transformation will take place at different speeds in the core, semiperiphery and periphery. The core and semiperiphery countries are already experiencing some of these changes earlier and faster due to their greater innovation potential, stronger institutional support and the proximity to large and affluent markets. It remains to be seen how these changes will affect the spatial structure of the European automotive industry.

6

Value Creation and Capture in the Automotive Industry

6.1 INTRODUCTION

The contemporary automotive industry is typified by vertically integrated production networks organized by large lead assembly firms, in which the majority of components production is outsourced to independent suppliers (Sturgeon et al., 2008). Component suppliers are hierarchically organized into supplier tiers that differ by the complexity of manufactured components and also by other firm-level characteristics, such as firm size and the corporate power they wield in production networks (Humphrey and Memedovic, 2003; Sturgeon and Lester, 2004; Pavlínek and Janák, 2007).

This chapter investigates how these distinct tiers of automotive firms contribute to value creation and value capture in the automotive industry by seeking answers to four questions. First, whether higher-tier firms create and capture higher value than lower-tier firms; second, whether higher-tier firms possess stronger and more diverse competencies than lower-tier firms; third, whether higher-tier firms import a higher or lower share of inputs from abroad than lower-tier firms; and fourth, whether domestic firms import lower shares of inputs than foreign-owned (henceforth foreign) firms (Frigant and Lung, 2002; Humphrey and Memedovic, 2003; Maxton and Wormald, 2004; Gereffi et al., 2005; Pavlínek and Janák, 2007; Mudambi, 2008; Sturgeon et al., 2008; Pavlínek, 2015a; Pavlínek and Žížalová, 2016).

These relationships between the firm's position in GPNs and its prospects for value creation and capture are explored in the context of the Czech automotive industry, which represents a typical example of the integrated periphery in the European automotive industry. As we could see in Chapters 3 and 4 of this book, these are peripheral automotive industry regions that have been integrated into core-based macro-regional automotive industry production networks through large inflows of FDI by foreign TNCs. Automotive TNCs seek to benefit there from low production costs, investment incentives and the advantages of regional economic blocs. The peripheral position of the Czech automotive industry in the European automotive industry is typified by its foreign control (see Table 5.7 in Chapter 5), with foreign firms accounting for 85.6 percent of employment, 95.5 percent of value added, 95.5 percent of production, 95.4 percent of turnover and 95.1 percent of gross investment in 2019 (Eurostat, 2022b; 2023c). It is also reflected by the limited presence of corporate headquarters and strategic higher-value-added functions, such as R&D (see Chapter 5 of this book) (Pavlínek and Ženka, 2011; Pavlínek, 2012).

The goal of this chapter is to develop an approach to measure value creation and capture in regional production networks based on firm-level indicators. Value creation is defined as firm-level activities that increase the value of final goods or services compared to the value of raw materials, intermediate goods, services and other expenses employed for their production. Value creation is measured at the firm level by value added in production and labor productivity. Value capture refers to the amount (or share) of created value that is retained by firms or subsidiaries that originally created it and that has not been transferred outside the host region of those firms or subsidiaries. As such, it is composed of two basic components: value captured by firms that created it and value that "leaks" from these firms to other subjects in the host region. Value capture is evaluated through wages, tax revenues, reinvestment and domestic sourcing. The measurements are done for different supplier tiers and for foreign and domestic suppliers in order to evaluate the contribution of different types of firms to value creation at the firm level and value capture at the firm and regional levels that will allow to assess the contribution of the automotive industry to regional economic development. The analysis confirms that higher-tier firms have greater economic effects than lower-tier firms because of the larger capital intensity of their production, higher corporate tax revenues and higher average wages per worker. However, lower-tier firms have larger direct employment and wage effects per unit of production.

This chapter begins with a brief discussion of value creation and capture in the contemporary economy. Second, I develop a firm-level approach to evaluate value creation and value capture in the context of the automotive industry. Third, I present five hypotheses about the distinct tiers of the automotive value chain that guide our empirical analysis of the Czech automotive industry. Fourth, I analyze value creation and capture in the Czech automotive industry. Finally, I summarize the findings in the conclusion.

6.2 VALUE CREATION, VALUE CAPTURE AND UNEVEN ECONOMIC DEVELOPMENT

The international spatial division of labor has been increasingly influenced by the investment activities of TNCs and their abilities to "slice up" the value chain and relocate its different functions to the potentially most profitable locations (Gereffi, 2005; Dicken, 2015). Economic geographers, among others, have been attempting to uncover where value is created and captured within GPNs in order to understand how GPNs contribute to economic development of particular countries and regions (Smith et al., 2002; Coe et al., 2004) and how flows and transfers of value contribute to uneven development (Hudson, 2011). It has been argued that in the contemporary economy the greatest value creation and capture come from the production of intangible goods rather than from the production of tangible goods and standardized services. Both upstream and downstream knowledge-intensive activities along the value chain, such as R&D on one side and brand management, marketing, advertising, distribution and after-sales service on the other side, create and capture significantly greater value than manufacturing operations (Mudambi, 2008). Lead firms typically control the production of intangible goods and thus secure higher profits through creating high entry barriers into these activities (Shin et al., 2013). Empirical evidence was found in the electronics industry that brand owners, which are almost invariably large core-based TNCs, capture the majority of value that is created along a particular value chain, while firms that manufacture final products capture a much lower share (Shin et al., 2012).

The automotive industry represents an example of increasingly complex transnational production networks and value chains (Sturgeon et al., 2008). While it differs from the electronics industry in that lead (assembly) firms have not outsourced the final vehicle assembly to subcontractors or contract manufacturers, external suppliers have increased their share of the total value of finished vehicles to 75–80 percent (Frigant, 2011a). This does not mean, however, that external suppliers also capture the same share of the created value in the value chain. Lead firms along with leading component suppliers have been increasingly shifting production to lower-cost "emerging" economies while maintaining crucial knowledge-intensive and high-value-added activities in their home countries (Sturgeon et al., 2008; Sturgeon and Van Biesebroeck, 2011; Pavlínek, 2012). Since automotive production networks are no longer predominantly organized at the national scale (Hudson and Schamp, 1995b; Dicken, 2015), the international flows of value within the automotive industry have increased rapidly in the form of trade, FDI and profit-shifting strategies.

The spatial distribution of economic activities with different value creation and capture potential has important regional development implications. Economic geographers and economists have demonstrated that higher-value-added knowledge-intensive activities and corporate control functions tend to concentrate in more developed core regions while lower-value-added production activities tend to concentrate in less developed peripheral regions (Hymer, 1972; Massey, 1979; Dicken, 2015). This spatial division of labor is closely related to the patterns of corporate ownership and control (Firn, 1975; Dicken, 1976; Schackmann-Fallis, 1989). In the context of manufacturing, it means that peripheral externally controlled branch plants typically specialize in the high-volume manufacturing while having very limited nonproduction functions. Such truncated branch plants have limited regional development benefits for their host regions and, in the long run, might contribute to technological underdevelopment of host economies (Britton, 1980; Hayter, 1982). In the automotive industry, this continues to be the case despite its reorganization of production and supplier relations in the 1980s and 1990s (Sheard, 1983; Womack et al., 1990), which allowed some peripheral branch plants to acquire nonproduction functions and upgrade into "performance/ networked branch plants" (Phelps, 1993a; Amin et al., 1994; Pike, 1998; Dawley, 2011). Although branch plants and firms based in peripheral regions might develop various competencies over time (Phelps, 1993a), functional upgrading resulting in a significantly improved position of such firms in the automotive industry value chain has been extremely difficult to achieve (Pavlínek and Ženka, 2011; Pavlínek and Žížalová, 2016).[1] Therefore, especially domestic automotive suppliers based in peripheral regions and less developed countries have been increasingly relegated to the bottom of the supplier hierarchy, which translates in the production of simple, low-value-added, standardized and slow-changing components (Barnes and Kaplinsky, 2000; Humphrey et al., 2000; Humphrey, 2003). Overall, the prevailing spatial division of labor in the automotive industry suggests that less developed peripheral regions, both at the national and international scale, are typified by lower value creation within GVCs and GPNs than more developed core regions. Furthermore, external control contributes to a potential value transfer from peripheral branch plants to corporate headquarters in the form of various profit-shifting strategies, including profit remittances and transfer pricing (Dischinger et al., 2014a; 2014b).

6.3 VALUE CREATION AND VALUE CAPTURE IN GLOBAL PRODUCTION NETWORKS

The precise measuring of value creation and capture in GPNs has proven to be extremely difficult because it requires access to the internal accounting data of individual firms, such as invoice-level internal data (Seppälä et al., 2014). Firms are generally unwilling to provide this information and even if they do, this level of detail would likely limit the analysis to a single product produced by a single TNC. Because of the unavailability of precise data, analyses of value creation and capture in GPNs of particular products in electronic industries, such as Apple's iPods, notebook computers and smartphones, had to rely on rough estimates (Dedrick et al., 2010; 2011). It would be difficult to apply these approaches in the context of complex production networks with thousands of suppliers, such as the automotive industry, unless we focus on only a few of the most important suppliers. Alternatively, econometric methods have been used to measure value capture at the national level using firm-level financial data in

---

[1] See Chapter 2 of this book for a more detailed discussion of this issue.

the electronic industry (Shin et al., 2013). This chapter develops an alternative way to measure value creation and capture in regional production networks based on firm-level indicators.

In the GPN perspective, created value refers to various forms of economic rent (Coe et al., 2004), which is conceptualized as the super-profit of an entrepreneur who is able to exploit either resources of above-average productivity or ubiquitous resources more effectively than his or her competitors (Kaplinsky, 1998), while preventing them from exploiting these resources by creating high barriers of entry (Kaplinsky and Morris, 2008). Profits therefore represent a plausible way to measure value creation (Kaplinsky, 2000; Henderson et al., 2002; Coe et al., 2004).[2] However, profits are highly volatile as they are affected by various investment projects, corporate tax reliefs, profit repatriations, transfer pricing and other profit-shifting strategies (Dischinger et al., 2014b). Profits can be reinvested in production in order to upgrade a firm's or subsidiary's production processes, which might increase its overall productivity, wages and corporate tax revenues in the long run. The (geographical) distribution of profits along the hierarchical value chain (Gereffi et al., 2005) does not necessarily correspond with the distribution of value added. Through transfer pricing, TNCs can allocate the largest share of their profits to subsidiaries with simple low-value-added assembly, while subsidiaries with high-value-added production may show a negligible or even negative profitability (Seppälä et al., 2014). Therefore, from the perspective of regional development, created value needs to be understood more broadly and should not be limited to profits. In addition to profits, created value is also reflected in technological and organizational innovations, effective collaboration with local suppliers, knowledge spillovers, agglomeration economies and the local presence of strategic high-value-added functions.

Different automotive firms are linked through complex supplier relationships and flows of information within automotive production networks that encourage the spatial proximity of certain automotive suppliers to assembly operations (Frigant and Lung, 2002; Larsson, 2002). The need for proximity and the resulting savings that accrue to individual suppliers lead to their clustering around assembly plants (Pavlínek and Janák, 2007; Sturgeon et al., 2008). Therefore, the value creation and capture of individual firms might be affected by the fact of whether they are located within such clusters. For the purpose of this chapter, therefore not only value created in an individual automotive firm is considered, but also value creation and capture in the network of the firm's regional suppliers, which are induced by domestic sourcing, knowledge spillovers and other mechanisms.

---

[2] This approach is different from that of Shin et al. (2012), who used gross profit to measure value capture rather than value creation.

Since there is no simple and established way to measure value creation, the gross value added is employed as the best available accounting indicator for quantifying the abstract and directly nonmeasurable category of created value. Gross value added includes not only pre-tax profits that are highly volatile, difficult to trace and interpret, but it also measures wages and the consumption of fixed capital. As such, it is a more complex, territorially bounded and stable indicator than profits that can be more easily interpreted. Gross value added per employee (labor productivity) is a key indicator of economic upgrading (Milberg and Winkler, 2011) in terms of productivity and profitability.

What is the difference between value added and created value? The conceptualization of value inspired by the resource-based theory (Peteraf, 1993) distinguishes between the perceived use value and exchange value. The former refers to specific qualities of the product (component, material, machine, service etc.) as subjectively perceived by customers and the price he or she is prepared to pay for it (Bowman and Ambrosini, 2000). The latter is the actual price paid by the buyer for this perceived use value. Therefore, value creation represents the accumulation, transformation and appropriation of valuable resources (machines, materials, components, know-how, technologies, licenses, management practices etc.) that increase the perceived use value of a firm's products. When these products are sold, perceived use value is transformed into (exchange) value added (Bowman and Ambrosini, 2000).

From a host region perspective, captured value is a part of value created by the resident firm or subsidiary that is retained and appropriated for host region benefits (Coe et al., 2004). Regional captured value is composed of two parts. First is value captured for the benefits of the resident firm or subsidiary, which is the share of profits that a firm invests in its upgrading in order to maintain or increase its competitiveness (Szalavetz, 2015). It has multiple forms, such as reinvested profits, employee skills, collaborative relationships with local suppliers, technological innovation and all other sources of economic rents that are retained by the resident firm or subsidiary and are not transferred to other regions. Second is value that "leaks" to other subjects in the host region, such as households, suppliers and universities, through various channels, including employee compensation, corporate taxes, regional sourcing or localized knowledge spillovers. Value is captured at various geographic scales. Profits reinvested into the establishment of a new plant or the expansion and upgrading of an existing plant affect the factory site at the local scale; jobs and wages affect the labor market at the regional scale through labor commute; corporate taxes are collected at the national scale; and domestic sourcing affects value capture at various scales from local to national, depending on the sourcing patterns of individual firms. Therefore, if we subtract this captured value from the total created value, we get the amount of "lost" value, which is transferred outside the region through various mechanisms, such as profit repatriation, transfer pricing and the transfer of a subsidiary's perceived used value and its commercialization by the parent company (Barrientos et al., 2011; Pavlínek and Ženka, 2011; Milberg and Winkler, 2011).

Wages, corporate tax revenues, reinvested profits and domestic sourcing are four directly measurable components of value capture that are interrelated in complex and often contradictory ways (Table 6.1). For example, rising wages might decrease a firm's profitability and, therefore, undermine the corporate tax base and vice versa. An increase in the corporate tax rate may lead to decreasing wages in an open economy because of falling marginal labor productivity and the consequent outflow of capital to lower-tax countries (Felix, 2009). There is also a trade-off between corporate tax revenues and profit reinvestments into expansions and/or upgrading of individual plants that reduce the corporate tax base. At the same time, profit reinvestments, which increase capital and technology intensity of production, should lead to increases in marginal labor productivity and, therefore, wages. Profit reinvestments may also increase the embeddedness of plants in particular locations (Wren and Jones, 2009) by fostering local linkages and developing nonproduction functions.

6.3.1 Wages

A monopoly position that is derived mostly from technological or branding innovations generates an excess rent (Kaplinsky, 1998). In an integrated monopoly firm, the excess rent is likely to translate into higher wages for all workers, including unskilled workers who are employed in routine low-value-added activities (Nathan and Sarkar, 2011). When routine low-value-added and easily replaceable activities are outsourced to external suppliers, there is no excess rent and wages tend to be lower for workers in supplier firms that take on outsourced activities (Nathan and Sarkar, 2011). Therefore, if we were to control for size, industry and regional specifics, we would expect the corporate power and the presence or absence of strategic nonproduction functions to be key factors that influence wage levels at the firm level in the context of a particular economy. Lower-tier firms that are engaged in routine low-value-added activities with low entry barriers have generally the lowest wages and worst prospects for wage increases (Ženka and Pavlínek, 2013).

6.3.2 Profits and Corporate Tax Revenues

Profits generated in the host economy can be reinvested or used to pay for corporate income taxes there or can be repatriated and invested abroad (UNCTAD, 2013). Reinvestment and corporate taxes contribute to value capture in the host economy while profit repatriation transfers the value abroad. The share of repatriated profits is affected by the nature of the activities conducted by foreign firms in host economies and by the position of foreign subsidiaries in the corporate hierarchy. The value is also transferred from host economies by TNCs through various profit-shifting strategies, including transfer pricing (Dunning and Lundan, 2008; Huizinga and

Laeven, 2008; Dicken, 2015). Overall, approximately 60 percent of global FDI income on equity was transferred back to home countries of foreign investors in 2010 (UNCTAD, 2013). Regions that host corporate headquarters tend to capture a higher share of value than those hosting subsidiaries because corporate headquarters concentrate on the production of intangible goods. As such, they tend to be more profitable than their subsidiaries and tend to pay higher taxes (Mudambi, 2008; Dischinger et al., 2014a; 2014b). The headquarters and their geographic vicinity also benefit from high expenditures of gross profits on high-value-added functions, such as R&D and corporate support functions, including strategic planning, marketing, management and administration (Dedrick et al., 2011; Pavlínek, 2012). Overall, countries and regions benefit significantly more from hosting TNC headquarters than from hosting subsidiaries that have similar firm characteristics (Dischinger et al., 2014a).

Reinvested profits can increase value capture in host regions in several ways. For example, the investment in a more advanced technology should translate into higher marginal labor productivity and higher wages (Szalavetz, 2005). Repeat investments can also enhance ties of foreign-owned plants to particular regional economies and extend the survival time durations of foreign-owned plants in host regions (Wren and Jones, 2009). In this chapter, reinvested profits are measured indirectly through the annual change in tangible assets, which includes repeated investment into buildings, machines and equipment, and also their depreciation. Tangible assets are used as a proxy measure of reinvested profits due to their spatial fixity and even though reinvested profits are only partially reflected in the annual change in tangible assets. The annual change in tangible assets represents a part of value captured in the host region, while the depreciation of tangible assets represents value that is sunk and, therefore, lost both for the region and for the firm (Melachroinos and Spence, 1999). In addition to tangible assets, reinvested profits may also flow into the employee training, licenses, software and other intangibles.

To the best of my knowledge, there is no coherent theoretical framework linking the position of firms within GPNs with the amount of value captured through corporate tax revenues. There is no systematic evidence that higher-tier firms are more prone to profit-shifting and tax avoidance than lower-tier firms. Therefore, I assume that the distribution of corporate tax revenues along the value chain follows the distribution of profits. Highly profitable assemblers and tier-one suppliers should pay higher taxes per employee than lower-tier firms. At the same time, I assume that foreign firms are more likely to engage in profit-shifting and tax avoidance strategies than domestic firms. The concentration of domestic firms among tier-two and tier-three suppliers should therefore translate into their higher relative corporate tax revenues as a share of total production than among higher-tier firms.

6.3.3 Domestic Sourcing

I consider the extent of domestic sourcing a measure of value capture for two basic reasons (Table 6.1). First, domestic procurement stimulates job creation among local suppliers and linkages between foreign and domestic firms that might help facilitate spillovers and knowledge transfer from foreign to domestic firms (Blomström and Kokko, 1998; UNCTAD, 2001; Görg and Strobl, 2005; Scott-Kennel, 2007; Santangelo, 2009; Pavlínek and Žížalová, 2016). Second, increased production by domestic suppliers improves their internal scale economies, while the spatial concentration of suppliers in the proximity of assembly plants can contribute to the development of external scale (localization) economies (Frigant and Lung, 2002; Larsson, 2002). In the contemporary automotive industry, spatial proximity to assembly operations is especially important for module and tier-one suppliers that produce modules and components dedicated to a particular automaker and supply them sequentially just in time (Frigant and Lung, 2002; Klier and Rubenstein, 2008). The geographic proximity of tier-one suppliers to assembly operations decreases transportation and logistical costs, allows for the better synchronization of their production, improves the ability of tier-one suppliers to quickly react to changes in the production scheduling of assemblers, increases the reliability of just-in-time delivery and speeds up the delivery of technical assistance by tier-one suppliers to assembly firms (Frigant and Lung, 2002; Larsson, 2002; Pavlínek and Janák, 2007). A large-volume vehicle assembly should therefore translate into a high share of preassembled modules and dedicated components being sourced by assembly firms from the host economy in which the assembly plant is located, as evidenced in Chapter 3 of this book.

TABLE 6.1 *Firm-level indicators for measuring value creation and value capture*

Indicator	Definition	Value created	Value captured
Value added in production	Value added/production (%)	Yes	No
Labor productivity	Value added per employee (thousand CZK)	Yes	No
Monthly wages	Average monthly wages per employee (CZK)	No	Yes
Tax revenues	Corporate tax revenues per employee (thousand CZK)	No	Yes
Wages in production (%)	Total wages/production (%)	No	Yes
Taxes in production (%)	Corporate tax revenues/ production (%)	No	Yes
Repeat investment	Tangible assets per employee – growth index	No	Yes
Domestic sourcing	The share of total value of materials and services sourced from Czechia of total value sourced annually (%)	No	Yes

Notes: Tangible assets = financial value of land, buildings, machines and equipment.
Source: author.

Tier-one suppliers supply preassembled highly customized modules that are often color- and model-specific in the just-in-time regime to a particular automaker. I expect tier-one suppliers to import more components from abroad than vehicle assemblers. This is because high-value-added and sophisticated components for tier-one suppliers may not be available from domestic firms and standardized, nondedicated and simple components supplied by tier-three to tier-one suppliers can be supplied from larger distances. The sourcing patterns of simple components are therefore more affected by scale economies and labor costs than geographic proximity. Tier-two suppliers should be positioned somewhere between tier-one and tier-three suppliers (see Pavlínek and Žížalová, 2016). At the same time, the globalization of the supplier base (Sturgeon and Lester, 2004) has relegated the majority of domestic suppliers to the supply of simple, low-value-added components in less developed countries (Barnes and Kaplinsky, 2000; Freyssenet and Lung, 2000; Humphrey et al., 2000). As a result, domestic suppliers may lack capabilities to supply certain specialized or sophisticated components or are uncompetitive because of their small scale of production, which necessitates the import of such components from abroad (Crone and Watts, 2003; Pavlínek and Žížalová, 2016) (2009–2011 interviews).[3]

However, the position of firms in GPNs has to be controlled for contingent characteristics that may affect the relationship between the tier and the extent of local sourcing, such as plant size and its age, the mode of entry of foreign firms, the firm's nationality and its corporate sourcing strategies (Barkley and McNamara, 1994; Crone and Watts, 2003; Tavares and Young, 2006). Larger plants tend to source domestically relatively less than smaller ones because it is often difficult to find local suppliers capable of supplying the large volumes required. In those cases when assembly firms and tier-one suppliers are significantly larger than tier-two and tier-three suppliers, the plant size may negatively affect their level of domestic sourcing. The linkages and sourcing relationships between foreign and domestic firms typically develop over time (Dicken, 2015). Older plants and plants acquired by TNCs show a generally higher propensity to source domestically than more recently established greenfield factories (Tavares and Young, 2006). However, local content requirements and follow sourcing often result in high levels of local content as the outcome of the localization of foreign-owned suppliers around new greenfield assembly plants, which do not have to translate in extensive supplier linkages between foreign firms and domestic suppliers (Pavlínek and Žížalová, 2016; Pavlínek, 2018).

---

[3] Detailed firm-level data have been collected through personal interviews with senior managers of selected automotive firms based in Czechia. The interviews with 100 foreign and domestic automotive firms were carried out by the author and members of his research team between December 2009 and August 2011.

6.4 HYPOTHESES

Based on the discussion of the literature, I present five hypotheses about different tiers and firm ownership of the automotive value chain that will be tested on the Czech automotive industry. First, higher-tier (e.g., tier-one) firms create higher value than lower-tier (e.g., tier-three) firms and, therefore, they gradually increase their share of the total value added in the automotive industry. This is because higher-tier firms produce more complex and higher-value-added components than lower-tier firms (Humphrey and Memedovic, 2003; Maxton and Wormald, 2004; Pavlínek and Janák, 2007). Together with assemblers, they wield greater corporate power in automotive value chains, which they use to maintain their privileged position and to squeeze lower-tier firms (Ravenhill, 2014; Sturgeon et al., 2008; Pavlínek, 2015a). Second, domestic suppliers import a lower share of inputs from abroad than foreign suppliers because foreign suppliers are more affected by the centralized sourcing strategies of TNCs (Pavlínek and Žížalová, 2016; Pavlínek, 2018). Third, higher-tier firms and assemblers import a lower share of inputs from abroad than lower-tier firms because they are forced to source greater shares of their inputs locally in order to satisfy the imperatives of modular and just-in-time production (Frigant and Lung, 2002; Pavlínek and Janák, 2007). Fourth, higher-tier firms possess stronger and more diverse competencies that are reflected in the presence of more nonproduction (strategic) higher-value-added functions than in lower-tier firms. Lower-tier firms produce simple components and are often captive suppliers that depend on higher-tier buyers for various nonproduction functions (Gereffi et al., 2005; Pavlínek and Žížalová, 2016). Fifth, higher-tier firms capture a greater share of created value than lower-tier firms because they conduct more nonproduction higher-value-added functions (Mudambi, 2008) and because they are able to offer higher wages than lower-tier firms in order to attract skilled labor. This is because jobs in nonproduction functions create greater value and tend to be better paid than production jobs. Furthermore, the presence of nonproduction functions increases the chances for the reinvestment of profits in a particular locality. Better-paid jobs and increased chances for reinvestment have potentially important implications for regional and national economies.

6.5 THE CZECH AUTOMOTIVE INDUSTRY

Before turning to the empirical analysis, I first need to provide a brief context of the Czech automotive industry. Since the early 1990s, the Czech automotive industry has been integrated in the European production networks through large inflows of FDI (Pavlínek, 2017a).

Czechia had the second-largest automotive FDI stock (€10 billion) in Eastern Europe in 2019. Large FDI inflows resulted in rapid increase in production from 197,000 vehicles in 1991 to 1.46 million in 2019 (AIA, 2022).

Here, I will only briefly characterize the structure of the Czech automotive industry, since I have analyzed its foreign capital-driven restructuring, growth and upgrading elsewhere (e.g., Pavlínek, 2008; 2015a; 2017a). The classification of Czech-based automotive firms into assemblers and three basic supplier tiers illustrates its hierarchical structure, in which the number of firms in individual tiers increases with the decreasing tier, while the average firm size, measured by the number of workers, decreases (Tables 6.2 and 6.3). When measured by employment, assemblers are on average four times larger than tier-one suppliers, eleven times larger than tier-two suppliers and almost twenty times larger than tier-three suppliers. The data also reveal large differences between lead firms and their suppliers. On average, assemblers have a much higher capital and technological intensity of production than suppliers, which translates into higher labor productivity, high shares of overall production, value added, tangible assets and R&D expenditures of the Czech automotive industry (Table 6.2). However, there is a significant variability within individual tiers. Mean values for assemblers are distorted by Škoda Auto because it accounts for 27 percent of production, 25 percent of value added, 67 percent of R&D expenditures, 18 percent of wages and 40 percent of corporate tax revenues of the total Czech automotive industry. Overall, the difference between Škoda Auto and the rest of the Czech-based automotive industry is larger than differences between individual supplier tiers (Ženka and Pavlínek, 2013). Škoda Auto is also unique in the context of the Czech automotive industry because it is what I call a tier-two lead firm, a firm that has many attributes of lead firms and possesses important nonproduction functions. However, strategic functions and autonomy of tier-two lead firms are limited because they are foreign-owned, which also affects their value capture by profit repatriation. The ultimate strategic functions are missing and conducted abroad by foreign owners, which is Volkswagen in the case of Škoda Auto (Pavlínek and Janák, 2007; Pavlínek, 2012). Still, Škoda Auto possesses significantly more nonproduction functions and competencies than a typical foreign assembly firm, such as Hyundai at Nošovice and Toyota at Kolín (the former Toyota–Peugeot–Citroën joint venture) in the case of Czechia, because Škoda is a distinct brand within the Volkswagen group.

TABLE 6.2 *Shares of individual supplier tiers on selected indicators of the total Czech automotive industry, 2008–2010*

Tier	Number of firms	Employment	Production	Value added	Wages	Corporate tax revenues	Tangible assets	R&D expenditures
Total	475	157,950	677,797	128,812	49,054	5,051	199,138	9,458
Assembly	9	20.9%	40.0%	33.4%	25.1%	52.6%	35.0%	59.2%
Tier one	49	25.3%	24.4%	24.6%	26.6%	14.6%	25.5%	17.5%
Tier two	148	26.4%	18.2%	21.3%	24.2%	15.3%	22.1%	10.9%
Tier three	269	27.4%	17.5%	20.7%	24.2%	17.6%	17.4%	12.4%

Notes: Financial indicators in million CZK; shares are calculated as mean values for 2008, 2009 and 2010 with the exception of corporate tax revenues, which are mean values for 2008–2009, and R&D expenditures, which are mean values for 2005, 2006 and 2007.
Source: calculated by the author based on data from CSO (2011).

TABLE 6.3 *Descriptive statistics for different tiers of Czech-based automotive firms (mean values for 2006, 2007 and 2008) (value creation and value capture)*

Tier	Employment per firm		Production per worker		Value added per worker		Wages per worker		Taxes per worker		Tangible assets per worker	
	MEAN	STDEV	MEAN	STDEV	MEAN	STDEV	MEAN	STDEV	MEAN	STDEV	MEAN	STDEV
Assembly	3,581	7,697	5,463	3,972	952	391	309	55	79	69	1,397	1,384
Tier one	879	1,224	3,996	3,567	670	415	272	60	36	60	927	653
Tier two	318	418	2,395	2,836	559	359	240	62	26	56	683	658
Tier three	184	341	1,824	1,580	474	287	231	61	18	33	461	499
Total	362	1,231	2,295	2,466	530	338	240	63	24	46	596	622

Notes: STDEV = standard deviation. Taxes refer to corporate tax revenues.
Source: calculated by the author based on data from CSO (2011).

6.6 VALUE CREATION AND VALUE CAPTURE IN THE CZECH AUTOMOTIVE INDUSTRY

The analysis of value creation and value capture in the Czech automotive industry draws on a unique 2011 dataset of 475 Czech-based automotive firms with 20 or more employees that was constructed from the data provided by the Czech Statistical Office (CSO, 2011). In addition to narrowly defined automotive industry firms (NACE 29), the database includes employment and financial indicators for firms in related supplier sectors, such as iron and steel, rubber and plastic, electronics, and machinery industries, for 1998, 2002 and 2005–2011. Additional data, such as the share of automotive products in sales, sourcing patterns and high-value-added functions conducted at the firm level, were collected through a 2009 telephonic survey of 475 firms in our database, which was administered by the author and members of his research team and yielded a response rate of 34.6 percent (274 firms). Finally, the interpretation of data analysis benefited from 100 firm-level interviews with the directors and top managers of Czech-based automotive firms conducted by the author the author and members of his research team between 2009 and 2011.

Individual firms were classified into five categories according to the share of automotive products in their sales (0–24.9 percent, 25.0–49.9 percent, 50.0–74.9 percent, 75.0–99.9 percent and 100 percent). The data for every firm were then weighted by a corresponding weight (0.125, 0.375, 0.625, 0.875 and 1) in order to reduce distortions resulting from the inclusion of firms that are only partially engaged in the automotive industry. In the next step, all 475 firms were classified according to their position in the automotive value chain into lead firms (assemblers) and three supplier tiers according to the technological complexity of their components (Veloso and Kumar, 2002; Humphrey and Memedovic, 2003; Maxton and Wormald, 2004; Pavlínek and Janák, 2007; Pavlínek et al., 2009).[4] Tier-one suppliers supply the most complex components, such as sophisticated parts of engines (compressors, turbochargers), transmissions and brakes, and complex preassembled modules, such as dashboards, door systems or seats. Tier-three suppliers produce the least complex parts and components, such as car bodies and their parts, metal and plastic pressings, exhaust pipes, windscreen wipers and simple interior parts such as seat upholstery. Weighted data for raw materials suppliers are included among tier-three suppliers. Tier-two suppliers produce the rest, that is, medium complex parts, such as simple engine parts, lights or locks. I am aware that large suppliers, such as Bosch, supply various components that differ in terms of their sophistication. As such, these suppliers may play different roles in the value chain as tier-one, tier-two and tier-three suppliers, or as system integrators (Pries, 1999; Frigant, 2011b). In those cases, individual

---

[4] See Pavlínek and Janák (2007) and Pavlínek et al. (2009) for a more detailed description.

suppliers were classified based on the highest tier into which at least some of their components would fall since I was unable to determine what proportion of supplier activity falls under different tiers. These three levels of the complexity of components are related to their value added. Generally, I assume that the production of the most complex and sophisticated components adds more value than the production of simple parts and components.

6.6.1 Value Creation

I start with testing the first hypothesis. Higher-tier firms create higher value than lower-tier firms and, therefore, they gradually increase their share of the total value added in the automotive industry. Based on the data in Tables 6.3 and 6.4, we can arrive at two important conclusions related to the position of firms in the supplier hierarchy and their value creation potential. First, higher-tier firms create a greater value per employee (show higher labor productivity) than lower-tier firms. Second, the share of value added (created value) of the total value of production is lower in higher-tier firms than in lower-tier firms (Table 6.4).

The stronger economic performance of assemblers and tier-one suppliers compared to the rest of the automotive industry supports the theoretical assumptions of GVC/GPN literature that link their "super-profits" in terms of economic rent to strategic functions and privileged position in value chains (e.g., Kaplinsky, 1998). Empirical studies have also illustrated how assemblers and the so-called megasuppliers wield their corporate power and exercise control over strategic functions within automotive production networks, which effectively discourages lower-tier suppliers from functional upgrading (e.g., Rutherford and

TABLE 6.4 *Change in the share of value added (value creation), wages and corporate tax revenues (value capture) of the total value of production by supplier tier*

Tier	Value added in production (%)		Wages in production (%)		Corporate tax revenues in production (%)	
	1998	2010	1998	2010	1998	2009
All firms	22.3	19.1	7.2	6.6	1.6	0.6
Assembly	17.1	16.6	4.4	4.1	1.4	0.8
Tier one	25.2	18.0	9.2	7.1	1.9	0.1
Tier two	31.5	23.4	10.1	9.6	1.7	0.5
Tier three	28.7	22.6	11.2	9.1	1.7	0.7

Note: Other components of the total value of production, such as the value of purchased materials, components, energy and services, are not included in the table.
Source: calculated by the author based on data from CSO (2011).

Holmes, 2008; Pavlínek and Ženka, 2011). They also squeeze lower-tier suppliers often to the brink of bankruptcy, especially during economic crises, in order to maximize their own profits (Pavlínek and Ženka, 2010; Pavlínek, 2015a). This was reflected in a very uneven decrease in the profitability in the Czech automotive industry during the economic crisis in 2008 as it fell on average by 19 percent for assemblers, 59 percent for tier-one suppliers, 73 percent for Tier-two suppliers and 71 percent for tier-three suppliers (Pavlínek, 2015a).

6.6.2 Changes in Value Creation by Supplier Tiers

In the next step, I consider changes in the value creation indicators by individual tiers during the 1998–2010 period. My previous research on upgrading in the Czech automotive industry has identified the two prevailing trends (Pavlínek and Ženka, 2011). The first one was the highly selective functional upgrading that was limited mostly to Škoda Auto and a few of the largest tier-one suppliers. It contributed to the increasing productivity and profitability gaps between assemblers and tier-one suppliers on one hand and lower-tier suppliers on the other hand. The second trend was the widespread process and product upgrading among domestic tier-two and tier-three suppliers following their integration into GPNs and the pressure to increase the efficiency and quality of their production. As a result, domestic tier-two and tier-three suppliers outpaced foreign-owned firms in the rates of growth of labor productivity.

Labor productivity increased by 83 percent for the automotive industry as a whole between 1998 and 2010. It grew fastest among tier-one suppliers (by 108 percent) and assemblers (by 93 percent) (Table 6.5). The share of value added in production, which is an indicator of value creation, decreased by 14 percent for the automotive industry as whole between 1998 and 2010. The decrease was the most pronounced for tier-one and tier-two suppliers (Table 6.4). The decreasing share of value added in production does not indicate downgrading but the FDI-driven extensive growth of the Czech automotive industry between 1998 and 2010 (Ženka and Pavlínek 2013). During this period, the number of automotive firms increased from 257 to 475, their total employment increased by 68 percent, production by 259 percent and value added by 207 percent. Tier-two suppliers grew the fastest of all automotive tiers, with their production increasing more than four times (by 414 percent) and employment more than doubling (by 138 percent). The rapid growth of tier-two suppliers between 1998 and 2010 resulted especially from the establishment of new greenfield branch plants by global suppliers in Czechia.

Overall, the value creation in the Czech automotive industry significantly increased during the 1998–2010 period. Did this increased value creation lead to increased value capture in Czechia? I consider this question in the next section.

TABLE 6.5 *The development of labor productivity (value creation), annual wages and corporate tax revenues per employee (value capture) by supplier tier, 1998–2009/2010*

Tier	Labor productivity			Annual wages			Corporate taxes revenues		
	1998 (thousands of CZK)	2010 (thousands of CZK)	% change	1998 (thousands of CZK)	2010 (thousands of CZK)	% change	1998 (thousands of CZK)	2009 (thousands of CZK)	% change
Assembly	803	1,549	93%	207	385	86%	68	60	-12%
Tier one	429	892	108%	157	349	123%	29	4	-87%
Tier two	451	725	61%	145	298	105%	28	15	-46%
Tier three	380	714	88%	148	288	94%	23	18	-19%
Total	514	749	83%	165	327	99%	37	23	-37%

Source: calculated by the author based on data from CSO (2011).

6.6.3 Value Capture

Domestic suppliers source a higher share of components, materials and services in Czechia than Czech-based foreign suppliers (Table 6.6), which confirms the second hypothesis. The share of domestically sourced components and materials does not significantly differ by tier among domestic firms. Among foreign firms, however, higher-tier firms source a higher share of components, materials and services in Czechia than lower-tier firms (see also Pavlínek and Žížalová, 2016). This therefore confirms the third hypothesis that higher-tier firms and assemblers import a lower share of inputs from abroad than lower-tier firms only for foreign firms. The high share of domestically sourced components by foreign assembly firms and also tier-one suppliers is related to the imperatives of just-in-time production in the automotive industry (Sheard, 1983). Tier-three suppliers, who supply standardized, simple and slow-changing components, have the lowest share of domestic sourcing. This is because these components are not typically supplied in the just-in-time regime and, as such, could be supplied over long distances from lower-cost countries, such as China and India. The second reason for the lowest share of components that are sourced from the domestic economy by tier-three suppliers is the unavailability of some parts and raw materials in Czechia, such as electronic components, admixtures for special plastics and natural rubber (Pavlínek and Žížalová, 2016). The centralized procurement by TNCs strongly influences sourcing patterns of all foreign firms. Czech-based subsidiaries typically have no or very limited influence over sourcing decisions of the vast majority of components and materials they use in production (2009–2011 interviews). Overall, therefore, higher-tier foreign firms have the potential to generate greater regional economic effects than lower-tier foreign firms by sourcing more from the host economy.

Reinvested profits represent an important component of value capture in the Czech automotive industry. As of 2021, the total FDI stock in the narrowly defined Czech automotive industry (NACE 29) stood at €8 billion, of which

TABLE 6.6 *The percentage share of components sourced from Czechia in 2009 by supplier tier (value capture)*

Tier	Domestic (%)	Foreign (%)	Total (%)
Assembly	–	67.6	67.6
Tier one	61.9	49.5	49.8
Tier two	59.0	37.2	40.7
Tier three	64.3	34.6	44.2
Total	62.3	44.2	46.8

Source: 2009 author's survey.

€5.6 billion (70.8 percent) was in the form of reinvested profits. However, the 2021 figures were strongly affected by the effects of the COVID-19 pandemic. Before the pandemic, the total FDI stock was €10 billion in 2019, of which €7.3 billion (72.6 percent) was reinvested profits (Figure 6.1).

The share of corporate taxes of the value of total production decreased from 1.6 percent to 0.6 percent between 1998 and 2009 for three basic reasons (Ženka and Pavlínek, 2013). First, the Czech corporate tax rate decreased by 40 percent (from 35 percent to 21 percent) between 1998 and 2008. Second, Czechia introduced a generous system of investment incentives in 1998 (see Pavlínek and Ženka, 2011), which provided a corporate tax relief for foreign investors. Third, the annual profit repatriation abroad in the form of dividends increased rapidly in the automotive industry of Czechia from €2.5 million in 2000 to €813 million in 2008 and €754 million in 2009 during the economic crisis. It continued to grow in the 2010s, amounting to €1.9 billion in 2019 and €1.6 billion in 2020, and declining to €809 million in 2021 (CNB, 2023).

Total repatriated profits in the form of dividends stood at €15.2 billion in 2021 (Figure 6.1), meaning that the total amount of repatriated profits exceeded the total reinvested profits by almost 2.7 times as of 2021 (CNB, 2023). In other words, of the total profits created in the Czech automotive in industry by foreign firms between 1998 and 2021 (€20.9 billion), 27 percent was captured in Czechia in the form of reinvestment, while 73 percent was transferred abroad in the form of dividends. The share of total profits generated by foreign firms in

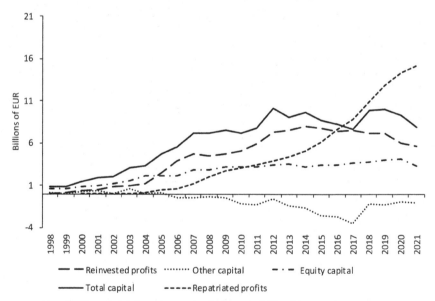

FIGURE 6.1 FDI stock in the automotive industry of Czechia, 1998–2021
Source: author, based on data in CNB (2023).

the automotive industry in Czechia during the 1998–2021 period that was transferred back to the home countries of foreign investors also significantly exceeded equity capital (by 4.6 times as of 2021). The 1998–2021 data thus suggest that the value capture in the Czech automotive industry decreased during this period despite large FDI inflows (Figure 6.1).

The share of wages of the value of total production did not change significantly between 1998 and 2010. The total value of wages increased at a similar rate to the overall volume of production during this period. The total employment grew more slowly (by 68 percent) than average nominal wages per employee (by 99 percent). Between 1998 and 2010, tier-one suppliers experienced the fastest increase in wages per employee (by 123 percent), while assemblers experienced the slowest (by 86 percent) (Table 6.5). Consequently, the wage gap between assemblers and suppliers slightly narrowed during this period. In contrast, the gap between assemblers and suppliers significantly increased in corporate taxes per employee (Table 6.5), which illustrates the ability of assemblers to concentrate increasing shares of profits at the expense of their suppliers. At the same time, assemblers, who accounted for 18.2 percent of the total automotive employment and 47.3 percent of total profits, accounted for 49.8 percent of corporate tax revenues between 2006 and 2008. Different tiers thus contribute to value capture and, consequently, regional development potential in different ways. While foreign assemblers and tier-one suppliers account for a disproportionately high share of total corporate tax revenues in the automotive industry, tier-two and tier-three suppliers are much more important in terms of the number of jobs they generate and related wage effects.

The data from the Czech automotive industry suggest that the stronger economic performance of assemblers and tier-one suppliers does not result solely from their corporate power, privileged position in the value chain, highly sophisticated production and control of high-value-added strategic functions. Many Czech-based foreign-owned assemblers and tier-one suppliers are typified by the low- to medium-value-added production in assembly branch plants with very limited or no strategic functions because these functions are concentrated in corporate headquarters in countries of their principal owners.

Overall, assemblers and tier-one suppliers in the Czech automotive industry do not generally perform more strategic nonproduction functions than lower-tier firms (Table 6.7). Instead, their strong position in the automotive value chain derives from the high capital and technology intensity of production, which is based on the transfer of highly advanced technology, machinery and production processes from their foreign parent companies. The capital intensity of production is considered to be a strong predictor of labor productivity and process upgrading (Szalavetz, 2005). Nevertheless, in the case of assemblers and to a lesser extent also tier-one suppliers, a low share of value-added wages and taxes of the overall value of production (Table 6.4) results from the combination of high capital intensity and intensive outsourcing of the production of components. Assemblers and large tier-one suppliers spend very high shares of their overall expenditures on the

TABLE 6.7 *The percentage of automotive firms conducting selected high-value-added functions in Czechia by supplier tier, 2009*

Functions and competencies	Assembly (%)	Tier one (%)	Tier two (%)	Tier three (%)
Strategic and marketing planning	42.9	44.0	58.9	67.3
Supplier selection	42.9	52.0	75.0	65.4
Decisions about what will be produced	42.9	48.0	63.6	64.7
Investment decisions	57.1	44.0	60.7	66.3
Market research	71.4	34.8	76.8	65.0
Price-setting for produced goods	71.4	56.0	73.2	67.3
Marketing of subsidiary products	71.4	44.0	67.9	62.5
R&D, design	71.4	58.3	63.6	64.0
Product distribution	71.4	87.5	87.5	69.9
Sale and after-sale services	71.4	59.1	76.8	64.4
Organization of production	85.7	100.0	100.0	91.1
Accounting and financial operations	85.7	100.0	100.0	90.9

Note: The number of firms answering individual questions ranged from 150 (for accounting and financial operations) to 192 (for strategic and marketing planning, decisions about what products will be produced, supplier selection, price setting for produced goods and marketing of subsidiary products).
Source: 2009 author's survey.

material, energy, components and services, while their share of wage expenditures is usually less than 10 percent (Table 6.4). It means that lower supplier tiers have larger direct employment and wage effects per unit of production, and also per unit of invested capital, than higher tiers. In 2010, the ratio of total annual wages per unit of tangible assets was 0.17 for assemblers, 0.20 for tier-one suppliers, 0.29 for tier-two suppliers and 0.34 for tier-three suppliers. At the same time, however, lower tiers have lower wages and lower corporate tax revenues per employee than higher tiers, which means that their ability to capture and appropriate value per employee is lower than for assemblers and higher-tier firms.

6.6.4   Strategic Nonproduction Functions and Competencies

Finally, I evaluate the presence of nonproduction functions and competencies in Czech-based automotive firms in order to test the fourth and fifth hypotheses. I assume that strategic nonproduction functions activities contribute to value creation and value capture more than production activities (Mudambi, 2008). The 2009 survey collected the data about strategic nonproduction functions conducted by individual firms. Depending on a particular function, between 150 and 192 firms replied as to whether they performed each of twelve different functions. These functions represent high-value-added activities that are typically associated with highly paid professional jobs. As such, the presence or absence of these functions at individual firms has potentially important implications for their value creation and value capture. However, I need to stress that the data refer only to the presence or absence of these functions and do not provide any information about their extent within individual firms. I am also aware that firms would tend to exaggerate rather than understate the presence and importance of these activities. Therefore, the survey data should be interpreted with caution as the representation of general trends rather than exact measurements.

The fourth hypothesis argues that higher-tier firms possess stronger and more diverse competencies, which are reflected in the presence of more nonproduction (strategic) higher-value-added functions than in lower-tier firms. However, the survey data revealed that on average, tier-one suppliers conduct the lowest number of nonproduction functions in Czechia (61 percent of "yes" answers of those who answered when asked about individual functions), followed by assemblers with 66 percent. Therefore, the fourth hypothesis must be rejected. The main reason for a slightly higher number of functions conducted by tier-two suppliers (75 percent) and tier-three suppliers (70 percent) is a higher share of domestic firms among these lower-tier suppliers (Table 6.7). The differences between domestic and foreign firms within individual tiers are more pronounced and, on average, 82 percent of domestic firms conduct strategic nonproduction functions in Czechia compared to 59 percent of foreign firms (Table 6.8).

There are important differences among individual supplier tiers and between foreign and domestic firms. Among foreign firms, higher-tier firms on average conduct fewer nonproduction functions than lower-tier firms, suggesting that higher-tier foreign suppliers are more tightly integrated into transnational corporate production networks and controlled from abroad. The opposite situation is true for domestic firms because higher-tier domestic firms conduct more functions than lower-tier firms (Table 6.8). Higher-tier domestic firms cannot stay competitive and survive without R&D and other nonproduction functions (2009–2011 interviews). Lower-tier domestic firms, especially tier-three suppliers, are often captive suppliers that depend for many nonproduction functions on buyers of their components (Gereffi et al., 2005; Pavlínek and Žížalová, 2016), which explains why domestic tier-three suppliers reported the lowest share of nonproduction functions of all tiers. Small sample size affects the results for foreign assemblers. There is a difference between foreign assemblers that were taken over by foreign TNCs and kept certain strategic functions in what has been previously called embedded path-dependent transformations (Pavlínek, 2002d), such as Škoda Auto and Iveco (former Karosa), and new greenfield assembly plants, such as Toyota and Hyundai, that lack these functions and have no plans to develop them (2009–2011 interviews). Although higher-tier firms capture a greater share of created value than lower-tier firms, it is not because they conduct more nonproduction functions. The data only confirm that assembly

TABLE 6.8 *The percentage of automotive firms conducting selected high-value-added functions in Czechia by ownership and supplier tier, 2009*

Functions and competencies	Assembly (%)		Tier one (%)		Tier two (%)		Tier three (%)	
	F	D	F	D	F	D	F	D
Strategic and marketing planning	0	100	33	100	34	92	60	73
Investment decisions	25	100	33	100	38	92	55	74
Supplier selection	0	100	43	100	59	96	55	73
Organization of production	75	100	100	100	100	100	93	90
Market research	50	100	25	100	63	96	54	73
Decisions about what will be produced	0	100	38	100	41	96	56	70
Price-setting for produced goods	50	100	48	100	56	96	57	74
Marketing of subsidiary products	50	100	33	100	50	92	50	71
Accounting and financial operations	75	100	100	100	100	100	92	90
R&D, design	50	100	50	100	45	88	53	71
Product distribution	50	100	85	100	81	96	66	73
Sale and after-sale services	50	100	50	100	66	92	57	69
Average	40	100	53	100	61	94	62	75

Notes: F denotes foreign firms; D denotes domestic firms. The number of firms answering individual questions ranged from 150 (for accounting and financial operations) to 192 (for strategic and marketing planning, decisions about what products will be produced, supplier selection, price setting for produced goods and marketing of subsidiary products).
Source: 2009 author's survey.

and tier-one firms pay significantly higher wages per employee than tier-two and tier-three firms (Table 6.5). Therefore, the fifth hypothesis, that higher-tier firms capture a greater share of created value than lower-tier firms because higher-tier firms conduct more nonproduction functions and offer higher wages than lower-tier firms, must be rejected.

6.7 CONCLUSION

This chapter set out to evaluate the value creation and capture in the Czech automotive industry by different tiers of automotive firms. It empirically tested whether two theoretical assumptions apply in the automotive industry in the context of integrated peripheries. First, whether higher-tier firms create and capture higher value than lower-tier firms because they produce more complex components and possess a strong bargaining power that allows them to squeeze their suppliers (Sturgeon et al., 2008). Second, whether intangible knowledge-based assets and strategic nonproduction functions represent a key source of value added for higher-tier firms (Mudambi, 2008).

The analysis suggests that the economic effects of the automotive industry largely depend on its capital intensity of production, especially in terms of wages and value added per employee, which tend to increase with the increasing capital intensity of production and vice versa. Since the highest capital intensity of production is found among assemblers and tier-one suppliers, these firms should have stronger economic effects than lower-tier suppliers. Additionally, assemblers and tier-one suppliers account for much higher corporate tax revenues than lower-tier suppliers and they have higher average wages per worker. This also points toward stronger economic effects of assemblers and tier-one suppliers than tier-two and tier-three suppliers. However, the vast majority of assemblers and tier-one suppliers are foreign-owned in the Czech automotive industry, which has two important implications. First, Czech-based subsidiaries of foreign lead firms and tier-one suppliers primarily concentrate on export-oriented assembly and production and their strategic nonproduction functions are weakly developed. Second, an increase in value creation by foreign firms does not necessarily have to translate into an increase in value capture because of profit repatriation, tax holidays and other profit-shifting strategies employed by foreign firms. At the same time, lower-tier suppliers have larger direct employment and wage effects per unit of production and investment capital than higher-tier suppliers. This is important for regional development since tier-two and tier-three suppliers are much more numerous, more spatially dispersed and received on average significantly lower investment incentives per newly created job than assemblers and tier-one firms.

The data analysis from the Czech automotive industry confirms the first hypothesis that higher-tier firms generate greater value per employee than lower-tier firms. As a result, their share of the total value added in the automotive industry has been increasing. The survey data also confirm the second hypothesis that domestic suppliers import a lower share of inputs than foreign suppliers. The third hypothesis that higher-tier firms import lower shares of inputs than lower-tier firms is confirmed for foreign but not domestic firms. Therefore, it must be rejected. Nevertheless, in the case of foreign firms, a higher share of domestic sourcing by assemblers and tier-one suppliers is another supporting evidence of higher-tier foreign firms creating and capturing greater value than lower-tier suppliers as confirmed by the first hypothesis.

The fourth hypothesis arguing that higher-tier firms possess stronger and more diverse competencies that are reflected in the presence of more nonproduction (strategic) higher-value-added functions than in lower-tier firms must be rejected, since higher-tier foreign firms conduct fewer nonproduction functions than lower-tier foreign firms in the Czech automotive industry. Parent companies typically conduct these functions for higher-tier foreign firms abroad. The fifth hypothesis must also be rejected. Higher-tier firms capture a greater share of created value than lower-tier firms because they offer higher wages than lower-tier firms but not because they conduct more nonproduction higher-value-added functions.

The rejection of the fourth and fifth hypotheses allows me to conclude that the high value creation and capture by assemblers and tier-one suppliers in the Czech automotive industry is not a function of the presence of valuable intangible assets and strategic nonproduction functions. Rather, it is a function of firm size and capital intensity of production. A significantly larger firm size contributes to high profitability by allowing higher-tier firms to capitalize on their internal scale economies and strong purchasing power, which translates into their very strong bargaining power. The capital intensity of production can at least partly explain the high labor productivity of higher-tier firms. The combination of a strong bargaining power with the high capital intensity of production and high labor productivity is probably the key explaining factor for relatively high wages, profitability and corporate tax revenues of higher-tier firms, especially assemblers. Further empirical research is needed to determine if this finding will hold in other integrated peripheries. If it does, we can expect a similar distribution of value creation and capture in countries with a similar or lower concentration of strategic nonproduction functions in the automotive industry, such as Spain, Portugal, Poland, Hungary, Slovakia, Mexico and Thailand.

The greater economic potential of higher-tier firms than lower-tier firms in the automotive industry has important policy implications for less developed countries. In the absence of a strong domestic automotive industry, it makes sense to attract foreign assembly firms because tier-one foreign suppliers will likely follow, which will also encourage foreign tier-two and tier-three suppliers to invest. Most Eastern European countries have followed this approach and engaged in aggressive bidding for foreign assembly plants in the 1990s and 2000s (Drahokoupil, 2009; Pavlínek, 2016). However, less developed countries with a weak domestic manufacturing sector need to factor in potential long-term less tangible costs of these FDI-oriented policies, such as increased economic dependence on foreign TNCs, outflow of profits and the danger of being locked in an unfavorable position in the international division of labor (Nölke and Vliegenthart, 2009).

It is reasonable to expect that the small and open Eastern European economies will continue to be heavily influenced by inflows of FDI and activities of foreign TNCs in the future. At the same time, the overwhelming economic dependence on foreign capital and economic control by foreign capital will make it extremely difficult for Eastern Europe to close the economic gap, including the gap in standards of living, with Western Europe as Eastern European countries are facing the danger of falling into the "middle income trap" (e.g., Ravenhill, 2014). A successful long-term development strategy of the automotive industry should therefore combine the presence of foreign firms with a simultaneous promotion of the strong domestic sector. A key policy issue is finding a balance between the degree of external control and dependence, and indigenous economic development based upon policies that would allow for a gradual upgrading of the position of Eastern European countries in the international division of labor.

7

The Transition toward the Production of Electric Vehicles in Eastern Europe

7.1 INTRODUCTION

The European automotive industry has embarked on a transition from the production of vehicles with internal combustion engines to the production of electric vehicles (i.e., battery electric vehicles (BEVs) and plug-in hybrid electric vehicles (PHEVs)), which will lead to the restructuring of the existing automotive industry in Europe. This transition has been necessitated by the adoption of strict CO_2 emission limits on newly produced vehicles by the European Commission with the goal of decreasing the release of CO_2 by the transport sector to limit global warming (Biresselioglu et al., 2018; EC, 2019; CLEPA, 2021; Pardi, 2021). The adoption of the "Fit for 55" package by the European Union, which aims to reduce European Union's emissions by at least 55 percent by 2030, will effectively ban internal combustion engines in all new cars and vans starting in 2035 (European Council, 2023a; 2023b). The automakers would be unable to meet these CO_2 emission standards with the existing internal combustion engine technologies and many view electric vehicles as the only viable alternative (Sigal, 2021; McKinsey&Company, 2021). However, different automakers have followed different strategies and different technological combinations to meet the emission limits.

The goal of this chapter is to analyze the impact of this transition in Eastern Europe to date in the context of the development of its automotive industry since the early 1990s and its relative position in the European automotive industry value chains and production networks. I argue that the course of the transition to the production of electric vehicles in Eastern Europe is strongly affected by the relative position of the Eastern European automotive industry in GVCs/GPNs and the international division of labor as the integrated periphery of the European automotive industry. I draw on the evolutionary economic geography perspective (e.g., Martin and Sunley, 2006; MacKinnon et al., 2019) to contend that this transition is strongly embedded in and constrained by the previous FDI-dependent development of the automotive industry in Eastern Europe (Pavlínek, 2017a) and its current integrated periphery position in the European automotive industry production system. This chapter draws on statistical data about the automotive industry in Eastern Europe, various automotive industry databases, press reports, specialized automotive industry media and additional secondary information. It also draws on firm-level interviews previously conducted by the author and members of his research team in Czechia and Slovakia.

The chapter is organized as follows. First, I briefly summarize the state of the automotive industry in Eastern Europe. Second, I characterize the relative position of Eastern Europe in the European automotive industry as the integrated periphery and briefly summarize its basic features. Third, I explain how the integrated periphery position affects the transition to the production of electric vehicles in Eastern Europe. Fourth, I discuss the uneven nature of the transition in Eastern Europe. Fifth, I analyze the development of the battery industry in Eastern Europe. Finally, I summarize the basic arguments in the conclusion.

7.2 THE AUTOMOTIVE INDUSTRY IN EASTERN EUROPE

A brief overview of the most important features of the automotive industry in Eastern Europe and its position in the European automotive industry division of labor is a necessary starting point of any analysis of its transition to the production of electric vehicles.

The opening of Eastern Europe to trade and investment in the early 1990s led to its integration in the European economy, including the rapid development of the export-oriented automotive industry (Van Tulder and Ruigrok, 1998; Havas, 2000; Pavlínek, 2002b; 2002d). Low production costs, market potential, geographic proximity, European Union membership or European Union preferential trading arrangements, labor surplus in the 1990s and early 2000s, large investment incentives that lowered the set-up sunk costs and thus the investment risk for foreign firms, and other location-specific factors attracted foreign automakers and component producers to set up production in Eastern Europe after 1990 (Pavlínek, 2002d; 2008; 2016; 2017a; 2020; Adăscăliței and Guga, 2020).

By 2019, the FDI stock in the narrowly defined automotive industry (the manufacture of motor vehicles, trailers and semitrailers – NACE 29) reached €45 billion in Eastern Europe (Eurostat, 2022a) (Figure 7.1a). FDI stock in NACE 29 is highly concentrated in Central Europe (Figure 7.1b). Poland, Czechia, Hungary and Slovakia together accounted for 80 percent of the total in 2021, reflecting their geographic, economic and political location advantages for the automotive industry compared to the rest of Eastern Europe. As a result of FDI inflows, the production of vehicles and components grew rapidly in Eastern Europe. Between 1991 and 2019, the output increased 6.6 times from

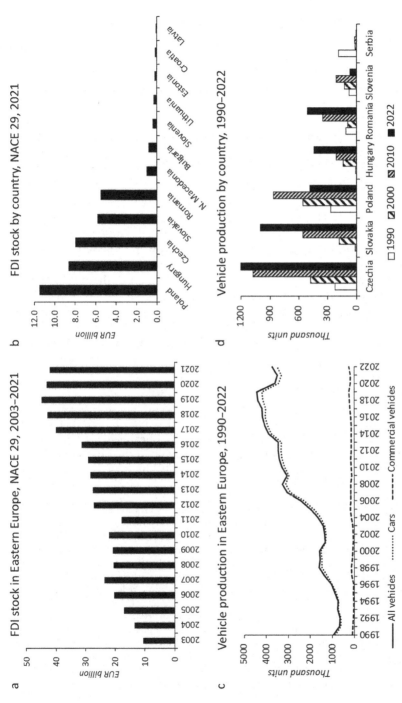

FIGURE 7.1 FDI and vehicle production in the Eastern European automotive industry

Note: NACE 29 = manufacture of motor vehicles, trailers and semi-trailers

Source: author, based on data in Pavlínek (2002b), Eurostat (2022a), OICA (2023).

670,000 to 4.4 million vehicles (Figure 7.1c), accounting for 24.9 percent of total vehicles produced in the European Union in 2019 (OICA, 2023). The 2020 production of vehicles decreased by 805,000 (of which 762,000 were cars) to 3.6 million in Eastern Europe because of the COVID-19 pandemic, but the Eastern European share of the total European Union output increased to 26.2 percent (OICA, 2023). Czechia, Slovakia and Poland were the largest vehicle producers in 2020 (Figure 7.1d). COVID-19 ripple effects, including the shortages of semiconductors, continued to negatively affect the vehicle production in 2021 and 2022. The 2022 production was also negatively affected by the war in Ukraine.[1]

Prior to the COVID-19 pandemic, the growth was concentrated in the export-oriented production of passenger cars (henceforth cars), which increased almost sevenfold from 863,000 to 4.2 million between 1991 and 2019 (Figure 7.1c). The assembly of cars takes place in Czechia, Slovakia, Romania, Hungary, Poland, Slovenia and Serbia (Figure 7.2a). Central Europe accounted for 85 percent of the total car production in Eastern Europe in 2022. Czechia and Slovakia alone accounted for 63 percent (OICA, 2023). Compared to cars, the interest of foreign capital in the production of commercial vehicles has been limited in Eastern Europe. FDI has been concentrated in Poland in the production of light commercial vehicles and heavy trucks. Poland and Czechia are the only two Eastern European countries with a surviving bus production, mainly due to FDI. Czech SOR remains the last significant domestic bus maker in Eastern Europe because Polish Solaris was sold to Spanish CAF in 2018.

The value of production in the car industry (NACE 29) increased almost eightfold between 1999 and 2020 (ninefold between 1999 and 2019) and the value of manufactured parts and components (NACE 29.3) increased fourteenfold between 1999 and 2020 (nineteenfold between 1999 and 2019) (Figure 7.2b). The biggest growth was in the 2000s. In the 2010s, the rate of growth slowed, and the value of production doubled between 2000 and 2019.

---

[1] The European automotive industry was disrupted by Russia's invasion and war in Ukraine in February 2022 (ANE, 2022c; Harrison, 2022). There are twenty-two foreign companies producing parts and components for the automotive industry in thirty-eight factories and employing over 60,000 workers in Ukraine. Many are producing wire harnesses. The production of wire harnesses by Leoni, Fujijura and Nexans has been particularly affected. For example, in early March 2022, the halting of assembly of cable harnesses at two large Leoni factories in Ukraine in Stryi and Kolomyja, which employ 7,000 workers, led to drastic reductions in production at Volkswagen, Audi, Porsche, BMW and Mercedes-Benz in Germany (ANE, 2022b; Eddy, 2022). Ukraine is also the source of 70 percent of the world's supply of neon, which is needed to produce semiconductors, as is palladium, of which about one third is supplied by Russia. Many foreign automakers halted their Russian factories and suspended business in Russia, including Ford, Honda, Toyota, Volkswagen, Jaguar, Aston Martin, Volvo, General Motors and Daimler Truck (ANE, 2022c). Foreign automotive suppliers have also suspended their operations in Russia. For example, Magna suspended production in its six factories in Russia, which employ 2,500 people (Irwin, 2022).

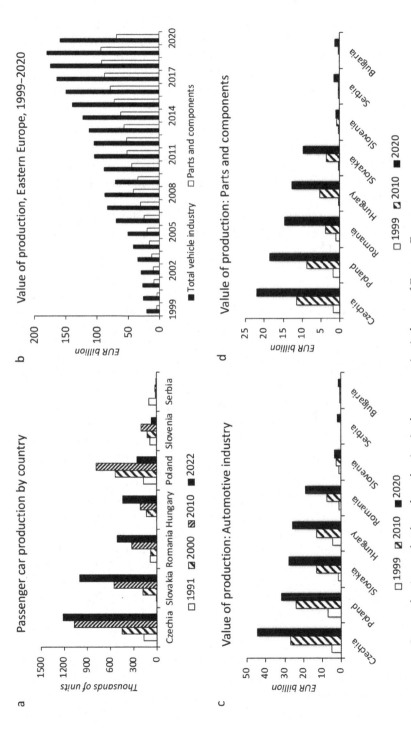

FIGURE 7.2 Car production and value of production in the automotive industry of Eastern Europe
Source: author, based on data in Pavlínek (2002b), Eurostat (2023c), OICA (2023).

In 2020, the production value of parts and components was higher only by 55 percent than in 2010 because of the decrease by 26 percent in 2020 compared to 2019, which was caused by the effects of the COVID-19 pandemic. The distribution of the value of production by country corresponds with the distribution of the car production (Figure 7.2c). The largest vehicle producing countries also have the largest production of components (Figure 7.2d).

7.2.1 Limits to Growth Due to Exhausted Labor Surplus

The declining rates of growth in the 2010s, especially in Central Europe well before the COVID-19 pandemic, reflect the exhaustion of labor surplus by the rapid growth of the automotive industry. It led to labor shortages in the 2010s that pushed wages up, which undermined the rate of profit. For example, in Czechia, which has had the lowest unemployment rate in the European Union since 2016, the unemployment rate has been below 3 percent since 2017 (2.9 percent in 2017, 2.2 percent in 2018, 2.0 percent in 2019, 2.6 percent in 2020, 2.8 percent in 2021, 2.2 percent in 2022) (Eurostat, 2023e). Czechia has also consistently had the highest vacancy rate in manufacturing in the European Union since 2016 (4.7 percent in the fourth quarter of 2022) (Eurostat, 2023b). Central Bohemia, which hosts the main production complex of Škoda Auto in Mladá Boleslav, the Toyota factory in Kolín and many component suppliers, recorded a consistently lower share of unemployed persons than the national average (2.1 percent in 2017, 2.0 percent in 2018, 1.3 percent in 2019, 1.9 percent in 2020 and 2.5 percent in 2021). Similarly, the region of Hradec Králové, which hosts the second Škoda assembly complex at Kvasiny and the Škoda factory at Vrchlabí, recorded a below-national average unemployment rate (2.2 percent in 2017, 2.3 percent in 2018, 1.6 percent in 2019, 2.6 percent in 2020 and 2.9 percent in 2021). The Moravia-Silesia region, which hosts the Hyundai assembly complex, had an unemployment rate slightly higher than the national average but it was still very low and made it difficult for automotive firms to find the needed workers (4.7 percent in 2017, 3.7 percent in 2018, 3.7 percent in 2019, 3.6 percent in 2020 and 4.6 percent in 2021) (CSO, 2022). Labor surplus in the Moravia-Silesia region, which was indicated by a high unemployment rate (14.7 percent in 2003, 14.5 percent in 2004, 13.9 percent in 2005) was an important factor in Hyundai's decision to locate its assembly factory in the Moravia-Silesia region (Pavlínek, 2008; CSO, 2022). Among forty-four foreign-owned automotive firms in Czechia interviewed between 2009 and 2011, 73 percent reported difficulties in hiring qualified workers despite the economic crisis (e.g., Pavlínek and Ženka, 2010; Pavlínek, 2015a).

Poland (2.9 percent) and Hungary (3.6 percent) had the second- and sixth-lowest unemployment rates in the European Union in 2022 (Eurostat, 2023e). Hungary has had the second-highest vacancy rate in manufacturing in Central Europe (2.7 percent in the fourth quarter of 2022), while Poland's vacancy rate has been much lower (0.9 percent in the fourth quarter of 2022) (Eurostat, 2023b). However, the national-level data do not reveal large regional differences in labor availability that are accentuated by the clustering of the automotive industry in regional production complexes (e.g., Sturgeon et al., 2008). For instance, the national unemployment rate in Slovakia has been higher than in the rest of Central Europe (6.1 percent in 2022) and its vacancy rate in manufacturing has been among the lowest in the European Union (0.8 percent in the fourth quarter of 2022) (Eurostat, 2023b; 2023e). Still, the Slovak automotive industry has experienced severe labor shortages in regions targeted by automotive FDI, especially in western Slovakia, which, along with the Bratislava region, hosts the largest share of FDI in the Slovak automotive industry, including four assembly factories and hundreds of component suppliers (e.g., Jacobs, 2016; Pavlínek, 2016). In 2001, the unemployment rate of West Slovakia (NUTS 2) was 17.5 percent. It decreased to 4.0 percent in 2022 (Eurostat, 2023f). The Bratislava region, which hosts a large Volkswagen assembly factory complex and many automotive suppliers, had an unemployment rate of 2.3 percent in 2022 (Eurostat, 2023f). The very low unemployment rate translated into severe labor shortages for automotive firms in western Slovakia and became a barrier for the further development of the automotive industry. Interviews with twenty-seven foreign-owned automotive industry firms conducted by the author in western Slovakia between 2011 and 2015 revealed that 96 percent of the interviewed firms had major difficulties hiring qualified workers in Slovakia. Only one supplier argued that it did not face major difficulties, but at the expense of busing workers to its factory from places located up to 100 kilometers away. In 2018, 82 percent of sixty-one surveyed automotive suppliers in Slovakia identified the lack of available qualified workers on the job market as a risk factor affecting their future growth prospects, 78 percent considered the unavailability and low quality of labor a major issue for their company, and 53 percent (up from 37 percent in 2016) argued that the lack of skilled labor restricted their ability to win or accept new contracts (PwC, 2018).

Similar widespread labor shortages in the automotive industry have been reported from other Eastern European countries, including Hungary (HIPA, 2020; Szabo et al., 2022) and Romania (Guga, 2019; Adăscăliței and Guga, 2020) and are considered the most important barrier to future investment across Eastern Europe, which also holds for Western Europe (Slačík, 2022). Labor shortages have forced automotive firms to increasingly rely on foreign workers and agency employment. More importantly, in line with theories of uneven economic development (e.g., Harvey, 2005b), some automakers and component suppliers, especially those engaged in labor-intensive production, have been increasingly looking for new, potentially more profitable locations with labor surplus and low labor costs for future investments in countries such as Serbia, Moldova, Bosnia and Herzegovina, and North Macedonia (Pavlínek, 2018; 2020). PSA and Renault have set up assembly plants in Morocco, with a projected capacity to reach 700,000 cars by the end of 2022 and Morocco is aiming for 1 million assembled vehicles per year by the mid-2020s (Bolduc, 2017b; Henry, 2020).

7.2.2 Upgrading and Higher-Value-Added Functions

FDI in the Eastern European automotive industry has led to the development of a distinct division of labor in the European automotive industry. By investing in Eastern Europe, foreign firms have mainly pursued cost-cutting to increase their profitability and competitiveness (Pavlínek, 2002d; 2020). This has translated in the focus on setting up production functions, while higher-value-added functions have remained concentrated in the home countries of foreign investors (Pavlínek, 2016; 2022a; Pavlínek and Ženka, 2016). In the 1990s, the focus in Eastern Europe was on the low-value-added labor-intensive assembly operations, often based on cross-border investment in the production of components and car assembly (Pavlínek, 1998; Pavlínek and Smith, 1998). Over time, however, there has been the gradual upgrading of the production to more sophisticated and capital-intensive automotive production of high-quality cars and components (Pavlínek et al., 2009; Pavlínek and Ženka, 2011), in which low labor costs continue to play an important role in keeping production costs under control and thus contributing to the overall competitiveness of finished products and also of lead automotive firms (Boyer and Freyssenet, 2002) (Table 7.1). Foreign assembly firms and many component suppliers are now making cars and components in state-of-the-art factories based on advanced technologies in Eastern Europe (Layan, 2006). There is therefore no doubt about FDI-driven process and product upgrading (Humphrey and Schmitz, 2002) in the automotive industry of Eastern Europe since the 1990s (Layan, 2006; Pavlínek et al., 2009; Szalavetz, 2019), although not all foreign firms have been successful in Eastern Europe, as evidenced, for example, by the failure of Daewoo investments (Pavlínek, 2006). Process and product upgrading has also been crucial for the competitiveness and survival of local (domestic) firms (Pavlínek and Ženka, 2011). Some surviving or newly established local automotive firms have successfully internationalized (Micek et al., 2021), although many domestic firms did not survive because the most successful ones were taken over by foreign firms (Pavlínek, 2002c), while unsuccessful ones ended in bankruptcy (Pavlínek, 2000; 2002a; 2003) and the overall growth of domestic firms has been much slower than the growth of foreign firms (Pavlínek, 2020). These processes have contributed to the overwhelming foreign control of the automotive industry in Eastern Europe (Table 7.2).

At the same time, foreign firms have invested disproportionately less in functional upgrading and the development of the higher-value-added functions in the automotive industry, including R&D in Eastern Europe (Pavlínek, 2004; 2012; 2020; Domański and Gwosdz, 2009; Darteyre and Guga, 2022) (Figures 7.3a and 7.3b). Foreign-controlled R&D employment and R&D investment gradually

TABLE 7.1 *Labor cost per employee full-time equivalent in thousands of EUR (at exchange rate parity) in the European automotive industry (NACE 29) by country, 2020*

	Thousands of EUR	Germany = 100
Switzerland	84.4	101.2
Ireland	84.4	101.2
Germany	83.4	100.0
Sweden	81	97.1
Belgium	78.6	94.2
Netherlands	70.5	84.5
Austria	69.2	83.0
Denmark	66.7	80.0
France	66.6	79.9
Italy	65.7	78.8
Norway	60.2	72.2
Iceland	55.3	66.3
Britain	54.6[a]	65.5
Finland	48.7	58.4
Spain	45.4	54.4
Slovakia	25.7	30.8
Czechia	25.5	30.6
Estonia	24.8	29.7
Portugal	22.6	27.1
Greece	22.5	27.0
Hungary	22.5	27.0
Poland	19.5	23.4
Latvia	18.5	22.2
Cyprus	18.3	21.9
Lithuania	16.9	20.3
Croatia	14.6	17.5
Romania	14.2	17.0
Turkey	14.0[b]	16.8
Bosnia and Herzegovina	10.7	12.8
Bulgaria	9.3	11.2
North Macedonia	5[c]	6.0

Notes: [a]2018, [b]2014, [c]2012.
Source: Eurostat (2023c).

TABLE 7.2 *The index of foreign control in the European automotive industry, 2019*

Slovakia	97.9
Hungary	96.3
Romania	94.2
Czechia	93.4
Bulgaria	92.0
Poland	89.7
Spain	85.9
Portugal	84.5
Britain	83.6[b]
Lithuania	83.6
Slovenia	83.3
Austria	80.1
Bosnia and Herzegovina	79.9[a]
Belgium	74.9
Sweden	63.5
Netherlands	58.1[a]
Estonia	57.2
Croatia	54.4[a]
Ireland	49.2
Denmark	44.6
Finland	31.3
Norway	25.1
France	24.1
Italy	23.6
Germany	14.9

Note: The average value of the share of foreign-controlled enterprises of five indicators in the manufacture of motor vehicles, trailers and semitrailers (NACE_R2): production value, value added at factor cost, gross investment in tangible goods, number of persons employed and turnover or gross premiums written.
[a] 2018, [b] 2017.
Source: calculated by author from data available in Eurostat (2022b; 2023c).

increased in Eastern Europe as the low cost of the R&D labor force attracted FDI and there are numerous examples of a successful automotive R&D developed by foreign firms in Eastern Europe (Pavlínek et al., 2009; Pavlínek, 2012; Szalavetz,

2019; Markiewicz, 2020; Guzik et al., 2020). However, important barriers exist, which are related to the organization of corporate R&D in the automotive industry (Pavlínek, 2012), as well as the shortages of the qualified R&D labor in Eastern Europe (Pavlínek, 2018; Szalavetz, 2022). Consequently, the share of R&D employment and R&D expenditures in the Eastern European automotive industry remains low compared to Western Europe (Tables 7.3 and 7.4) (Pavlínek, 2022a). While Eastern Europe accounted for 32 percent of jobs in the European Union automotive industry in 2020, its share of R&D jobs was 8.7 percent and the share of R&D business expenditures was only 3.6 percent in 2019 (Figure 7.3d). The overall weakness of automotive R&D in Eastern Europe is also illustrated by the very low number of patents compared to Western Europe (Delanote et al., 2022). Although selective functional upgrading in functions other than R&D in foreign subsidiaries has gradually developed (Sass and Szalavetz, 2013; Szalavetz, 2022), empirical firm-level research has uncovered the weak presence of strategic and high-value-added functions in the foreign subsidiaries of automotive firms in the Eastern European automotive industry (Pavlínek, 2016; Pavlínek and Ženka, 2016), which is closely related to the distribution of functions in the corporate hierarchy (Hymer, 1972; Pavlínek, 2012).

7.3 THE INTEGRATED PERIPHERY OF THE EUROPEAN AUTOMOTIVE INDUSTRY

The uncritical and simplistic accounts of the development of the automotive industry in Eastern Europe view it as an unqualified success by emphasizing short-term capital, employment and production effects of FDI (Jakubiak et al., 2008; Kureková, 2012; Kureková Mýtna, 2018; Markiewicz, 2020). These accounts tend to present the growth of the automotive industry as a success of the national economy by ignoring the fact that it is mainly the result of large FDI inflows and has very little to do with the nature and the level of development of the national economy. At the same time, these accounts either underplay or completely ignore the potential long-term effects of the foreign-capital-driven development in the form of newly created dependencies (capital, technological, financial, decision-making) and the outflow of value in the form of dividends and profit repatriation (Dischinger et al., 2014b; 2014a) that will affect the ability of Eastern European countries to improve their position in the international division of labor and close the development gap with the more developed countries of Western Europe (Pavlínek, 2022b).

For example, in Slovakia, the government agencies, politicians and media frequently argue that the country is a global automotive industry "superpower" because it has achieved the highest production of cars per capita in the world (e.g., Sario, 2022; ZAP, 2022). This simplistic account of the automotive industry in Slovakia based on a single indicator ignores the fact that the automotive industry is almost completely controlled by foreign capital and

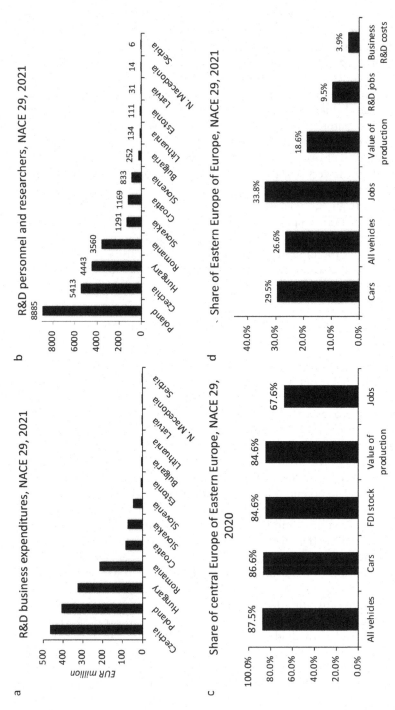

FIGURE 7.3 R&D in the automotive industry of Eastern Europe and regional shares of the automotive industry.
Note: Data for Europe exclude data for Russia, Ukraine, Belarus and Turkey, which are not available.
Source: author, based on data in Eurostat (2023c); OICA (2023).

Slovakia has the highest index of foreign control in the European Union, at 97.9 percent in 2019 (Table 7.2). The share of foreign capital of production value, value added at factor cost and turnover exceeds 99 percent (Eurostat, 2022b; 2022c). All cars are assembled in foreign-owned factories based on foreign technology, work organization and management and R&D (see Pavlínek, 2016). The foreign-controlled automotive industry is mostly isolated from the Slovak economy because it has only tenuous linkages with domestic firms, which diminishes a potential for spillovers from foreign to domestic firms (Pavlínek, 2018). By far the most important production factor Slovakia contributes to the automotive industry is its relatively low-cost labor compared to Western Europe (Table 7.1). Instead of being the global automotive industry superpower and despite the highest per-capita production of cars in the world, an empirical analysis has demonstrated Slovakia's peripheral position in the European automotive industry production system, which is almost totally controlled from the core areas of the global automotive industry. Other countries of the Eastern European integrated periphery are in a similar highly dependent peripheral position in the automotive GVCs/GPNs (Table 7.2) (Pavlínek, 2022a).

It is, therefore, important to understand the course of the current and future transition to the production of electric vehicles in Eastern Europe from an evolutionary perspective and in the context of its relative position as the integrated periphery in the European automotive industry GVCs/GPNs (Pavlínek, 2018; 2020; 2022a). Since the concept of the integrated periphery has been theoretically and conceptually developed in Chapters 3 and 4 of this book, its discussion here is limited to a brief summary of basic features applied to the automotive industry of Eastern Europe. At the general level, I have defined an integrated periphery in Chapter 3 as "a dynamic area of relatively low-cost (industrial) production that is geographically adjacent to a large market and has been integrated within a core-based macro-regional production network through FDI. In an integrated periphery, production, organization and strategic functions in a given industry are externally controlled through foreign ownership." Accordingly, I have identified the basic features of the integrated periphery of the European automotive industry in Eastern Europe in Chapters 3 and 4 as follows.

1. There are substantially lower labor costs than in the core regions of the European automotive industry (Pavlínek, 2022a), such as Germany, France and Italy, despite a smaller wage gap in 2020 than in the 1990s when wages in Eastern Europe were about 90 percent lower than in Western Europe (Table 7.1).[2]

---

[2] In 2001, compared to Germany, average personnel costs (personnel costs per employee) in the automotive industry (NACE 29) were lower by 86 percent in Slovakia, 85 percent in Czechia,

2. There is a sizeable labor surplus at the initial stages of growth of the automotive industry, which, however, becomes exhausted over time because of the FDI-driven growth of the automotive industry, leading to labor shortages that undermine the future growth prospects (e.g., PwC, 2019; HIPA, 2020).

3. There is geographic proximity to large and lucrative markets in core regions of Western Europe, especially Germany. It lowers transportation costs of automotive products from integrated peripheries to core areas and vice versa and is further supported by the development of modern transport infrastructure in integrated peripheries, such as divided highways and modernized high-speed railways.

4. Membership in the European Union or preferential trading arrangements with the European Union in the cases of non-European Union countries provide tariff-free access to European Union markets.

5. There is a high degree of foreign ownership and control over the automotive industry through FDI, which is the highest in the European Union. It usually exceeds 90 percent for the most important automotive industry countries of Eastern Europe (Table 7.2).

6. An export-oriented high-volume production focuses on standardized cars and generic automotive components, along with low-volume production of niche-market vehicles (Havas, 2000; Pavlínek, 2002d; Layan, 2006). Typically, more than 90 percent of assembled vehicles are exported (Pavlínek, 2018; WTEx, 2021; OEC, 2023).

7. There is regional specialization based on the spatial division of labor resulting from the strategy of complementary specialization (Kurz and Wittke, 1998), in which the integrated periphery has a greater share of low-value-added labor-intensive production tasks compared to the automotive industry in Western Europe (Pavlínek, 2002d; Jürgens and Krzywdzinski, 2009a; Stöllinger, 2021; Slačík, 2022).

8. There is a weak presence of high-value-added and strategic functions, such as R&D and strategic decision-making, compared to the extent of production functions in integrated peripheries (Tables 7.3 and 7.4, Figure 7.3d) (Pavlínek, 2012; 2016; 2022a; Pavlínek and Ženka, 2016; Stöllinger, 2021; Delanote et al., 2022; Slačík, 2022), resulting in the truncated development of the automotive industry (Pavlínek, 2017b).

9. FDI-friendly state policies, large investment incentives, low corporate taxes and an active state competition over strategic automotive FDI with other countries contribute to a "race to the bottom" in the integrated periphery (Drahokoupil, 2008; 2009; Pavlínek, 2016).

10. Compared to the automotive industry in core countries, especially Germany, labor unions are weaker, labor codes are more liberal and

---

84 percent in Poland, 82 percent in Hungary, 96 percent in Bulgaria and 95 percent in Romania (Eurostat, 2016a).

labor practices are more flexible (Jürgens and Krzywdzinski, 2009a; 2009b; Drahokoupil and Myant, 2017; Martišková et al., 2021).

11. The domestic automotive industry is weakly developed compared to the foreign-controlled automotive sector (Table 7.2, Chapters 3 and 4) resulting in the integration of domestic firms into macro-regional GVCs/GPNs at an inferior and subordinate position mainly as low-cost tier-three suppliers of niche products and simple parts and components (Pavlínek and Janák, 2007; Pavlínek and Žížalová, 2016; Pavlínek, 2018).

Overall, there is no doubt that the post-1990 development of the automotive industry in Eastern Europe has been very successful when measured by production volumes, jobs created, capital invested, the contribution to GDP and foreign trade and other quantitative indicators (Figures 7.1 and 7.2) (e.g., Delanote et al., 2022; Slačík, 2022). At the same time, however, the foreign-controlled automotive industry in Eastern Europe has been articulated into automotive GVCs/GPNs via FDI and trade in a dependent and subordinated position through what the GPN perspective calls the structural mode of strategic coupling between regional assets and the needs of TNCs (Coe and Yeung, 2015; Coe, 2021). More specifically, it has been mostly articulated as an "assembly platform" that concentrates on production functions and has weakly developed strategic functions (Pavlínek, 2016; Pavlínek and Ženka, 2016; Stöllinger, 2021; Delanote et al., 2022; Slačík, 2022). It is also typified by weak linkages of foreign-owned automotive firms with host country economies that translate into weak spillovers from foreign firms to host country economies (Chapter 3 of this book, Pavlínek and Žížalová, 2016). This situation contributes to a low value capture from the automotive industry compared to the automotive industry in Western Europe and has long-term structural consequences for the Eastern European integrated periphery, especially for its ability to close the development gap, wage levels and the standard of living with more developed Western Europe.

7.4 THE INTEGRATED PERIPHERY AND THE TRANSITION TO THE PRODUCTION OF ELECTRIC VEHICLES IN EASTERN EUROPE

The relative position of the Eastern European integrated periphery in the European automotive industry GVCs/GPNs will influence the course of its transition to the production of electric vehicles. The starting point of my analysis is the assumption of inevitability of the transition away from the production of internal combustion engine vehicles, which is based on three points. First, the emission limits imposed on the European Union automotive industry by the European Commission (EC, 2019; CLEPA, 2021; Pardi, 2021) cannot be met without shifting the production away from internal combustion engine vehicles. Second, feasible technological options for the automotive industry to meet these limits by the deadline specified in the European Union regulations are currently limited. Consequently, a consensus has emerged in the automotive industry about meeting the emission limits and regulations by shifting to the production of electric vehicles (BEVs, PHEVs and hybrids) (Jetin, 2020; McKinsey&Company, 2021; Sigal, 2021). Third, the automotive industry trends in the direction of electric vehicles in China (Yeung, 2019; Schwabe, 2020a) and the USA (Slowik and Lutsey, 2018), the largest and third-largest (after the European Union) automobile markets in the world, generate regulatory and competitive pressures on the European automakers to embrace the electric vehicle technology. This pressure applies in foreign markets (especially in China) in the form of state regulation (Yeung, 2019; Schwabe, 2020a) and the growing competition from local (Chinese and American) carmakers in electric vehicles. It also applies in the European Union markets because of the growing competition in electric vehicles from foreign firms, especially the American Tesla, electric vehicles made by foreign firms in China that will be imported to Europe (e.g., the Mini electric vehicle made by GM at Wuling) and from Chinese automakers (Manthey, 2021a; Sigal, 2022b).[3] At the same time, the transition to the production of electric vehicles is risky and extremely costly for the automotive industry (Dijk et al., 2016; Delanote et al., 2022) and involves many uncertainties for automotive firms and suppliers (CLEPA, 2021). The failure of European Union-based automakers to succeed would have serious repercussions not only for the European automotive industry but for the entire European economy (ACEA, 2022a).

In terms of the Eastern European automotive industry, several general observations can be made about how its position in GVCs/GPNs and the international division of labor in the automotive industry will affect its transition to the production of electric vehicles.

7.4.1 Eastern Europe is Not the Center of Innovation for Electromobility

First, Eastern Europe is not and will not be the center of innovation for electromobility. R&D for electric vehicles is mainly conducted in the home countries of assembly firms and large "global" tier-one suppliers, which are mostly located in Western Europe, the USA, Japan and South Korea. Škoda Auto in Czechia and Dacia in Romania represent a partial exception, which is related to their position as tier-two lead firms (Pavlínek and Janák, 2007; Pavlínek, 2015b). A tier-two lead firm has a significant autonomy to produce, manage and develop a distinct brand within a larger group. As such, it has many attributes of typical automotive lead firms, including its own international production and

---

[3] In 2022, China was the third-largest exporter of vehicles to the European Union market (after Britain and Turkey), while the USA was the seventh-largest. The imports of Chinese vehicles grew from 81,000 in 2015 to 196,000 in 2020 and 561,000 in 2022. The imports of American vehicles increased from 245,000 in 2015 to 394,000 in 2020, before declining to 271,000 in 2022 (ACEA, 2022a; 2023a).

distribution network, which it coordinates and controls. It has the power to select suppliers and thus determine who will be included or excluded from its supplier network and under what conditions suppliers deliver components for the assembly. Most importantly, however, tier-two lead firms are foreign-owned, which means that their power and autonomy are limited. Ultimate decisions and control are in the hands of their ultimate owners, the tier-one lead firms, which are Volkswagen in the case of Škoda Auto and Renault in the case of Dacia.

Despite a few additional examples of R&D developed by assembly firms, such as 400 R&D workers working in technical development at Audi Hungária (Audi, 2021), R&D competencies of car makers are very limited or completely absent in Eastern Europe (Pavlínek, 2012). It also applies to the supplier sector despite the selective development of R&D activities by foreign TNCs in Eastern Europe (Pavlínek et al., 2009; Pavlínek, 2012; Guzik et al., 2020), as reflected in the low share of business R&D expenditures of the total value of production and the low share of R&D personnel and researchers of total persons employed in the automotive industry (Tables 7.3 and 7.4).

TABLE 7.3 *The share of business R&D expenditures of the total value of production in the automotive industry (NACE 29) of selected European countries, 2020*

	Percent	Germany = 100
Sweden	7.42[a]	106.2
Germany	6.99	100.0
Austria	4.88	69.8
Britain	4.54[b]	64.9
Italy	3.37	48.2
France	3.04	43.5
Finland	2.92	41.8
Norway	2.45	35.1
Netherlands	2.10[c]	30.0
Belgium	1.62	23.2
Latvia	1.29	18.4
Slovenia	1.24	17.7
Hungary	1.21	17.3
Poland	1.10	15.7
Spain	1.01	14.4
Romania	1.00	14.3
Czechia	0.90	12.8
Estonia	0.88[a]	12.5
Ireland	0.83	11.9
Lithuania	0.73	10.5

(continued)

TABLE 7.3 *(continued)*

	Percent	Germany = 100
Denmark	0.73	10.5
Portugal	0.46	6.6
Bulgaria	0.27	3.8
Slovakia	0.21	3.0
North Macedonia	0.03	0.4
Greece	0.00	0.0
Cyprus	0.00	0.0
Bosnia and Herzegovina	0.00	0.0
Serbia	0.00	0.0

Notes: [a]2019, [b]2018, [c]2012. The value for Sweden is calculated from the total for NACE 29 and NACE 30 (NACE 29 data not available).
Source: calculated by author based on data in Eurostat (2023a; 2023c), Statistics Sweden (2023).

TABLE 7.4 *The share of R&D personnel and researchers of total persons employed in the automotive industry (NACE 29) of selected European countries, 2020*

	Percent	Germany = 100
Sweden	18.61	111.5
Germany	16.68	100.0
Austria	11.99	71.8
Britain	11.58[a]	69.4
Italy	10.67	64.0
Netherlands	10.14[b]	60.8
Norway	9.24	55.4
France	7.31	43.8
Finland	5.46	32.7
Slovenia	5.30	31.8
Hungary	4.14	24.8
Spain	4.05	24.3
Belgium	4.01	24.1
Portugal	3.90	23.4
Poland	3.63	21.8
Czechia	3.01	18.0
Ireland	2.51[c]	15.1
Denmark	2.25[c]	13.5

(continued)

TABLE 7.4 (*continued*)

	Percent	Germany = 100
Romania	1.92	11.5
Lithuania	1.91	11.5
Estonia	1.55	9.3
Latvia	1.46	8.8
Slovakia	1.26	7.6
Greece	0.73	4.4
Bulgaria	0.71	4.2
North Macedonia	0.07	0.4
Serbia	0.00	0.0
Bosnia and Herzegovina	0.00	0.0

Notes: [a]2018, [b]2012, [c]2019. For Belgium, Germany and Greece the 2020 number of R&D personnel and researchers is calculated as the average of 2019 and 2021 figures and for Poland as the average of 2018 and 2021 figures. The value for Sweden is calculated from the total for NACE 29 and NACE 30 (NACE 29 data not available).
Source: calculated by author based on data in Eurostat (2023c; 2023d), Statistics Sweden (2023).

This situation is a typical feature of "truncated development," which refers to the absence or low share of high-value-added activities, such as R&D functions, strategic planning and decision-making about major investments in foreign-owned factories in host regions, and the concentration in home countries of foreign investors, usually at corporate headquarters and corporate R&D centers (see Chapter 2) (Britton, 1980; 1981; Hayter, 1982; Pavlínek, 2017b). The truncated development is strongly pronounced in the Eastern European automotive industry because of the very high degree of foreign ownership and control (Table 7.2) (Pavlínek, 2016; Pavlínek and Ženka, 2016). It is the case despite the fact that innovation activities in the core–periphery regional systems, such as the one in the European automotive industry, gradually and selectively spread from core areas to the integrated peripheries, including some R&D functions related to electromobility (Friedmann, 1967; Pavlínek et al., 2009; Pavlínek, 2022a; 2012).

For example, Škoda Auto has been developing new R&D competencies in Czechia related to the transition to the production of electric vehicles (Škoda Auto, 2021c), although these R&D competencies are much weaker than the ones performed by Volkswagen's corporate R&D center in Germany. Despite the gradual and selective development of innovative activities mostly driven by cheaper R&D labor in Eastern Europe than in Western Europe, the intensity and size of innovation activities will continue to be much stronger in the core areas than in the integrated periphery. The main reason is better conditions for innovation activities in core areas, as argued in Chapter 5 of this book (Tödtling and Trippl, 2005; Isaksen and Trippl, 2017), which is reflected in higher automotive industry R&D employment and R&D spending in Western Europe compared to Eastern Europe (Tables 7.3 and 7.4).

7.4.2   A Slower Pace of Transition to the Production of Electric Vehicles than in Western Europe

The second general observation about the transition to the production of electric vehicles in Eastern Europe is its slower speed than in Western Europe, especially when compared to the core countries of the European automotive industry (Germany, France and Italy). For example, Renault plans 90 percent of its sales to be of battery electric vehicles by 2030 but its Romanian-based low-cost brand Dacia might reach only 10 percent battery electric vehicles according to the Renault Group's director of R&D (Randall, 2021), and it plans to sell internal combustion engines "for as long as it can," according to Dacia's chief executive officer (ANE, 2022a). While fully dedicated factories for the large-scale production of electric vehicles have been opened in Western Europe (e.g., Volkswagen's factories at Zwickau and Emden, Tesla's factory near Berlin) or are being planned (e.g., Volkswagen's Trinity factory near Wolfsburg), Eastern European factories have so far employed the strategy of mixed production, in which electric vehicles are assembled along with internal combustion engine vehicles in the same factory. This strategy will make it more difficult to achieve scale economies and, therefore, lower production costs of electric vehicles. To make this kind of mixed production viable in the short and medium run, Eastern European factories plan to compensate with lower production costs and high labor flexibility. In the long run, however, this strategy is not competitive with the production in fully dedicated electric vehicle factories and the production model in which each assembly line is fully dedicated to one platform (Gibbs, 2019b). Consequently, the mixed production strategy may become a major disadvantage for the competitive position of Eastern European factories in the future.

As of now, there are only three known exceptions to the mixed production strategy in Eastern Europe (Table 7.7). The first is the BMW factory, which is under construction in Debrecen, Hungary, and which should be completed in 2025. The Debrecen factory was originally also planned for the mixed production of models with internal combustion engines and electrified drivetrains (BMW, 2018). However, after first delaying the factory construction and the production launch by three years, it was decided to fully dedicate the factory to the production of electric vehicles (BMW, 2020). The second exception is the Volvo factory announced in 2022 that will be built in Slovakia between 2023 and 2026 (Hampel, 2022c). The third exception is the BYD factory that will be built in Hungary, which might also assemble plug-in hybrid electric vehicles (Westerheide, 2024). These three cases suggest that factories fully dedicated to electric vehicles will eventually be developed in Eastern Europe to serve the European Union markets and will likely exist alongside the factories producing vehicles based on internal combustion engines for non-European Union markets.

7.4.3 Longer Production of Internal Combustion Engine Vehicles and Internal Combustion Engines than in Western Europe

Third, the production of internal combustion engine cars and internal combustion engines will continue longer in Eastern Europe than in Western Europe. The restructuring of the internal combustion engine production in Europe will entail either the closure of internal combustion engine factories or their conversion to the production of electric engines or batteries in the high-wage European automotive industry core countries, such as Germany and France. The remaining internal combustion engine production will move to countries with lower wages in the integrated periphery, such as Eastern Europe (Sigal, 2022a). In some cases, the production of internal combustion engine vehicles and internal combustion engines is already being transferred to Eastern Europe from Western Europe, which might benefit the Eastern European locations in the short and medium run by additional investment, job creation and increased production. For example, Volkswagen is transferring the production of the Volkswagen Passat from Germany to Slovakia to make space for the production of electric vehicles in Germany (VW, 2021); Stellantis is increasing the production capacity of its engine factory by 50 percent in Szentgotthárd, Hungary to start the production of new 1.6-liter petrol engines in the first half of 2023 (Hungarian Insider, 2021); and Ford is transferring the production of 1.0-liter internal combustion engines from Cologne, Germany to its Craiova engine plant in Romania (Hampel, 2022a).

The production of internal combustion engine cars will continue longer in Eastern Europe than in Western Europe for at least five reasons. First, there are newer, more modern assembly factories than in Western Europe. Second, older technologies continue longer in peripheral locations than in core locations of spatial systems according to the product life cycle model (Vernon, 1966). Third, Eastern Europe has the advantage of lower production costs than in Western Europe (Table 7.1). Fourth, Eastern Europe will continue to produce internal combustion engine vehicles for non-European Union markets, such as Škoda Auto, which will produce internal combustion engine cars for the markets in less developed regions, such as India, Southeast Asia, South America and Africa (Škoda Auto, 2021b). Fifth, the transition to the production of electric vehicles in Eastern Europe will mainly be driven by foreign demand. More than

90 percent of cars produced in Eastern Europe are exported and the demand for electric vehicles has been low in Eastern Europe compared to Western Europe because of higher prices of electric vehicles compared to cars with internal combustion engines and limited subsidies for the purchase of electric vehicles (ACEA, 2021c; 2022b). It will make sense for the automakers to continue to make internal combustion engine cars close to the market in Eastern Europe where they also will be sold.

For all these reasons, we may assume that the Eastern European integrated periphery will be the last region in the European Union to completely shut down the production of internal combustion engine vehicles. The production of internal combustion engine cars will continue for at least an additional twenty years unless there will be a political decision by the European Commission banning the production and sale of internal combustion engine cars sooner. However, relying on the continuing production of internal combustion engine cars is a risky strategy for the Eastern European automotive industry, because the delay in the introduction of the large volume production of electric vehicles might undermine its long-term competitiveness. The continuing specialization in the internal combustion engine technology, which will rapidly become obsolete, instead of the cutting-edge battery electric vehicle technology, might result in a long-term disadvantage in the Eastern European automotive industry compared to countries and regions that undergo a rapid transition to the production of electric vehicles.

7.4.4   The Dependence of the Eastern European Automotive Industry's Future on Foreign TNCs

Fourth, the high degree of foreign control over the Eastern European automotive industry (Table 7.2) means that the future of the Eastern European automotive industry, including the course of the transition to the production of electric vehicles, will be decided abroad by large foreign-owned assembly firms and component suppliers through their corporate decisions about the allocation of production and investment. Flagship foreign investors have achieved the "corporate capture" of national and local institutions and resources in Eastern Europe, which primarily serve the needs of foreign TNCs, often at the expense of domestic firms and other local needs (Phelps, 2000; 2008; Drahokoupil, 2008; 2009; Pavlínek, 2016).

The role of Eastern European governments will be mostly limited to the efforts to influence these corporate decisions via the provision of various investment incentives to attract automotive FDI, especially flagship investors (Pavlínek, 2016), including FDI into battery manufacturing (e.g., €267 million in investment incentives to Volvo to build the assembly factory in Košice by Slovakia; €209 in million state aid to SK On for the construction of the battery plant in Iváncsa; €108 million awarded to Samsung SDI for the expansion of its battery cell plant in Göd by Hungary; €95 million in aid given to LG Energy

Solution to expand the battery plant in Wrocław by Poland; and large investment incentives promised by Czechia for the construction of a battery gigafactory) (Tables 7.5 and 7.6).

While Eastern European countries are willing to offer large investment incentives to flagship investors, especially assembly firms, large suppliers and battery manufacturers, they have otherwise followed a mostly wait-and-see strategy. Consequently, the support of the state for the transition to the production of electric vehicles beyond investment incentives has been limited so far. There has been uneven but mostly weak state support for the building of infrastructure (charging stations) (Transport & Environment, 2020; ACEA, 2021b; Grzegorczyk, 2021; Darteyre and Guga, 2022) and uneven state support for the purchase of electric vehicles. For example, as of 2023, Hungary, Romania and Croatia offer generous purchase incentives. Smaller incentives are provided in Estonia, Lithuania, Poland and Slovenia, and no incentives for individuals are in place in Bulgaria, Czechia, Latvia and Slovakia (ACEA, 2023b).

Poland represents an interesting exception. Its government has actively attempted to break out of FDI dependency in the transition to electric vehicles by launching the project of the national battery electric vehicle, the Izera, in 2020. The Izera will be produced by the state-owned company ElectroMobility Poland, although it will strongly depend on foreign technologies and know-how. Three Izera models (an SUV, a hatchback and a station wagon) will be designed by the Italian design company Pininfarina and built on Geely's SEA platform. However, the components are planned to be supplied mostly by Polish suppliers. The assembly was supposed to be launched in 2024 but was postponed until the end of 2025 (Đorđević, 2021; Hampel, 2022b; Randall, 2023a; 2023b).

In some cases, Eastern European governments have been hostile to European Commission regulations and the transition to electric vehicles. In Czechia, for example, Prime Minister Andrej Babiš argued in 2021, "We have repeatedly said that the [European Union's climate] goals must be set in a way not to harm our industry ... It must be done reasonably, not based on ideology" (Prague Morning, 2021). Following the 2021 elections, the new prime minister of Czechia Petr Fiala declared on December 19, 2021: "the proposal of the European Commission to ban the production and sales of [new] internal combustion engine cars after 2035 is unacceptable for the government of Czechia" (Aktuálně.cz, 2021). The new minister of industry and trade of Czechia added: "I think it's nonsense to ban the sale of internal combustion engines" (Prokeš, 2021). The weak role of the state in the transition to the production of electric vehicles as a mere facilitator (Horner, 2017) in Eastern Europe reinforces the assumption that the future of the Eastern European automotive industry will mainly depend on the corporate strategies of foreign TNCs.

TABLE 7.5 *Battery gigafactories in Eastern Europe, including announced projects*

Company and home country	2021 capacity (GWh)	Start date	Location	Notes
LG Energy Solution, South Korea	70.0	2018	Wrocław, Biskupice Podgórne, Poland	The expansion to 70 GWh in 2022, 115 GWh in 2025. Total investment: €1.5 billion; 6,000 full-time workers. Investment incentives: €95 million to expand the plant.
SK On (SK Innovation), South Korea	7.5	2020	Komárom Plant 1, Hungary	The expansion to 23.5 GWh by 2023, 1,300 workers. Investment: €688 million.
SK On, South Korea		2022	Komárom Plant 2, Hungary	9.8 GWh, option up to 16 GWh. Investment: €753 million.
Samsung SDI, South Korea	2.5	2017	Göd Plant 1, Hungary	2.5 GWh in 2020, expansion to 12 GWh by 2023 and 20 GWh by 2028.
Samsung SDI, South Korea	7.5	2021	Göd Plant 2, Hungary	Investment: €740 million. Investment incentives: €108 million. In partnership with Mercedes-Benz.
Sunwoda Electronics, China		2025	Nyíregyháza, Hungary	Investment: €1.5 billion.
Eve Energy, China		2026	Debrecen, Hungary	Planned capacity: 28 GWh. Investment: €1 billion; 1,000 jobs. Investment incentives: €38 million. Supply of the BMW Debrecen factory.
SK On, South Korea		2028	Iváncska Plant 3, Hungary	9.8 GWh, rising to 30 GWh in 2028; 2,500 jobs. Total investment by SK innovation in Hungary: €1.6 billion. Investment incentives: €209 million.
CATL, China		2028	Debrecen, Hungary	Planned capacity: 100 GWh. Investment: €7.34 billion; 9,000 jobs.
EIT InnoEnergy, Netherlands		2025	Subotica, Serbia	The first LFP lithium-ion battery gigafactory in Europe. 500 MWh planned in 2024, 8 GWh by the end of 2025, expansion to 16 GWh planned later. Based on the LFP technology developed by the Serbian company ElevenEs in Subotica.

(continued)

Company	Year	Location	Details
Avesta Battery and Energy Engineering, Belgium	2026	Galaţi, Romania	Planned capacity: 22 GWh. Investment: €1.4 billion; 8,000 jobs.
InoBat and Gotion High-Tech, Slovakia/China	2026	Šurany, Slovakia	A letter of intent to build a 20-GWh gigafactory was signed with the Slovak government in November 2023. Planned capacity to potentially increase to 40 GWh in the second stage.
InoBat, Slovakia	2025	Ćuprija, Serbia	A memorandum of understanding with Serbia's Ministry of Finance and the Municipality of Ćuprija signed in September 2023. Initial capacity: 4 GWh, which could grow up to 32 GWh. Investment incentives: €419 million.

Source: based on AMS (2021b), Harrison (2021), various news reports and company press releases.

TABLE 7.6 *Selected FDI into the battery industry in Eastern Europe, including the announced future investments*

Company, home country	Start year	Location	Notes
SK IE Technology (SK Innovation), South Korea	Plant 1: 2021, Plant 2: 2023, Plant 3: 2024, Plant 4: 2024	Dąbrowa Górnicza, Poland	Plants for separators used in electric car batteries; 1,000 new jobs. Total investment: €1.5 billion.
EcoPro BM, South Korea	2024–2025	Debrecen, Hungary	Cathode material factory for electric car batteries. Investment: €715 million.
Enchem, South Korea	N.A. (announced in 2021)	Komárom, Hungary	Lithium salt production facility for lithium-ion batteries with annual capacity of 20,000 tons.
Anodox Energy, Sweden	2022	Riga, Latvia	The assembly of battery packs for electric vehicles should start in December 2022. A second factory should follow. Investment: €50 million; 300 jobs. Status was unclear as of 2023.
Enchem, South Korea	2020	Biskupice Podgórne, Poland	Lithium salt production facility for lithium-ion batteries with annual capacity of 20,000 tons. The construction of the second factory in Kobierzyce announced in 2022.
Capchem, China	2022	Śrem, Poland	A €50-million electrolyte production factory for 40,000 tons of electrolyte per year; sixty jobs.
Daimler, Germany	2022	Jawor, Poland	Battery assembly facility, 100,000 batteries for BEVs and PHEVs per year.
Northvolt, Sweden	2022	Gdańsk, Poland	Production of battery modules. An initial capacity of 5 GWh in 2022 and potential for 12 GWh.
Umicore, Belgium	2022	Nysa, Poland	Cathode material factory; 400 jobs. Production capacity will grow to over 200 GWh/year to produce battery cells for 3 million electric vehicles after 2025.
Ionway (a JV between Volkswagen and Umicore) Belgium/Germany	N.A. (announced in 2023)	Nysa, Poland	The second cathode material factory at the same location announced in 2023. Investment: €1.7 billion; 900 jobs by 2030. Investment incentives: €350 million.

(*continued*)

Company, country	Location	Year	Details
SKC (SK Group), South Korea	Stalowa Wola, Poland	2024	Copper foils factory for use in electric vehicle batteries. Investment: €693 million, initial capacity of 50,000 tons per year.
Volkswagen (Škoda Auto), Germany	Mladá Boleslav, Czechia	2019	€130-million car battery assembly line for the Volkswagen Group's MQB platform. 205,784 batteries assembled in 2022. The annual capacity of 380,000 MEB battery systems achieved at the end of 2023; 250 jobs. Expansion to 1,500 batteries per day announced in 2023.
Stellantis, France	Trnava, Slovakia	2019	The assembly of car batteries (35,922 assembled in 2020).
Porsche, Germany	Horná Streda, Slovakia	2024	€195-million car battery modules assembly factory; sixty jobs. Investment incentives: €4.2 million.
Dräxlmaier, Germany	Timișoara, Romania	2022	Battery systems for hybrid cars. Investment: €200 million; more than 1,000 jobs.
BYD, China	Fót, Hungary	N.A. (announced in 2023)	Battery assembly plant. Investment: €27 million; 100 jobs. Investment incentives: €3.8 million.
Huayou Cobalt, China	Ács, Hungary	N.A. (announced in 2023)	Nickel-rich ternary lithium battery cathode material plant. Investment: €1.4 billion (€250 million in the first phase). Annual capacity of 100,000 metric tons (initial capacity of 25,000 metric tons).
Andrada, Slovenia	Alsózsolca, Hungary	N.A. (announced in 2023)	Recycling factory for electric car batteries. Investment: €26 million. Annual capacity 10,000 tons of recycled batteries per year. Investment incentives: €12 million; 200 jobs.
BMZ Group, Germany	Skopje, North Macedonia	N.A. (announced in 2023)	More than sixty production lines planned by 2028. Production will be relocated from Germany and Poland; up to 600 jobs.
Rock Tech Lithium, Germany/Canada	Romania	2029	A production plant for battery-grade lithium hydroxide. Investment: €715 million. A memorandum of understanding signed in March 2022. Location unknown.

Note: BEVs = battery electric vehicles, PHEVs = plug-in hybrid electric vehicles.
Source: based on various news reports and company press releases.

7.4.5   The Continuing Strong Location Advantages for the Automotive Industry in Eastern Europe

Fifth, Eastern Europe will continue to have strong location advantages for the automotive industry in the context of the European Union. These include low wages compared to Western Europe, the geographic location close to the large and affluent Western European markets and European Union membership. Eastern Europe will continue to be an attractive location for potential new electric vehicle assembly plants and the production of battery cells and components. In the long run, the drive for profit of automotive companies will prevail. As long as the wages in Eastern Europe continue to be significantly lower than in Western Europe, especially in Germany, Eastern Europe will be attractive for the continuing production and additional investment, including the investment in the battery industry and production of electric vehicles (Tables 7.5–7.7) (Pavlínek, 2020). However, as already discussed, this potential can be undermined by insufficient or exhausted labor surplus despite low labor costs, as has recently been the case in Central Europe and Romania (Pavlínek, 2015a; Guga, 2019; PwC, 2019; Adăscăliței and Guga, 2020; HIPA, 2020). The recent location decision of Japan's Nidec corporation illustrates this point. In December 2021, Nidec started the construction of a factory to produce electric engines in Novi Sad, Serbia, which will employ 1,000 workers. Nidec will also build a smaller factory for automotive inverters and engine control units that will create 200 jobs. Serbia has been selected for the location of these factories because of its low wages (Table 7.1), labor surplus (the total unemployment rate of 9.1 percent in 2020, down from 19.4 percent in 2014) and future European Union membership (Eurostat, 2021; Manthey, 2021b; Nidec, 2021). These factories will not be built in Poland or Hungary despite their greater recent experience in engine manufacturing (Table 7.8) and proximity to the market because of their higher wages (Table 7.1) and labor shortages that were considered more important for the location decision by Nidec. Ultimately, when the basic preconditions for automotive FDI are present, such as political stability, the absence of trade barriers with the European Union and the transportation access to the market, it is the combination of labor costs and labor availability that drives concrete location decisions in the Eastern European automotive industry (Pavlínek, 2020; HIPA, 2020; Nidec, 2021; Vesić and Vukša, 2021).

The most important limitations of these five general observations about the transition to the production of electric vehicles are related to the highly increased geopolitical risks and volatility caused by the 2022 war in Ukraine and by the unfolding energy crisis in Europe. Energy costs multiplied in Eastern Europe in 2022 compared to 2021. Combined with one of the highest dependencies of large Eastern European vehicle producers, such as Czechia, Slovakia and Hungary, on Russian natural gas, it may undermine one of Eastern Europe's competitive advantages in the automotive industry. For example, in

TABLE 7.7 *Production of electric vehicles in Eastern Europe in 2022, including the announced future production and investments as of 2023*

Lead firm	Brands	Models	Location	Notes
Next.e.GO Mobile	e.Go	Next generation e.Go Life	Lovech, Bulgaria	A German micro-factory for up to 30,000 electric vehicles per year should open at the beginning of 2024.
Rimac	Rimac	Electric supercars	Zagreb, Croatia	The majority owner (55 percent) of Bugatti since 2021 in the Bugatti-Rimac joint venture, in which Porsche holds 45 percent. Low-volume production.
Hyundai	Hyundai	Kona EV	Nošovice, Czechia	2022 output: 29,873 BEVs (9.3 percent of the total vehicle output), 33,177 PHEVs (10.3 percent of the total vehicle output); 50,000 BEVs planned for 2024.
Volkswagen Group	Škoda	Superb iV PHEV	Kvasiny, Czechia	2022 output: 14,681 PHEVs, including Octavia iV PHEV made in Mladá Boleslav (21 percent of the total Škoda vehicle output in Czechia).
Volkswagen Group	Škoda	Enyaq iV EV, Octavia iV PHEV	Mladá Boleslav, Czechia	2022 output: 57,213 BEVs (8.3 percent of the total Škoda vehicle output in Czechia). The series production of the Enyaq Coupé iV launched in February 2022. Six BEVs planned by 2026.
SOR	SOR	Electric buses	Libchavy, Czechia	2022 output: 42 BEVs (8.1 percent of the total vehicle output).
BMW	BMW	Third generation electric cars, the Neue Klasse	Debrecen, Hungary	Factory opening in 2025 to produce 150,000 electric vehicles per year.

(*continued*)

TABLE 7.7 (continued)

Lead firm	Brands	Models	Location	Notes
BYD	BYD	Buses	Komárom, Hungary	The production of 200 e-buses per year since April 2017. The expansion to 1,000 e-buses per year is expected to be completed in 2022.
BYD	BYD	N.A.	Szeged, Hungary	Electric car factory for the production of BYD electric cars for the European market will be built between 2024 and 2026.
Daimler	Mercedes-Benz	EQB	Kecskemét, Hungary	Series production of the all-electric Mercedes EQB since October 2021.
Suzuki	Suzuki	Vitara hybrid	Esztergom, Hungary	Suzuki plans to offer a BEV by 2025 but it is unclear whether it will be made in Hungary.
Volkswagen Group	Audi	Q3 PHEV	Győr, Hungary	The production started in December 2020 and is integrated into the existing production process of internal combustion engine cars.
Next.e.GO Mobile	e.Go	e.wave X	Tetovo, North Macedonia	A German micro-factory for up to 30,000 electric vehicles per year should open at the end of 2024.
Solaris	Solaris	e-bus	Owińska, Poland	The Polish brand owned by the Spanish CAF; 390 e-buses sold in 2021, 11.9-percent market share in Europe. Between 2012 and 2021, Solaris sold 1,132 electric buses or 13.3 percent of Europe's total. In 2020, 1,560 buses were produced, of which 44 percent were fully electric and one third were hybrids.
Volkswagen Group	MAN	Lion's City E bus, hybrid bus	Starachowice, Poland	Series production of the all-electric Lion's City e-bus started in October 2020.

(continued)

EMP Poland	Izera	SUV and hatchback BEVs	Jaworzno, Poland	The national BEV project, majority state-owned. Assembly launch pushed from 2023 to late 2025; 15,000 jobs, 3,000 in assembly, 12,000 among suppliers. Annual capacity: 150,000 BEVs.
Stellantis	Fiat	Jeep Avenger SUV, Fiat 600e	Tychy, Poland	Series production of all-electric Jeep Avenger SUV in February 2023 and of Fiat 600e in September 2023.
Ford	Ford	Puma mild hybrid	Craiova, Romania	The Puma mild hybrid produced since 2019. Production of an all-electric Ford E-Transit Courier panel van and the E-Tourneo Courier passenger car version will start in 2024. Production of an all-electric Puma will start in 2025.
Stellantis	Fiat	Compact EV	Kragujevac, Serbia	The start of production of small electric vehicles planned for 2024.
Kia	Kia	Ceed, XCeed, Sportage PHEV	Žilina, Slovakia	In 2020, 21,000 PHEVs (8 percent of the total output) and 31,916 units of mild hybrid versions of the Kia Sportage and Kia Ceed (12 percent of total output). A BEV model planned in 2025.
JLR	Land Rover	Defender, Discovery PHEVs	Nitra, Slovakia	The PHEV Defender since September 2021. The Defender and Discovery BEVs planned by 2030.
Stellantis	PSA	Peugeot e-208, batteries for all brands	Trnava, Slovakia	Peugeot e-208 BEV since 2019; 7,263 BEVs in 2019 (2 percent of the factory output), 33,334 in 2020 (10 percent); 35,922 batteries assembled in 2020. The assembly of Peugeot e-208 BEV transferred to Zaragoza, Spain in 2023.
Volkswagen Group	Audi, Seat, Škoda, Volkswagen, Porsche	Five SUV PHEVs (the Volkswagen Touareg, Porsche Cayenne, Porsche Cayenne Coupé, Audi Q7, Audi Q8).	Bratislava, Slovakia	In 2020, 42,275 BEVs and 28,875 PHEVs were assembled. BEVs accounted for 13.7 percent and PHEVs for 9.3 percent of the total vehicle production. Electrified vehicles accounted for 23 percent of the total vehicle output. Volkswagen e-up! BEV discontinued in 2023.

(continued)

TABLE 7.7 (*continued*)

Lead firm	Brands	Models	Location	Notes
Geely Volvo Cars	Volvo	Volvo EXC90, Polestar 3	Košice, Slovakia	Factory construction is planned to start in 2023 and series production in 2026. Annual capacity up to 250,000 BEVs; 3,300 jobs (5,000 jobs after the introduction of the second shift). Investment: €1.2 billion. Investment incentives: €400 million.
Renault-Nissan-Mitsubishi	Renault, Smart	Twingo Electric, Clio PHEV	Novo Mesto, Slovenia	The Renault Twingo Electric is being manufactured exclusively by Revoz and accounted for one third of its total output in 2021. The production of the Smart Forfour EQ electric vehicle ended in December 2021.

Note: BEVs = battery electric vehicles, PHEVs = plug-in hybrid electric vehicles.
Source: AMS (2021a), AIA (2022), various news reports and company press releases.

September 2022, Volkswagen warned that it might relocate production away from Germany and Eastern Europe to its factories in Southwestern Europe or coastal areas of Northern Europe because of their proximity to seaborne liquefied natural gas terminals (ANE, 2022d). Eastern Europe may also be impacted by the increased perceived investment risk due to its geographic proximity to Ukraine, which might negatively affect future investment decisions by TNCs in the Eastern European automotive industry.

7.5   UNEVEN EFFECTS OF THE TRANSITION TO THE PRODUCTION
      OF ELECTRIC VEHICLES IN THE AUTOMOTIVE INDUSTRY

The overall trend away from the production of internal combustion engine vehicles and toward electric vehicles will lead to the restructuring of the automotive industry in Europe (McKinsey&Company, 2021; Sigal, 2021). The main questions about the transition to the production of electric vehicles in Eastern Europe are about its speed and its effects, that is, how long it will take and how it will ultimately affect the automotive industry. However, in thinking about these effects, we need to keep in mind that the trend toward the production of electric vehicles is only one of several important megatrends that will affect the automotive industry in Eastern Europe. Other trends, such as those associated with the digitalization, robotization and automation of production (Industry 4.0), continuing investment, reinvestment and the relocation of production, will also impact the automotive industry in Eastern Europe and will likely have more important employment effects than the transition to the production of electric vehicles (e.g., Bauer et al., 2020; Drahokoupil, 2020; Szabo, 2020).

The shift to the production of electric vehicles will likely disrupt employment patterns but it will disrupt them unevenly in different sectors of the Eastern European automotive industry. The two most important sectors of the narrowly defined automotive industry employing the most workers are the production of parts and components (NACE 29.3) and the manufacture of vehicles and engines (NACE 29.1). NACE 29.3, which employed 671,590 persons in Eastern Europe in 2020 (Eurostat, 2023c), accounting for 78 percent of all automotive industry jobs, is likely to be most affected.[4] Within NACE 29.3, suppliers of components and parts for the internal combustion engine powertrain (e.g., components and parts for engines, gear boxes, fuel and exhaust systems) will be most affected as their products will become redundant in battery electric vehicles. For example, a combustion engine has 1,018 forged components, while a comparable fully electric engine has only 143

---

[4] The actual direct employment in the automotive industry is larger as the broadly defined automotive industry also includes firms from other industrial sectors that are involved in the automotive value chain but are not included in NACE 29, such as suppliers from the plastic industry, rubber industry, electrical equipment industry and iron and steel industry.

(Schwabe, 2020b). The drivetrain of a battery electric vehicle is less complex than in conventional vehicles and requires, for example, only half of its bearings (Davies et al., 2015). Therefore, even if the production of internal combustion engines is replaced with the production of electric engines, it might result in significant job loss, because the production of electric engines is less labor-intensive than the manufacture of internal combustion engines (Bauer et al., 2020; CLEPA, 2021). On the other hand, large segments of the supplier industry that are unrelated to internal combustion engines will experience no or small effects (e.g., seats, wheels, structure parts, air conditioning systems), and the new segments of the automotive industry related to the battery system will create new jobs (e.g., batteries, battery management systems, sensors). The entire battery industry, including the extraction of raw materials, manufacturing of battery cells, battery assembly and recycling, could create up to 4 million jobs in the European Union (Harrison, 2021).

The shift to electric vehicles might also disrupt employment patterns in NACE 29.1, which employed 160,000 people in Eastern Europe in 2020 (Eurostat, 2023c), because the assembly of battery electric vehicles is less labor-intensive than the manufacturing of traditional cars. There are fewer mechanical parts and, despite many new electric and electronic components and the battery, fewer workers will be needed in the final assembly. For example, to maintain the employment levels from before the transition to electric vehicles, Volkswagen's Zwickau BEVs factory integrated some processes that used to be outsourced to external suppliers, such as stamping work for the hood, fenders and doors. This ultimately translates into fewer jobs in the supplier sector (Gibbs, 2019a). NACE 29.1 will also be affected due to the fact that the production of electric engines is less labor-intensive than the manufacture of internal combustion engines (Bauer et al., 2020; CLEPA, 2021).

These effects will be geographically uneven across Eastern Europe since different Eastern European countries are specialized to a different degree in the production of distinct automotive products and components. For example, Poland and Hungary are more dependent on exports of internal combustion engines, engine parts and transmissions than other Eastern European countries (Figure 7.4a). The production of engines and gearboxes in Czechia and Slovakia is mainly for the large local assembly of cars and not for exports. Poland, the largest producer of engines, has six engine factories (Table 7.8) and exported engines worth €1.9 billion in 2021 (OEC, 2023). Poland, Hungary and Czechia are also the largest exporters of engine parts from Eastern Europe (Figure 7.4a), making them potentially vulnerable to the decrease in the production of internal combustion engines.

But even in the cases of internal combustion engines, the production will not necessarily end in 2035, because some Eastern European factories, such as Škoda Auto in Czechia and its suppliers, plan to continue to produce internal combustion engines for foreign markets that will undergo much slower transition to electromobility, such as India, Russia, South America and North Africa. The speed of the transformation will also differ for different segments of

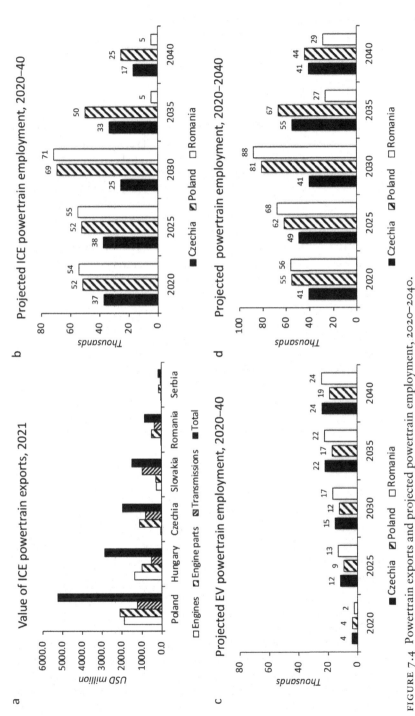

FIGURE 7.4 Powertrain exports and projected powertrain employment, 2020–2040.

Note: Engines refer to internal combustion engines, transmissions refer to transmissions for motor vehicles.

Source: author, based on data in CLEPA (2021), OEC (2023).

TABLE 7.8 *Engine and transmissions plants in Eastern Europe*

Country	Product	Parent company	Location
Poland	Engines	Volkswagen AG	Polkowice, Poland
	Engines	Daimler Group	Jawor, Poland
	Engines	Toyota Motor Europe	Wałbrzych, Poland
	Engines	Toyota Motor Europe	Jelcz-Laskowice, Poland
	Engines	Stellantis	Tychy, Poland
	Engines	Stellantis	Bielsko-Biała, Poland
	Transmissions	Toyota Motor Europe	Wałbrzych, Poland
Czechia	Engines	Volkswagen AG (Škoda)	Mladá Boleslav, Czechia
	Transmissions	Hyundai	Nošovice, Czechia
	Transmissions	Volkswagen AG (Škoda)	Mladá Boleslav, Czechia
	Transmissions	Volkswagen AG (Škoda)	Vrchlabí, Czechia
Romania	Engines	Renault SA	Mioveni (Pitești), Romania
	Engines	Ford Europe	Craiova, Romania
	Transmissions	Daimler	Sebeș, Romania
	Transmissions	Renault SA	Mioveni (Pitești), Romania
Hungary	Engines	Volkswagen AG	Györ, Hungary
	Engines	Stellantis	Szentgotthárd, Hungary
	Transmissions	ZF Friedrichshafen	Eger, Hungary
Slovakia	Engines	Kia (Hyundai Motor Group)	Žilina, Slovakia
	Transmissions	Getrag Ford	Kechnec, Slovakia
	Transmissions	Volkswagen AG	Bratislava, Slovakia

Source: based on ANE (2017), ACEA (2021a).

the supplier industry. In most cases, the change will not be abrupt, but it will be gradual and the existing engine factories might gradually transition to the production of electric engines. For example, Audi Hungária at Györ, Hungary, the largest engine factory in Eastern Europe and in the world, started to produce electric engines in 2018. Out of the total number of 1,677,545 engines produced in 2022, 108,097 (6.4 percent) were electric powertrains and their share will continue to increase in the future (Audi Hungaria, 2023) so that the factory may assemble only 271,000 internal combustion engines in 2029 (Sigal, 2022a).

Projections of changes in powertrain employment under the most likely scenario of the transition to electric vehicles prepared for selected European countries for the 2020–2040 period by CLEPA (2021) suggest for Eastern European countries the maximum employment in internal combustion engine powertrain technologies around 2030, followed by a steady decline to 2040 (Figure 7.4b), and a steady increase in the employment in electric vehicle powertrain technologies (Figure 7.4c), which, however, will not compensate for job losses in the internal combustion engine powertrain technologies. Overall, almost 50 percent of powertrain jobs are projected to be lost in Czechia, Poland and Romania between 2030 and 2040. Compared to 2020, the number of powertrain jobs is projected to be lower by one fourth in these three countries in 2040 (Figure 7.4d) (CLEPA, 2021).

Local automotive suppliers are mostly captive tier-three suppliers or niche suppliers in automotive GVCs/GPNs (Pavlínek and Žížalová, 2016; Pavlínek, 2018). As such, domestic firms will be in a weak position to effect any changes related to the transition to electric vehicles in Eastern Europe. Empirical research has suggested the weakening position of domestic firms in the Eastern European automotive industry because of their inability to benefit from and keep up with its rapid FDI-driven growth in the 2000s and 2010s (Pavlínek, 2020).

7.6 THE BATTERY INDUSTRY IN EASTERN EUROPE

Attracting FDI to battery and cell manufacturing is a feasible strategy to attract the assembly of electric vehicles, thus ensuring the future of the automotive industry in Eastern Europe and offsetting job losses caused by the decreases in the production of internal combustion engines, even though jobs in the electric vehicle battery assembly are not high-value-added jobs (Szalavetz, 2022) and the production of battery cells is highly automated (Schade et al., 2022). Since batteries are heavy and can account for up to one third of the total electric vehicle weight (Delanote et al., 2022), the geographic proximity of the battery assembly operations lowers transportation costs involved in transporting finished batteries to a vehicle assembly factory. There are also strong strategic reasons behind the development of the battery industry in Europe because batteries account for 30–50 percent of the value of battery electric vehicles (CLEPA, 2022). It has been estimated that twenty-four new battery gigafactories with annual capacity of 25 GWh will have to be built in Europe by 2030 to meet the European battery demand (McKinsey&Company, 2021). In December 2020, the European Union specified its local content requirements for the European lithium battery production, which include the location of key parts of its value chain in Europe between 2024 and 2027 (e.g., cathodes, anodes and chemicals), with the goal of achieving 100 percent European sourcing by 2027. The European Commission approved large subsidies for the development of the European battery industry (€3.2 billion in 2019 and €2.9 billion in 2020) (Harrison, 2021). These developments will support the growth of the battery industry in Eastern Europe, including an increase in high-value-added jobs in battery design and testing that has already been documented in a few celebrated cases of local startups, such as InoBat in Slovakia and ElevenEs in Serbia, and also in some foreign subsidiaries (Szalavetz, 2022) (Table 7.6). However, because the production of battery cells is very energy intensive, the future growth of the battery industry in Eastern Europe is likely to be negatively affected by drastically increased energy prices and the high degree of dependence on Russian natural gas, unless alternative sources of cheap energy are found.

Deposits of lithium, a crucial raw material to produce car batteries, have potentially been one of the locational advantages of Eastern Europe for the development of the battery industry. Two large deposits have been discovered in Eastern Europe: one in western Czechia in the Ore Mountains close to the German border, which is the largest lithium deposit in Europe (up to 3 percent of global lithium deposits), the other one in the Loznica region of western Serbia along the Drina River close to the Bosnia and Herzegovina border. Foreign mining TNCs, such as Australian European Metals Holdings in the case of Czechia and British-Australian Rio Tinto, in the case of Serbia, were interested in mining the lithium deposits. In both cases, however, mining projects became highly politicized. In the case of Czechia, after the political outcry about foreign capital control of the lithium deposit, the government-linked energy company ČEZ purchased a majority stake in Geomet, European Metals Holdings' subsidiary, for €32 million because it held exploration licenses for lithium deposits (Deloitte, 2021). ČEZ and European Metals Holdings are considering mining lithium but no decision about the mining has been made as of 2023, which, according to the Czech government, might start in 2026 (HN, 2019; 2021; 2023). In the case of Serbia, the government stopped the USD2.4 billion mining project in January 2022 following the strong resistance of local communities and environmentalists (Randall, 2022b).

Compared to Western Europe, the development of the battery industry in Eastern Europe has so far been limited (AMS, 2021b; Williams, 2021; Dunn, 2022). As of August 2022, only 13.3 percent of completed or planned installed capacity of lithium battery gigafactory projects were in Eastern Europe (Heines, 2022). Within Eastern Europe, the growth has so far been restricted to Hungary (5.5 percent of the European total) and Poland (4.9 percent) as of 2022 (Table 7.5). The recently announced large investments by Chinese CATL, Sunwoda Electronics and Eve Energy in three additional gigafactories in Hungary will strongly increase its European share. By 2030, Hungary's annual battery output has been projected to reach 250GWh, followed by Poland (120 GWh), Serbia (48GWh), Czechia (25GWh), Romania (22GWh), and Slovakia (10GWh) (Rzentarzewska and Cery, 2023).

In coming years, we might also expect investments in the Eastern European battery industry from European companies, whose rapidly growing investments have so far been limited to Western Europe (Beutnagel and Verpraet, 2021; Heines, 2022). It is likely that in addition to Hungary and Poland other Eastern European countries will be targeted by FDI in the battery production. Hungary and Poland have been more aggressive than other Eastern European countries in attracting the battery industry (Tables 7.5 and 7.6) perhaps because of their greater dependence on the production of internal combustion engines

(Figure 7.4a) and, therefore, greater vulnerability to potential job losses related to the decrease in the production of internal combustion engines compared to the rest of Eastern Europe.

Czechia, which has the largest production of cars in Eastern Europe (Figure 7.2a), has so far failed to attract any battery gigafactories. The Czech government has been actively attracting one of six planned Volkswagen gigafactories, which is supported by Škoda Auto, by offering investment incentives, including tax breaks, building of transportation infrastructure and retraining the thousands of workers (Liebreich, 2021; Charvát, 2022). Czechia's Eastern European locational advantages, such as low labor costs, the largest European lithium deposits and the proximity of other Volkswagen factories, are being undermined by the limited state support for the transition to electromobility, the weak promotion of future technologies and the rapidly rising energy costs since 2022 (Hampel, 2021; Škoda Auto, 2021a). Volkswagen has therefore also considered Poland and Hungary for its Eastern European gigafactory, which might be a way to extract the biggest possible investment incentives from one of these three governments, a typical strategy in location decisions by automotive TNCs in the European integrated periphery (Pavlínek, 2016). In November 2023, Volkswagen announced the indefinite postponement of its planned Eastern European gigafactory due to a lower-than-expected demand for its electric vehicles in Europe (Hovet, 2023).

In Slovakia, InoBat Auto, the Slovak startup, which is partially owned by Chinese Gotion High Tech (25 percent), and the California-based Wildcat Discovery Technologies, the owner of patented technology for car batteries, are building a €100 million 45-MWh pilot battery line close to the town of Trnava. Along with an R&D center for 150 R&D workers, it should be completed in 2024 and produce up to 50,000 high-performance battery cells for aircraft and racing cars (Manthey, 2019; Bolduc, 2021; Ehl, 2023). A separate JV of InoBat and Gotion plans to build a 20-GWh gigafactory to produce up to 150,000 smart batteries per year in the town of Šurany (Randall, 2022a; Ehl, 2023) (Table 7.5). Eastern Europe has also attracted a growing FDI into module and pack battery manufacturing, which bundles individual battery cells into modules and packs, as well as into material suppliers for battery production and battery recycling. A high share of these investments went to Poland (Table 7.7), whose government allocated €3.1 billion for investment incentives to the battery industry in 2019 (Strzałkowski, 2021).

7.7 CONCLUSION

This chapter considers the implications of the integrated periphery position of the Eastern European automotive industry in the European GVCs/GPNs and international division of labor for the course of the transition to the production of electric vehicles. It argues that the dependent position of Eastern Europe will strongly influence the course of this transition. Although there are many questions and uncertainties about this transition that have been greatly enhanced by the geopolitical and economic instability due to the war in Ukraine since 2022, several general conclusions about its nature in Eastern Europe can be made. First, the extremely high dependence of the East European automotive industry on foreign ownership and control means that the course of the transition will be driven by the corporate decisions of foreign automotive TNCs. Local firms will be unable to influence the course of the transition and play a significant role. Second, while the role of the CO_2 regulation imposed on the automotive industry at the European Union level has been instrumental in triggering the transition to the production of electric vehicles, the role of states and their policies in Eastern Europe will be severely limited. It will mainly focus on attracting additional FDI from flagship foreign investors through offering various investment incentives, engaging in the "race to the bottom" by competing with other states in the integrated periphery for these investments, and pursuing additional policies designed to meet the needs of flagship investors in the production of electric vehicles. Third, the transition to the production of electric vehicles will be slower in Eastern Europe than in Western Europe because of the continuing production of internal combustion engine vehicles, the slower introduction of fully dedicated electric vehicle factories and the greater reliance on the mixed production of electric vehicles and internal combustion engine vehicles than in Western Europe. While this slower transition will likely increase the employment in the Eastern European automotive industry in the short and medium run in the 2020s, it might weaken the position of Eastern Europe in the international division of labor of the European automotive industry in the long run by relying on the increasingly obsolete and less profitable internal combustion engine technologies and falling behind Western Europe, and because Western Europe will move to the full-scale production of electric vehicles in electric vehicle dedicated factories faster. Fourth, the impact of the transition to electric vehicles will be uneven within the automotive industry. In terms of jobs, there will be a greater potential for job losses in the production of parts and components than in the vehicle assembly. The creation of new jobs in the battery industry will depend on the abilities of Eastern European governments to attract foreign battery manufacturers. So far, however, the majority of battery gigafactories are built or planned to be built in Western Europe, not in Eastern Europe. Only Hungary and to a lesser extent Poland have so far attracted any significant investment in the battery industry. Fifth, the transition will be geographically uneven in Eastern Europe. The course of the transition and its outcome in individual Eastern European countries will depend on their ability to attract FDI in the production electric vehicles, the battery industry and battery components production, which will help offset potential losses related to phasing out the production of components for internal combustion engines.

The chapter has identified several risks for the future competitiveness of the automotive industry in the Eastern European integrated periphery based on the currently pursued strategies of the transition to electric vehicles. Most importantly, the reliance on the mixed production of internal combustion engine vehicles with electric vehicles and on the production of internal combustion engine cars for a longer period than in Western Europe, and the potential failure of some Eastern European countries to attract the battery industry, especially battery gigafactories, might undermine their long-term competitive position in the European automotive industry. To counteract these risks, the integrated periphery will continue to rely on its enduring competitive advantage of low production costs, especially low labor costs, to continue to attract FDI in the automotive industry, which is risky because of the exhausted labor surplus in many countries. Since the transition to the production of electric vehicles will mostly depend on foreign capital, it will continue to be dependent growth (Pavlínek, 2017a), which is unlikely to improve the highly dependent position of Eastern European countries in automotive GVCs/GPNs and the international division of labor in the European automotive industry.

The validity of these conclusions is generally supported by recent research (e.g., CLEPA, 2021; Delanote et al., 2022; Slačík, 2022; Szalavetz, 2022). However, it can be strongly undermined by the effects of the increased geopolitical instability and energy crisis in Europe. Eastern Europe is more vulnerable than Western Europe due to its geographic location close to Ukraine and Russia, the high dependence on Russian energy resources and the landlocked location of many Eastern European countries, which makes access to alternative sources of oil and liquified gas more difficult and expensive. This might negatively affect the future investment decisions of foreign TNCs in the Eastern European automotive industry and has already been manifested by the indefinite postponement of the construction of Volkswagen's battery gigafactory in Eastern Europe. Therefore, given the analysis presented in this chapter and significant risks identified above, the best outcome of the transition to the production of electric vehicles the Eastern European automotive industry can hope for is to maintain its integrated peripheral position in the European automotive industry division of labor and GVCs/GPNs that has developed since the early 1990s.

8

Conclusion

In this book, I have analyzed the changes in the European automotive industry since the 1990s through the conceptual lenses of the GVC/GPN approach by focusing on the spatial strategies of automotive lead firms. I have examined the consequences of these changes for regional economic development and for the spatial division of labor in the European automotive industry. The goal of this final chapter is to summarize the findings and highlight the conceptual contribution of the book not only for the understanding of the changing European automotive industry, but also to evaluate its contribution to the GVC/GPN perspective.

8.1 FDI AND ECONOMIC DEVELOPMENT

Given the sharply increased importance of FDI in the world economy since the 1970s, I began this book with a critical review and explanation of the developmental effects of FDI in less developed countries and in peripheral regions of more developed countries because of its direct relationship to the recent growth of the automotive industry in the peripheral regions of Europe. The GVCs/GPNs approach considers the automotive industry to be a typical example of producer driven GVCs/GPNs and, more specifically, of captive value chains, in which large firms organize and coordinate, increasingly at the international scale, investment-based vertical production networks of component suppliers. Lead firms' internationalization strategies in the automotive industry have been based on FDI and the direct ownership of production facilities abroad. A basic explanation of long-term economic effects of automotive FDI in host countries and regions has therefore been an important starting point for the analysis of the European automotive industry.

I have suggested that the empirical data and analyses from existing literature on less developed countries point toward very uneven effects of FDI and the overall limited evidence of positive impacts of FDI on long-term economic development in less developed countries. The empirical evidence does not support the overly optimistic arguments about the long-term positive impacts of FDI in less developed countries maintained by the mainstream economic perspective on FDI. However, the empirical evidence neither fully supports the dependency and world-systems perspectives, which mostly emphasize the negative long-term developmental effects of FDI in less developed countries. I have explained the different conclusions of these two perspectives on FDI in less developed countries by their focus on different time periods. The mainstream perspective tends to focus on the immediate short-term effects of FDI in host economies, which are often positive. The dependency and world-systems perspectives tend to emphasize long-term effects of FDI and argue that negative effects tend to prevail in less developed countries in the long run. At the same time, both perspectives tend to ignore the spatial unevenness and variation of FDI impacts across less developed countries.

Overall, I have argued that the heterodox perspective, which is drawing on institutional and evolutionary economics, is more attuned to consider geographically varied and uneven experiences of less developed countries with FDI. Based on the experience of the most successful less developed countries, the heterodox perspective emphasizes the importance of strong state industrial policies and institutions supporting the development of domestic firms alongside the FDI-driven development. The variation in state capacity, industrial policies and policies toward foreign and domestic firms strongly affect the potential contribution of FDI to a successful economic development in less developed countries.

In Chapter 2, I have extended the review of FDI effects in less developed countries from Chapter 1 to FDI effects in peripheral regions of more developed countries by arguing that the economic development effects of FDI differ between core and peripheral regions. I have attributed these different regional development outcomes of FDI to different mechanisms of FDI in core and peripheral regions, which lead to a greater concentration of horizontal FDI in core regions and of vertical FDI in peripheral regions. I have argued that this difference between core and peripheral regions explains the greater development potential of FDI in core regions than in peripheral regions in the long run through the development of more and better-quality linkages between foreign and domestic firms. Since FDI spillovers from foreign to domestic firms occur through FDI linkages, enabling the diffusion of more advanced foreign technology in host economies, a greater quantity and better quality of linkages translate into greater diffusion and absorption of foreign technology in core regions than in peripheral regions. This explanation of FDI mechanism in core and peripheral regions is important for the understanding the regional development effects of automotive FDI in the European automotive industry, especially in its integrated peripheries.

Chapter 2 also critically reviewed conceptual approaches to FDI in peripheral regions of developed countries elaborated by economic geographers since the 1970s, namely the branch plant economy and truncation, new regionalism, new international division of labor and spatial divisions of labor, and the GPN perspective. Despite the changing nature of the capitalist economy since the 1970s and rapidly progressing economic globalization, all these conceptual approaches, including the critique of new regionalism, came to similar conclusions about the limited long-term development effects of FDI in peripheral regions of developed countries.

8.2 REGIONAL DEVELOPMENT EFFECTS OF AUTOMOTIVE FDI IN INTEGRATED PERIPHERIES

I have applied and further developed the conceptual insights from Chapters 1 and 2 by focusing on the European automotive industry in the rest of the book. In Chapter 3, I introduced the concept of integrated peripheries as peripheral spatial zones that have experienced rapid development of their automotive industry. By drawing on Harvey's theory of spatiotemporal fix and uneven development (Harvey, 1982; 2005b), and by combining it with the concept of strategic coupling from the GPN perspective, I have explained the profit-seeking spatial strategies of automotive lead firms and their large FDI in the development of the automotive industry in integrated peripheries. Integrated peripheries have been conceptualized as lower-cost production areas located in the proximity of core automotive industry regions and large lucrative markets, which have been integrated into the existing automotive GVCs/GPNs through FDI, trade and production linkages. This transnational integration has been made possible by the inclusion of new peripheries in trade blocs or free-trade arrangements allowing for tariff-free movement of raw materials, components and finished vehicles, and by technological changes that have lowered their transportation costs.

By drawing on the GPN approach, I have argued that integrated peripheries are articulated in GPNs via the assembly type of the structural mode of strategic coupling. The structural strategic coupling between TNCs and host country regions is typified by very uneven power distribution, in which power and control is concentrated in the hands of lead firms, while coupled regions are in a dependent and subordinate position. The uneven power distribution in structural couplings translates into greater economic benefits for TNCs than for coupled peripheral regions. As such, it is the least advantageous mode of strategic coupling from the position of coupled regions, which is typified by limited long-term positive economic effects in peripheral regions.

Empirically, I have examined automotive industry development in integrated peripheries in Eastern Europe by investigating FDI linkages in the Slovak automotive industry. The case study was based on firm-level data collected through the survey of 299 firms and face-to-face interviews with fifty firms. These data allowed me to evaluate both the quantity and quality of supplier linkages in the automotive industry of Slovakia.

The data revealed weak backward and forward supplier linkages between domestic firms and foreign subsidiaries. Foreign automotive firms operating in Slovakia are strongly integrated in transnational GVCs/GPNs, which are however mostly made of other foreign firms located abroad as Slovakia-based foreign subsidiaries heavily rely on imports of raw materials and components from abroad. Foreign component suppliers that invested in Slovakia to satisfy the follow sourcing requirements of assembly firms have strong forward linkages with assembly firms in Slovakia. However, they have weak backward linkages with other foreign subsidiaries in Slovakia and almost nonexistent backward linkages with domestic Slovak firms, which also applies to the remaining foreign subsidiaries in Slovakia. Weak linkages of foreign firms with domestic suppliers translate into weak spillovers from foreign to domestic firms in Slovakia, which strongly undermines any potential long-term benefits of automotive FDI in Slovakia.

The firm-level empirical data collected in Slovakia have also allowed for the evaluation of the quality of linkages in those rare cases when linkages between foreign subsidiaries and domestic firms exist. The analyses of these linkages have revealed that developmental linkages are absent, and that most linkages are either dependent or detrimental. This further underscores the very limited potential for automotive FDI to generate FDI spillovers in Slovakia and therefore strongly points to limited long-term positive regional development effects of automotive FDI. The findings from Slovakia thus underscore the nature and weak long-term development potential of the structural mode of strategic coupling of integrated peripheries into GPNs.

8.3 INTERNATIONALIZATION AND RESTRUCTURING OF THE EUROPEAN AUTOMOTIVE INDUSTRY

In Chapter 4, I have argued that from the mid-1960s, the European automotive industry was progressively internationalized through the investment strategies of automotive industry lead firms, which were eager to increase or maintain their rate of profit by developing production in peripheral locations that had a labor surplus and lower labor costs than in the established core regions of the automotive industry. Lead firms, which are large automotive industry TNCs mostly from the automotive industry core countries, could pursue these transnational investment strategies in Europe for two fundamental reasons. The first was an economic integration in the European Union allowing for the free movement of capital across the European Union, which is an example of what I have called an institutional fix. The second was a technological change allowing for the rapid and low-cost movement of raw materials, parts, components, preassembled modules, partially assembled vehicles and finished vehicles, which is an example of what I have called a technological fix.

Building on Chapter 3, Chapter 4 has conceptualized the uneven development of the European automotive industry through the formation of spatiotemporal fixes in peripheral lower-cost regions as automotive TNCs are eager to invest in these areas because of their potential for higher rates of profit than in existing locations. The formation of spatiotemporal fixes in peripheral regions is made possible by the development of technological, organizational and institutional fixes. These peripheral regions, which I have called integrated peripheries in Chapter 3, are then integrated through FDI, trade and production linkages in the transnational European automotive industry system and experience a rapid growth in output of vehicles and components. Eastern Europe represents the latest spatiotemporal fix that has been developed and exploited by lead firms in the European automotive industry.

However, as explained in Chapter 4, the growth of the automotive industry in integrated peripheries does not last because, over time, it exhausts the labor surplus, which pushes wages up and ultimately undermines the rate of profit. A decreasing rate of profit eventually forces lead firms to start looking for new areas with lower wages and surplus labor for new investments, resulting in the gradual territorial expansion of integrated peripheries over time and in the growth bouncing from region to region.

At the same time, I have explained how the growth of the automotive industry in integrated peripheries affects the existing production locations in core areas and in older integrated peripheries. Since the higher rate of profit achieved by investing in integrated peripheries contributes to the profitability of an entire automotive TNC, it supports the continuation of production in existing less-profitable high-wage core locations. Despite their higher costs and lower rates of profit, these core locations continue to hold strong advantages compared to integrated peripheries, such as their proximity to existing suppliers, large markets, skilled labor force and innovation capabilities. Additionally, large sunk costs in existing locations often make potential closures and relocations prohibitively expensive. Therefore, the restructuring of operations in existing locations is much more likely to lead to more labor-intensive and lower-value-added activities being relocated to integrated peripheries, while more skill-intensive and higher-value-added activities are being retained in core locations. The resulting more fine-grained division of labor and greater territorial specialization may contribute to the increased efficiency and profitability of an entire TNC and of the transnationally organized automotive industry as whole. Still, the existing locations might experience factory closures and job losses because some production might be relocated from core areas and older integrated peripheries to new integrated peripheries.

The empirical analysis of 2,124 restructuring events during the 2005–2016 period has supported this conceptual explanation of spatial change in the European automotive industry. It has revealed that the European automotive industry has been in a constant spatial flux and its spatial restructuring has been driven by the transnational investment and disinvestment strategies of automotive lead firms from automotive industry core countries. The increased role of foreign firms in creating and eliminating jobs and the decreased role of large domestic firms at the same time point to an increasing level of internationalization in the European automotive industry. The data have also revealed a marginal role played by domestic firms in the rapid growth of the automotive industry in the Eastern European integrated periphery. This growth has almost exclusively been driven by foreign firms. These findings support the conclusions about the limited long-term effects of FDI in less developed countries and peripheral regions, which were presented in Chapters 1, 2 and 3 of this book.

8.4 THE CORE–PERIPHERY STRUCTURE OF THE EUROPEAN AUTOMOTIVE INDUSTRY

Chapter 5 has further extended the analysis of the European automotive industry by considering its core–semiperiphery–periphery structure. In the context of the GVC/GPN perspective, Chapter 5 has built on Friedmann's core–periphery model, Harvey's theory of the spatiotemporal fix and uneven development, and on spatial divisions of labor in spatial systems to develop, justify and test an innovative methodology to determine the relative positions of countries in the European automotive industry, and how their relative positions change over time.

The proposed methodology has been developed in several steps. First, the positional power of countries in automotive industry GVCs/GPNs is estimated as the average of their producer-driven and buyer-driven power, which is calculated from bilateral national trade data with automotive industry products. Second, the positional power of each country is normalized by its ownership and control power, which is measured by the index of foreign control in the automotive industry. Third, this normalized positional power of countries is further normalized by the index of innovation, which measures the innovation capacity of each country in the automotive industry. The resulting index, which I refer to as "automotive industry power," has been calculated for each country and every year between 2003 and 2017. In the final step, a cluster analysis has been applied on the descendent order of the natural logarithm of the average values of automotive industry power of European countries for the 2003–2017, 2003–2007, 2008–2012 and 2013–2017 periods to determine five clusters for each of these periods. The five clusters correspond with five spatial categories of a higher-order core, lower-order core, semiperiphery, periphery and lower-order periphery of the European automotive industry. The changes in the position of countries in these spatial categories over time point toward their unstable positions, while unchanged positions over time point toward their stable positions in the core–semiperiphery–periphery system.

The empirical analysis has revealed the dominant position of Germany as a higher-order stable core of the European automotive industry during the 2003–2017 period. France and Italy represent a much weaker but still stable lower-order core. Sweden and Britain have been delimited as being unstable core countries close to the core–semiperiphery borderline position and trending toward the semiperiphery. The stable semiperiphery is concentrated in Western Europe and includes some formerly integrated periphery countries that advanced into the semiperiphery over time, such as Spain and Belgium. The unstable semiperiphery includes countries in the borderline position between the periphery and semiperiphery, such as Czechia, which is likely to slip back into the peripheral position rather than to consolidate its position in the stable semiperiphery. Most European countries have been classified in the peripheral position, of which most are located in Eastern Europe. Some of these peripheral countries, such as Poland and Slovakia, have seen strong improvements in their positional power during the study period, due to the rapid development of the export-oriented automotive industry, both vehicle assembly and components production. In the case of Poland, for example, this might lead to its gradual advancement in the European semiperiphery over time.

The results of the analysis of relative positions of countries in the European automotive industry based on the estimated network position of firms in this system validate the analyses and conclusions about the restructuring and spatial change of the European automotive industry that were presented in Chapters 3 and 4 of this book.

8.5 VALUE CREATION AND VALUE CAPTURE IN THE AUTOMOTIVE INDUSTRY

Chapter 6 has turned to the question of value creation and capture in GVCs/GPNs, which is one of the crucial issues for the GVCs/GPNs approach when considering the implications of the integration of countries and regions in GVCs/GPNs for their long-term economic development. More specifically, Chapter 6 has explored relationships between a firm's position in GVCs/GPNs and its prospects for value creation and capture. Consequently, by building on and further developing conceptual thinking from preceding chapters of this book, Chapter 6 has developed an approach to measure value creation and capture in regional production networks based on firm-level indicators. The gross value added is used to measure value creation. Value capture is measured by wages, corporate tax revenues, reinvested profits and domestic sourcing.

The chapter then explored how the network position of firms in automotive industry GVCs/GPNs affects their value creation and capture. In other words, it investigated how different tiers of suppliers contribute to value creation and capture in GVCs/GPNs. The empirical study has been conducted by analyzing firm-level data from the Czech automotive industry.

The empirical analysis conducted in Chapter 6 has validated the theoretical assumptions of potential greater economic effects of vehicle assemblers and large tier-one component suppliers in automotive industry GVCs/GPNs. Larger firms create greater value in GVCs/GPNs than smaller firms because of their larger capital intensity of production compared to smaller firms, which constitute the bulk of tier-two and especially of tier-three suppliers. This is because wages and value added per employee tend to increase with the increasing capital intensity of production and decrease with the declining capital intensity of production. There is also a greater potential for value capture from vehicle assemblers and large tier-one suppliers because they account for significantly higher corporate tax revenues and have higher average wages per worker compared to lower-tier suppliers. At the same time, the importance of lower-tier suppliers in terms of value capture is in their larger direct employment and wage effects per unit of production and investment capital compared to higher-tier suppliers. Additionally, lower-tier suppliers are more numerous and spatially dispersed than assembly firms and tier-one suppliers, which increased their potential regional development effects.

However, while this interpretation explains the value creation and capture of different tiers of automotive firms in core regions of the automotive industry, value capture in peripheral regions is negatively affected by foreign ownership and control in producer-driven GVCs/GPNs, and by the international division of labor in the automotive industry. Foreign firms repatriate profits from their foreign affiliates, exploit tax holidays and employ various profit-shifting strategies, which significantly undermines the value capture potential from the automotive industry in regions and economies hosting these firms. Additionally, automotive lead firms conduct strategic nonproduction functions, which constitute a key source of value added for higher-tier firms, mostly in core regions and in their home economies rather than in foreign locations. Consequently, these high value-added nonproduction functions are usually weakly developed compared with lower-value-added production functions in peripheral automotive industry regions, such as integrated peripheries. This situation increases value capture potential in core regions compared to peripheral regions of the automotive industry.

A potential strategy to partially address this situation is through greater state support for the development of domestic firms through industrial policies in peripheral regions. In the Eastern European integrated periphery, however, state support has largely been aimed at the development of the foreign-controlled automotive industry through various forms of investment incentives. The state support for the domestic sector has been either nonexistent or very limited (Pavlínek, 2016).

8.6 THE TRANSITION TO THE PRODUCTION OF ELECTRIC VEHICLES

Chapter 7 of the book has considered the implications of the transition to the production of electric vehicles for the European automotive industry. By building on conceptual arguments developed in preceding chapters, it has focused on this transition in the Eastern European integrated periphery.

The transition to the production of electric vehicles in Eastern Europe has been considered from the evolutionary perspective as being embedded in the nature and growth of the Eastern European automotive industry since the early 1990s, including the position of Eastern Europe in automotive GVCs/GPNs and in the international division of labor in the European automotive industry. The chapter has argued that the transition in Eastern Europe is also strongly affected by its peripheral position in the European automotive industry, which will affect its course in several important ways. First, it will mean that Eastern Europe is not and will not be the center of innovation for electromobility in Europe. This is because innovation activities related to electromobility already follow the spatial pattern of existing automotive industry innovations by being mostly concentrated in core areas of the European automotive industry. Some innovation activities related to electromobility are being selectively developed by automotive lead firms in Eastern Europe mostly for cost-cutting reasons. Overall, however, Eastern Europe lags and will likely continue to lag in innovation activities behind automotive industry regions in the core of the European automotive industry because, as explained in Chapter 5, core regions are typified by more favorable conditions for innovative activities compared to peripheral regions, which will ensure their higher rates of innovation related to electromobility than in the Eastern European integrated periphery.

Because of its peripheral position, Eastern Europe will experience the transition to the production of electric vehicles more slowly than the core and semiperipheral automotive industry regions of Western Europe. As a result, vehicles with internal combustion engines will be produced longer in Eastern Europe than in Western Europe. I have explained this situation based on the product life cycle model, according to which older technologies are exploited for longer in peripheral regions, while core regions more rapidly abandon more obsolete products and technologies and move toward the production of new products based on new technologies. A longer production of vehicles with internal combustion engines in Eastern Europe will be further reiterated by the existence of modern and efficient assembly factories for cars with internal combustion engines and engine factories built in the region mostly since the early 2000s. It will also be reinforced by a steadily high demand for cars with internal combustion engines and low demand for electric vehicles in Eastern

Europe because of their higher prices and lower purchasing power in the region. Finally, lower wages in Eastern Europe will contribute to the longer production of lower-priced and lower-profit-margin vehicles with internal combustion engines compared to higher-priced and higher-profit-margin electric cars. For all these reasons, we are likely to see a gradual transition to the production of electric cars in Eastern Europe, which will be based on the mixed production of cars with internal combustion engines and electric vehicles rather than on fully dedicated factories for electric cars. However, I have argued that this nature and gradual pace of transition toward electric vehicles might ultimately undermine the long-term competitive position of Eastern Europe in the European automotive industry by increasing the gap behind Western Europe, which will move to the production of electric cars in fully dedicated factories faster.

I have also argued that the transition to the production of electric vehicles is unlikely to change the peripheral position of Eastern Europe in European GVCs/GPNs and its overwhelming dependence on foreign capital and foreign automotive lead firms. Because of its continuing locational advantages, the Eastern European integrated periphery will continue to be attractive for automotive FDI, although there might be important changes in the structure of FDI source countries. This can already be seen in large investments in the battery industry by Chinese and South Korean lead firms in Hungary and Poland. I have argued that all these trends will ultimately ensure the continuing highly dependent peripheral position of Eastern Europe in European automotive industry GVCs/GPNs in the foreseeable future.

8.7 THE UNCERTAIN FUTURE OF THE EUROPEAN AUTOMOTIVE INDUSTRY

The overall picture of the European automotive industry developed in this book from the economic geography perspective has emphasized its relentless restructuring. This continual spatial change has been driven by investment and disinvestment strategies of global lead firms. Since the 1960s, these strategies have led to the geographic expansion of the automotive industry into new peripheral countries and regions in search of higher rates of profit while, at the same time, triggering the restructuring in the existing core and semiperipheral countries and regions. These spatial strategies of automotive lead firms have therefore played an important role in the competitive strategies of European and non-European lead firms and contributed to the continuing competitiveness of the European automotive industry.

However, the European automotive industry faces several important challenges, which will affect its long-term future, competitiveness and sustainability. While the trend toward the production of electric cars seems to be entrenched, the success of European automotive firms in this transition is far from certain. European lead firms face the danger of being outcompeted in both

European and foreign markets by Asian and American automotive firms and electric battery companies. An unsuccessful transition of European automotive firms to the production of electric cars would not necessarily mean the collapse of the European automotive industry but might undermine the position of Europe as one of the core areas of the global automotive industry and lead to its increased dependence on foreign capital and technologies. This might weaken the value capture from the automotive industry and its regional development benefits in Europe. Additionally, as I have mentioned in Chapter 5, the automotive industry is being affected by other important trends, including automation, robotics, digitalization (Industry 4.0), autonomous driving and new forms of car ownership, which are beyond the scope of this book, but which have the potential to affect the future structure, employment and the geography of production of the European automotive industry.

Finally, the war in Ukraine has sharply increased geopolitical risks for the European automotive industry and negatively affected its future prospects by triggering rapid geopolitical decoupling (Pavlínek, 2024) of European automotive lead firms from Russia. Geopolitical decoupling led to exit of automotive lead firms from Russia and disrupted automotive GVCs and GPNs, leading to large financial losses. Among European lead firms, Renault, Volkswagen, Mercedes-Benz and Stellantis collectively lost USD5.7 billion because of exit or the suspension of operations in Russia in 2022 and 2023 (Renault lost USD2.3 billion, Volkswagen USD2.2 billion, Mercedes-Benz USD693 million and Stellantis USD470 million). Additional large financial losses were recorded by European automotive suppliers, such as Bosch, Continental, Faurecia, Michelin, Siemens, Valeo and ZF (Sonnenfeld, 2023). The automotive industry in Eastern Europe is more susceptible to these increased geopolitical risks because of its relative proximity to Ukraine and Russia, its high dependence on Russian natural gas and oil and the landlocked location of many Eastern European countries that makes alternative supplies of oil and liquified natural gas more expensive than in Western Europe. Higher perceived geopolitical risks and higher energy costs might negatively affect future investment and location decisions of automotive lead firms.

Given these challenges, the future of the European automotive industry will largely depend on the ability of European lead firms to maintain their competitive position in the global automotive industry, ideally with the help of strong but sensible industrial policies at the national and European Union levels. Given the importance of spatial strategies of automotive lead firms in previous decades, there is no doubt they will continue to play an important role in the European automotive industry in the future as well.

References

ACEA (2021a) Interactive map: Automobile assembly and production plants in Europe. Available at: www.acea.auto/figure/interactive-map-automobile-assembly-and-production-plants-in-europe/ (accessed March 12, 2022).

ACEA (2021b) Interactive map: Correlation between electric car sales and charging point availability (2021 update). Available at: www.acea.auto/figure/interactive-map-correlation-between-electric-car-sales-and-charging-point-availability-2021-update/ (accessed October 3, 2022).

ACEA (2021c) *Making the transition to zero-emission mobility: 2021 progress report.* Brussels: European Automobile Manufacturers' Association.

ACEA (2022a) *The automotive industry pocket guide 2021/2022.* Brussels: European Automobile Manufacturers' Association.

ACEA (2022b) *Electric vehicles: Tax Benefits & purchase incentives in the 27 member states of the European Union (2022).* Brussels: European Automobile Manufacturers' Association.

ACEA (2023a) *The automotive industry pocket guide 2023/2024.* Brussels: European Automobile Manufacturers' Association.

ACEA (2023b) *Tax benefits and purchase incentives, electric passenger cars, 27 EU member states (2023).* Brussels: European Automobile Manufacturers' Association.

Adăscăliței D and Guga Ș (2020) Tensions in the periphery: Dependence and the trajectory of a low-cost productive model in the Central and Eastern European automotive industry. *European Urban and Regional Studies* 27(1): 18–34.

AfDB, OECD and UNDP (2014) *African economic outlook 2014: Global value chains and Africa's industrialisation.* Abidjan: African Development Bank.

Agosin MR and Machado R (2005) Foreign investment in developing countries: Does it crowd in domestic investment? *Oxford Development Studies* 33(2): 149–162.

AIA (2022) Annual time series of vehicle production and sales. Available at: www.autosap.cz (accessed December 15, 2022).

Aktuálně.cz (2021) Auto není žádný luxus nebo zábava. Dle Fialy je zákaz spalovacích motorů nepřijatelný. Aktuálně.cz, December 19.

Akyüz Y (2017) *Playing with fire: Deepened financial integration and changing vulnerabilities of the Global South.* Oxford: Oxford University Press.

Aláez-Aller R and Barneto-Carmona M (2008) Evaluating the risk of plant closure in the automotive industry in Spain. *European Planning Studies* 16(1): 61–80.

Aláez-Aller R, Gil C and Ullibarri M (2015) FDI in the automotive plants in Spain during the great recession. In Galgóczi B, Drahokoupil, J, Bernaciak M (eds.) *Foreign investment in Eastern and Southern Europe after 2008: Still a lever of growth?* Brussels: ETUI, pp. 139–170.

Alfaro L, Chanda A, Kalemli-Ozcan S and Sayek S (2010) Does foreign direct investment promote growth? Exploring the role of financial markets on linkages. *Journal of Development Economics* 91(2): 242–256.

Alguacil M, Cuadros A and Orts V (2011) Inward FDI and growth: The role of macroeconomic and institutional environment. *Journal of Policy Modeling* 33(3): 481–496.

Allan T, Keulertz M, Sojamo S and Warner J (2013) *Handbook of land and water grabs in Africa: Foreign direct investment and food and water security.* Abingdon: Routledge.

Alon I, Apriliyanti ID and Henríquez Parodi MC (2021) A systematic review of international franchising. *Multinational Business Review* 29(1): 43–69.

Alvarado R, Iñiguez M and Ponce P (2017) Foreign direct investment and economic growth in Latin America. *Economic Analysis and Policy* 56: 176–187.

Amendolagine V, Boly A, Coniglio ND, Prota F and Seric A (2013) FDI and local linkages in developing countries: Evidence from sub-Saharan Africa. *World Development* 50: 41–56.

Amendolagine V, Presbitero AF, Rabellotti R and Sanfilippo M (2019) Local sourcing in developing countries: The role of foreign direct investments and global value chains. *World Development* 113: 73–88.

Amin A (1999) An institutionalist perspective on regional economic development. *International Journal of Urban and Regional Research* 23(2): 365–378.

Amin A, Bradley D, Howells J, Tomaney J and Gentle C (1994) Regional incentives and the quality of mobile investment in the less favoured regions of the EC. *Progress in Planning* 41(1): 1–112.

Amin A and Thrift N (1994) Living in the global. In Amin A and Thrift N (eds.) *Globalization, institutions and regional development in Europe.* Oxford: Oxford University Press, pp. 1–22.

Amin S (1976) *Unequal development: An Essay on the social formations of peripheral capitalism.* Hassocks: The Harvester Press.

AMS (2021a) Electric vehicle and hybrid vehicle plant database. *Automotive Manufacturing Solutions*, June 3.

AMS (2021b) Lithium-ion battery gigafactory database. *Automotive Manufacturing Solutions*, 3 June 2021.

Amsden AH (1989) *Asia's next giant: South Korea and late industrialization.* Oxford: Oxford University Press.

Amsden AH (2001) *The rise of "the rest": Challenges to the West from late-industrializing economies.* Oxford: Oxford University Press.

Amsden AH (2007) *Escape from empire: The developing world's journey through heaven and hell.* Cambridge, MA: The MIT Press.

Amsden AH and Chu W-w (2003) *Beyond late development: Taiwan's upgrading policies.* Cambridge, MA: The MIT Press.

Andreoni A and Chang H-J (2019) The political economy of industrial policy: Structural interdependencies, policy alignment and conflict management. *Structural Change and Economic Dynamics* 48: 136–150.

ANE (2017) ANE guide provides details on nearly 100 engine and transmission factories. Available at: https://europe.autonews.com/ane-guide-provides-details-nearly-100-engine-and-transmission-factories (accessed March 12, 2022).

ANE (2022a) Dacia to stick with combustion engines beyond 2030. *Automotive News Europe*, September 16.

ANE (2022b) Europe's auto production crashes as flow of wire harnesses dries up. *Automotive News Europe*, March 2.

ANE (2022c) How Russia's invasion of Ukraine is impacting the auto industry. *Automotive News Europe*, March 2.

ANE (2022d) VW may shift output from Germany over gas shortage. *Automotive News Europe*, September 23.

Aoyama Y, Murphy JT and Hanson S (2011) *Key concepts in economic geography*. London: Sage.

Arias M, Atienza M and Cademartori J (2014) Large mining enterprises and regional development in Chile: Between the enclave and cluster. *Journal of Economic Geography* 14(1): 73–95.

Arrighi G and Drangel J (1986) The stratification of the world-economy: An exploration of the semiperipheral zone. *Review (Fernand Braudel Center)* 10(1): 9–74.

Ascani A and Gagliardi L (2020) Asymmetric spillover effects from MNE investment. *Journal of World Business* 55(6): 101–146.

Audi (2021) Audi at the Győr site. Available at: www.audi-mediacenter.com/en/audi-at-the-hungary-site-gyor-5570 (accessed March 14, 2022).

Audi (2023) Successful year in 2022 at Audi Hungary: More cars and powertrains produced than ever before. Available at: www.audi-mediacenter.com/en/press-releases/successful-year-in-2022-at-audi-hungaria-more-cars-and-powertrains-produced-than-ever-before-15162 (accessed November 6, 2023).

Bair J and Werner M (2011a) Commodity chains and the uneven geographies of global capitalism: A disarticulations perspective. *Environment and Planning A: Economy and Space* 43(5): 988–997.

Bair J and Werner M (2011b) The place of disarticulations: Global commodity production in La Laguna, Mexico. *Environment and Planning A: Economy and Space* 43(5): 998–1015.

Baran PA (1957) *The political economy of growth*. London: Monthly Review Press.

Barkley DL and McNamara KT (1994) Local input linkages: A comparison of foreign-owned and domestic manufacturers in Georgia and South Carolina. *Regional Studies* 28(7): 725–737.

Barnes J and Kaplinsky R (2000) Globalization and the death of the local firm? The automobile components sector in South Africa. *Regional Studies* 34(9): 797–812.

Barrientos S, Gereffi G and Rossi A (2011) Economic and social upgrading in global production networks: A new paradigm for a changing world. *International Labour Review* 150(3–4): 319–340.

Basu P and Guariglia A (2007) Foreign direct investment, inequality, and growth. *Journal of Macroeconomics* 29(4): 824–839.

Bathelt H and Glückler J (2013) Institutional change in economic geography. *Progress in Human Geography* 38(3): 340–363.

Bauer W, Riedel O and Herrmann F (2020) *Employment 2030: Effects of electric mobility and digitalisation on the quality and quantity of employment at Volkswagen.* Stuttgart: Fraunhofer Institute for Industrial Engineering IAO.

Bellak C (2004) How domestic and foreign firms differ and why does it matter? *Journal of Economic Surveys* 18(4): 483–514.

Benabdejlil N, Bounya N, Layan J-B, Lung Y and Piveteau A (2015) Renault in northern Morocco: The emergence of an automobile cluster in Tangier. *23rd GERPISA Colloquium*, Paris, June 10.

Benabdejlil N, Lung Y and Piveteau A (2016) L'émergence d'un pôle automobile à Tanger (Maroc). *Cahiers du GREThA 2016-04.* Bordeaux: Université de Bordeaux, 1–23.

Benadbdejlil N, Lung Y and Piveteau A (2017) L'émergence d'un pôle automobile à Tanger (Maroc). *Critique économique* 35(winter–spring): 31–57.

Benito GRG (2005) Divestment and international business strategy. *Journal of Economic Geography* 5(2): 235–251.

Bermejo Carbonell J and Werner RA (2018) Does foreign direct investment generate economic growth? A new empirical approach applied to Spain. *Economic Geography* 94(4): 425–456.

Beutnagel W and Verpraet I (2021) German carmakers race to secure European battery cell production. *Automotive manufacturing solutions*, February 15.

Bilbao-Ubillos J and Camino-Beldarrain V (2008) Proximity matters? European Union enlargement and relocation of activities: The case of the Spanish automotive industry. *Economic Development Quarterly* 22(2): 149–166.

Biresselioglu ME, Demirbag Kaplan M and Yilmaz BK (2018) Electric mobility in Europe: A comprehensive review of motivators and barriers in decision making processes. *Transportation Research Part A: Policy and Practice* 109: 1–13.

Blalock G and Gertler PJ (2008) Welfare gains from foreign direct investment through technology transfer to local suppliers. *Journal of International Economics* 74(2): 402–421.

Blažek J (2016) Towards a typology of repositioning strategies of GVC/GPN suppliers: The case of functional upgrading and downgrading. *Journal of Economic Geography* 16(4): 849–869.

Blažek J and Hejnová T (2020) Geography, ownership and uneven trends in the economic performance of small banking centres in Europe during the financial crisis. *European Urban and Regional Studies* 27(4): 359–378.

Blomström M and Kokko A (1998) Multinational corporations and spillovers. *Journal of Economic Surveys* 12(3): 247–277.

Blomström M and Kokko A (2001) Foreign direct investment and spillovers of technology. *International Journal of Technology Management* 22(5–6): 435–454.

Blomström M, Kokko A and Zejan M (2000) *Foreign direct investment: Firm and host country strategies.* New York: MacMillan Press.

BMW (2018) *BMW Group to expand production network in Europe.* BMW. Available at: www.press.bmwgroup.com/global/article/detail/T0283624EN/bmw-group-to-expand-production-network-in-europe (accessed April 18, 2022).

BMW (2020) *BMW Group paves the way for production network of the future.* BMW. Available at: www.press.bmwgroup.com/global/article/detail/T0320954EN/bmw-group-paves-the-way-for-production-network-of-the-future (accessed March 13, 2022).

Bohle D (2006) Neoliberal hegemony, transnational capital and the terms of the EU's eastward expansion. *Capital & Class* 30(1): 57–86.

Bohle D and Greskovits B (2006) Capitalism without compromise: Strong business and weak labor in Eastern Europe's new transnational industries. *Studies in Comparative International Development* 41(1): 3–25.

Bolduc DA (2017a) After attracting top suppliers, Macedonia eyes bigger prize. *Automotive News Europe*, May 10.

Bolduc DA (2017b) Morocco aims to add 2 more car plants. *Automotive News Europe*, August 14.

Bolduc DA (2021) How InoBat aims to stand out from VW, Tesla, CATL in battery cell sector. *Automotive News Europe*, May 15.

Bordenave G and Lung Y (1996) New spatial configurations in the European automobile industry. *European Urban and Regional Studies* 3(4): 305–321.

Borensztein E, De Gregorio J and Lee JW (1998) How does foreign direct investment affect economic growth? *Journal of International Economics* 45(1): 115–135.

Borgatti SP and Everett MG (1999) Models of core/periphery structures. *Social Networks* 21(4): 375–395.

Bornschier V and Chase-Dunn C (1985) *Transnational corporations and underdevelopment*. New York: Praeger.

Bowman C and Ambrosini V (2000) Value creation versus value capture: Towards a coherent definition of value in strategy. *British Journal of Management* 11(1): 1–15.

Boyer R and Freyssenet M (2002) *The productive models: The conditions of profitability*. Houndmills, Basingstoke: Palgrave Macmillan.

Bridge G (2008) Global production networks and the extractive sector: Governing resource-based development. *Journal of Economic Geography* 8(3): 389–419.

Bridge G and Bradshaw M (2017) Making a global gas market: Territoriality and production networks in liquefied natural gas. *Economic Geography* 93(3): 215–240.

Brincks C, Domański B, Klier T and Rubenstein J (2018) Integrated peripheral markets in the auto industries of Europe and North America. *International Journal of Automotive Technology and Management* 18(1): 1–28.

Brincks C, Klier T and Rubenstein J (2016) The role of national champions in the evolving footprint of vehicle production in Europe – 1990–2013. *International Journal of Automotive Technology and Management* 16(2): 130–146.

Britton JNH (1976) Influence of corporate organization and ownership on linkages of industrial plants: Canadian inquiry. *Economic Geography* 52(4): 311–324.

Britton JNH (1980) Industrial dependence and technological underdevelopment: Canadian consequences of foreign direct investment. *Regional Studies* 14(3): 181–199.

Britton JNH (1981) Industrial impacts of foreign enterprise: A Canadian technological perspective. *Professional Geographer* 33(1): 36–47.

Brucal A, Javorcik B and Love I (2019) Good for the environment, good for business: Foreign acquisitions and energy intensity. *Journal of International Economics* 121: 1–17.

Bruton HJ (1998) A reconsideration of import substitution. *Journal of Economic Literature* 36(2): 903–936.

Buckley PJ and Casson M (1976) *The future of the multinational enterprise*. London: The Macmillan Press.

Buckley PJ, Doh JP and Benischke MH (2017) Towards a renaissance in international business research? Big questions, grand challenges, and the future of IB scholarship. *Journal of International Business Studies* 48(9): 1045–1064.

Calabrese GG (2020) The Italian automotive industry: Between old and new development factors. In Covarrubias VA and Ramírez Perez SM (eds.) *New frontiers of the automobile industry: Exploring geographies, technology, and institutional challenges*. Cham: Palgrave Macmillan, pp. 163–201.

Carkovic M and Levine R (2005) Does foreign direct investment accelerate economic growth? In Moran TH, Graham EM and Blomström M (eds.) *Does foreign direct investment promote development?* Washington, DC: Institute for International Economics, Center for Global Development, pp. 195–220.

Carrillo J (2004) Transnational strategies and regional development: The Case of GM and Delphi in Mexico. *Industry and Innovation* 11(1–2): 127–153.

Carrillo J, Lung Y and van Tulder R (2004) *Cars, carriers of regionalism?* London: Palgrave Macmillan.

Carrincazeaux C, Lung YN and Rallet A (2001) Proximity and localisation of corporate R&D activities. *Research Policy* 30(5): 777–789.

Casella B and Formenti L (2018) FDI in the digital economy: A shift to asset-light international footprints. *Transnational Corporations* 25(1): 101–130.

Castillo JC and de Vries G (2018) The domestic content of Mexico's maquiladora exports: A long-run perspective. *The Journal of International Trade & Economic Development* 27(2): 200–219.

Cattaneo O, Gereffi G and Staritz C (eds) (2010) *Global value chains in a postcrisis world: A development perspective*. Washington, DC: The World Bank.

Caves RE (1971) International corporations: Industrial economics of foreign investment. *Economica* 38(149): 1–27.

CB (2016) *International comparisons of hourly compensation costs in manufacturing, 1996–2015*. New York: The Conference Board, Inc.

CB (2018) *International comparisons of hourly compensation costs in manufacturing and sub-manufacturing*. New York: The Conference Board, Inc.

Chang H-J (2004) Regulation of foreign investment in historical perspective. *The European Journal of Development Research* 16(3): 687–715.

Chang H-J (2008) *Bad Samaritans: The guilty secrets of rich nations and the threat to global prosperity*. London: Random House.

Chang H-J and Andreoni A (2020) Industrial policy in the 21st century. *Development and Change* 51(2): 324–351.

Charnock G, Purcell TG and Ribera-Fumaz R (2016) New international division of labour and differentiated integration in Europe: The case of Spain. In Charnock G and Starosta G (eds.) *The New International Division of Labour: Global Transformation and Uneven Development*. London: Palgrave Macmillan, pp. 157–180.

Charvát O (2022) Devět miliard na areál pro Gigafactory. Vláda chystá finanční injekci, která má přilákat VW. *Hospodářské noviny*, July 27.

Chase-Dunn C (1975) The effects of international economic dependence on development and inequality: A cross-national study. *American Sociological Review* 40(6): 720–738.

Chase-Dunn C and Hall TD (eds.) (1991) *Core/periphery relations in precapitalist worlds*. London: Routledge.

Chase-Dunn C and Hall TD (1997) *Rise and demise: Comparing world-systems*. Boulder, CO: Westview Press.

Chen C (2018) The liberalisation of FDI policies and the impacts of FDI on China's economic development. In Garnaut R, Song L and Fang C (eds.) *China's 40 years of reform and development: 1978–2018*. Acton: ANU Press, pp. 595–617.

Chew SC and Lauderdale P (eds.) (2010) *Theory and methodology of world development: The writings of Andre Gunder Frank*. New York: Palgrave Macmillan.

Chiappini R (2012) Offshoring and export performance in the European automotive industry. *Competition & Change* 16(4): 323–342.

Chu W-w (2017) Inductive method and development perspective: Alice Amsden on Taiwan and beyond. *Cambridge Journal of Regions, Economy and Society* 10(1): 15–34.

Clark GL and Wrigley N (1995) Sunk costs: A framework for economic geography. *Transactions of the Institute of British Geographers* 20(2): 204–223.

Clark GL and Wrigley N (1997) Exit, the firm and sunk costs: Reconceptualizing the corporate geography of disinvestment and plant closure. *Progress in Human Geography* 21(3): 338–358.

CLEPA (2021) *Electric vehicle transition impact assessment report 2020–2040: A quantitative forecast of employment trends at automotive suppliers in Europe*. Etterbeek: European Association of Automotive Suppliers.

CLEPA (2022) *The role of batteries in the transition*. Available at: https://clepa.eu/who-and-what-we-represent/suppliers-eu-employment-footprint/batteries/ (accessed October 2, 2022).

CNB (2023) *Foreign direct investment*. Available at: www.cnb.cz/analytics/saw.dll?Portal.

Coe NM (2014) Missing links: Logistics, governance and upgrading in a shifting global economy. *Review of International Political Economy* 21(1): 224–256.

Coe NM (2021) *Advanced introduction to global production networks*. Cheltenham: Edward Elgar.

Coe NM, Dicken P and Hess M (2008) Global production networks: Realizing the potential. *Journal of Economic Geography* 8(3): 271–295.

Coe NM and Hess M (2011) Local and regional development: A global production network approach. In Pike A, Rodríguez-Pose A and Tomaney J (eds.) *Handbook of local and regional development*. London: Routledge, pp. 128–138.

Coe NM, Hess M, Yeung HWC Dicken P and Henderson J (2004) "Globalizing" regional development: A global production networks perspective. *Transactions of the Institute of British Geographers* 29(4): 468–484.

Coe NM, Lai KPY and Wójcik D (2014) Integrating finance into global production networks. *Regional Studies* 48(5): 761–777.

Coe NM and Yeung HWC (2015) *Global production networks: Theorizing economic development in an interconnected world*. Oxford: Oxford University Press.

Coe NM and Yeung HWC (2019) Global production networks: Mapping recent conceptual developments. *Journal of Economic Geography* 19(4): 775–801.

Coffey D and Thornley C (2020) Britain's car industry: Policies, positioning, and perspectives. In Covarrubias VA and Ramírez Perez SM (eds.) *New frontiers of the automobile industry: Exploring geographies, technology, and institutional challenges.* Cham: Palgrave Macmillan, pp. 137–161.

Cohen WM and Levinthal DA (1989) Innovation and learning: The 2 faces of R-and-D. *Economic Journal* 99(397): 569–596.

Contreras OF, Carrillo J and Alonso J (2012) Local entrepreneurship within global value chains: A case study in the Mexican automotive industry. *World Development* 40(5): 1013–1023.

Crone M (2002) Local sourcing by multinational enterprise plants: Evidence from the UK regions and the implications for policy. *Environment and Planning C-Government and Policy* 20(1): 131–149.

Crone M and Watts HD (2003) The determinants of regional sourcing by multinational manufacturing firms: Evidence from Yorkshire and Humberside, UK. *European Planning Studies* 11(6): 717–737.

CSO (2011) *Annual survey of economic subjects in selected industries.* Prague: The Czech Statistical Office.

CSO (2022) *Basic characteristics of activity status of population aged 15 or more.* Prague: The Czech Statistical Office.

Cui L, Meyer KE and Hu HW (2014) What drives firms' intent to seek strategic assets by foreign direct investment? A study of emerging economy firms. *Journal of World Business* 49(4): 488–501.

Cumbers A, MacKinnon D and McMaster R (2003) Institutions, power and space: Assessing the limits to institutionalism in economic geography. *European Urban and Regional Studies* 10(4): 325–342.

Curwin KD and Mahutga MC (2014) Foreign direct investment and economic growth: New evidence from post-socialist transition countries. *Social Forces* 92(3): 1159–1187.

Danyluk M (2018) Capital's logistical fix: Accumulation, globalization, and the survival of capitalism. *Environment and Planning D: Society and Space* 36(4): 630–647.

Darteyre P and Guga Ş (2022) The future of the European automobile industry: Poland and Romania. In Galgóczi B (ed.) *The future of the automotive sector.* Brussels: ETUI.

Davies H, Cipcigan LM, Donovan C Newman D and Nieuwenhuis P (2015) The impact of electric automobility. In Nieuwenhuis P and Wells P (eds.) *The global automotive industry.* Chichester: John Wiley & Sons, pp. 185–198.

Dawley S (2007a) Fluctuating rounds of inward investment in peripheral regions: Semiconductors in the North East of England. *Economic Geography* 83(1): 51–73.

Dawley S (2007b) Making labour-market geographies: Volatile "flagship" inward investment and peripheral regions. *Environment and Planning A: Economy and Space* 39(6): 1403–1419.

Dawley S (2011) Transnational corporations and local and regional development. In Pike A, Rodríguez-Pose J and Tomaney J (eds.) *Handbook of local and regional development.* London: Routledge, pp. 394–412.

Dawley S, MacKinnon D and Pollock R (2019) Creating strategic couplings in global production networks: Regional institutions and lead firm investment in the Humber region, UK. *Journal of Economic Geography* 19(4): 853–872.

De Backer K and Sleuwaegen L (2003) Does foreign direct investment crowd out domestic entrepreneurship? *Review of Industrial Organization* 22(1): 67–84.

Dedrick J, Kraemer KL and Linden G (2010) Who profits from innovation in global value chains? A study of the iPod and notebook PCs. *Industrial and Corporate Change* 19(1): 81–116.

Dedrick J, Kraemer KL and Linden G (2011) The distribution of value in the mobile phone supply chain. *Telecommunications Policy* 35(6): 505–521.

Delanote J, Ferrazzi M, Hanzl-Weiß D, et al. (2022) *Recharging the batteries: How the electric vehicle revolution is affecting Central, Eastern and South-Eastern Europe.* Luxembourg: European Investment Bank.

Deloitte (2021) *Rozvoj výroby baterií v Česku.* Prague: Deloitte.

Demena BA (2015) Publication bias in FDI spillovers in developing countries: A meta-regression analysis. *Applied Economics Letters* 22(14): 1170–1174.

Demena BA and Afesorgbor SK (2020) The effect of FDI on environmental emissions: Evidence from a meta-analysis. *Energy Policy* 138: 111192.

Dicken P (1976) The multiplant business enterprise and geographical space: Some issues in the study of external control and regional development (Volume 10, Number 4, 1976). *Regional Studies* 10(4): 401–412.

Dicken P (1994) The Roepke lecture in economic geography global-local tensions: Firms and states in the global space-economy. *Economic Geography* 70(2): 101–128.

Dicken P (2015) *Global shift: Mapping the changing contours of the world economy.* New York: The Guilford Press.

Dicken P, Forsgren M and Malmberg A (1994) The local embeddedness of transnational corporations. In Amin A and Thrift N (eds.) *Globalization, institutions and regional development in Europe.* Oxford: Oxford University Press, pp. 23–45.

Dijk M, Wells P and Kemp R (2016) Will the momentum of the electric car last? Testing an hypothesis on disruptive innovation. *Technological Forecasting and Social Change* 105: 77–88.

Dimitratos P, Liouka I and Young S (2009) Regional location of multinational corporation subsidiaries and economic development contribution: Evidence from the UK. *Journal of World Business* 44(2): 180–191.

Dischinger M, Knoll B and Riedel N (2014a) The role of headquarters in multinational profit shifting strategies. *International Tax and Public Finance* 21(2): 248–271.

Dischinger M, Knoll B and Riedel N (2014b) There's no place like home: The profitability gap between headquarters and their foreign subsidiaries. *Journal of Economics & Management Strategy* 23(2): 369–395.

Domański B, Guzik R and Gwosdz K (2014) The changing position of Central Europe in the European automotive industry. In Medina LÁ, Carrillo J and González Marín ML (eds.) *El auge de la industria automotriz en México en el siglo XXI: Reestructuración y Catching Up.* Mexico City: UNAM FCA Publishing, pp. 47–67.

Domański B and Gwosdz K (2009) Toward a more embedded production system? Automotive supply networks and localized capabilities in Poland. *Growth and Change* 40(3): 452–482.

Domański B and Lung Y (2009) Editorial: The changing face of the European periphery in the automotive industry. *European Urban and Regional Studies* 16(1): 5–10.

Đorđević N (2021) When will Poland's much-heralded electric car hit the streets? *Emerging Europe*, September 2.

Drahokoupil J (2008) The investment-promotion machines: The politics of foreign direct investment promotion in Central and Eastern Europe. *Europe-Asia Studies* 60(2): 197–225.

Drahokoupil J (2009) *Globalization and the state in Central and Eastern Europe: The politics of foreign direct investment.* London: Routledge.

Drahokoupil J (ed.) (2020) *The challenge of digital transformation in the automotive industry: Jobs, upgrading and the prospects for development.* Brussels: ETUI.

Drahokoupil J and Myant M (2017) Dependent capitalism and employment relations in East Central Europe. In Delteil V and Kirov VN (eds.) *Labour and social transformation in Central and Eastern Europe: Europeanization and beyond.* London: Routledge, pp. 42–59.

Dunford M and Liu W (2017) Uneven and combined development. *Regional Studies* 51(1): 69–85.

Dunn J (2022) Northvolt selects northern Germany for its third European gigafactory. *Automotive Manufacturing Solutions*, March 16.

Dunning JH (1977) Trade, location of economic activity and the MNE: A search for an eclectic approach. In Hesselborn P-O, Ohlin B and Wijkman PM (eds.) *The international allocation of economic activity.* London: Holmes and Meier, pp. 395–418.

Dunning JH (2000) The eclectic paradigm as an envelope for economic and business theories of MNE activity. *International Business Review* 9(2): 163–190.

Dunning JH and Lundan SM (2008) *Multinational enterprises and the global economy.* Cheltenham: Edward Elgar.

Dunning JH and Rugman AM (1985) The influence of Hymer's dissertation on the theory of foreign direct investment. *The American Economic Review,* 75(2): 228–232.

Dussel Peters E (2016) Mexico's new industrial organisation since the 1980s: Glocal challenges from export-orientation and polarisation. In Weiss J and Tribe M (eds.) *Routledge handbook of industry and development.* London and New York: Routledge, pp. 320–334.

EC (2019) *The European green deal.* Brussels: European Commission.

Eddy N (2022) German automakers hit by Ukraine disruption helped by key supplier Leoni's task force. *Automotive News Europe,* March 5.

Ehl M (2023) Od míchačky po zrání ve skladu. Unikátní pohled na vznik evropské továrny na baterie do aut a letadel. *Hospodářské noviny,* October 10.

Ellingstad M (1997) The maquiladora syndrome: Central European prospects. *Europe-Asia Studies* 49(1): 7–21.

Enderwick P and Buckley PJ (2020) Rising regionalization: Will the post-COVID-19 world see a retreat from globalization? *Transnational Corporations Journal* 27(2): 99–109.

ERM (2017) European Restructuring Monitor. Available at: www.eurofound .europa.eu.

Ernst D and Kim L (2002) Global production networks, knowledge diffusion, and local capability formation. *Research Policy* 31(8-9): 1417–1429.

European Council (2023a) Fit for 55. Available at: www.consilium.europa.eu/en/policies/ green-deal/fit-for-55-the-eu-plan-for-a-green-transition/ (accessed March 20, 2024).

European Council (2023b) "Fit for 55": Council adopts key pieces of legislation delivering on 2030 climate targets. April 25. Available at: www.consilium .europa.eu/en/press/press-releases/2023/04/25/fit-for-55-council-adopts-key-pieces- of-legislation-delivering-on-2030-climate-targets/?utm_source=dsms-auto&utm_ medium=email&utm_campaign=%27Fit%20for%2055%27%3A%20Council% 20adopts%20key (accessed March 20, 2024).

Eurostat (2008) NACE Rev. 2: Statistical classification of economic activities in the European Community. *Eurostat Methodologies and Working Papers.* Luxembourg: Eurostat.

Eurostat (2016a) *Annual detailed enterprise statistics on manufacturing, subsections DF-DN and total* (NACE Rev. 1.1, D) [sbs_na_2a_dfdn]. Luxembourg: Eurostat.

Eurostat (2016b) *Structural business statistics: Annual detailed enterprise statistics – industry and construction.* Luxembourg: Eurostat.

Eurostat (2018) *Structural business statistics: Annual detailed enterprise statistics – industry and construction.* Luxembourg: Eurostat.

Eurostat (2020a) *Comext.* Luxembourg: Eurostat.

Eurostat (2020b) *Correspondence table NACE Rev. 2 – NACE Rev. 1.1.* Luxembourg: Eurostat.

Eurostat (2020c) *Foreign control of enterprises by economic activity and a selection of controlling countries.* Luxembourg: Eurostat.

Eurostat (2020d) *Structural business statistics: Annual detailed enterprise statistics – industry and construction.* Luxembourg: Eurostat.

Eurostat (2021a) Total R&D personnel and researchers in business enterprise sector by NACE Rev. 2 activity and sex [rd_p_bempoccr2]. Luxembourg: Eurostat.

Eurostat (2021b) *Total unemployment rate [TPS00203].* Luxembourg: Eurostat.

Eurostat (2022a) *EU direct investment positions, breakdown by country and economic activity (BPM6) [bop_fdi6_pos].* Luxembourg: Eurostat.

Eurostat (2022b) *Foreign control of enterprises by economic activity and a selection of controlling countries [fats_g1a_08].* Luxembourg: Eurostat.

Eurostat (2022c) *Structural business statistics: Annual detailed enterprise statistics – industry and construction [sbs_na_ind_r2].* Luxembourg: Eurostat.

Eurostat (2023a) *Business expenditure on R&D (BERD) by NACE Rev. 2 activity [rd_e_berdindr2].* Luxembourg: Eurostat.

Eurostat (2023b) *Job vacancy statistics by NACE Rev. 2 activity, occupation and NUTS 2 regions – quarterly data [[jvs_q_isco_r2].* Luxembourg: Eurostat.

Eurostat (2023c) *Structural business statistics: Annual detailed enterprise statistics – industry and construction [sbs_na_ind_r2].* Luxembourg: Eurostat.

Eurostat (2023d) *Total R&D personnel and researchers in business enterprise sector by NACE Rev. 2 activity and sex [rd_p_bempoccr2].* Luxembourg: Eurostat.

Eurostat (2023e) *Total unemployment rate [TPS00203].* Luxembourg: Eurostat.

Eurostat (2023f) *Unemployment rate by NUTS 2 regions [tgs00010].* Luxembourg: Eurostat.

EY (2010) *The Central and Eastern European automotive market: Industry overview.* Stuttgart and Detroit: Ernst & Young.

Fagerberg J and Srholec M (2008) National innovation systems, capabilities and economic development. *Research Policy* 37(9): 1417–1435.

Fan H, He S and Kwan YK (2020) FDI backward spillovers in China: What a meta-analysis tells us? *Emerging Markets Finance and Trade* 56(1): 86–105.

Farole T, Rodríguez-Pose A and Storper M (2010) Human geography and the institutions that underlie economic growth. *Progress in Human Geography* 35(1): 58–80.

Farole T, Staritz C and Winkler D (2014) Conceptual framework. In Farole T and Winkler D (eds.) *Making foreign direct investment work for sub-Saharan Africa:*

Local spillovers and competitiveness in global value chains. Washington, DC: The World Bank, pp. 23–55.

Farole T and Winkler D (2014) The role of mediating factors for FDI spillovers in developing countries: Evidence from a global dataset. In Farole T and Winkler D (eds.) *Making foreign direct investment work for sub-Saharan Africa: Local spillovers and competitiveness in global value chains.* Washington, DC: The World Bank, pp. 59–86.

Farrell R (2008) *Japanese investment in the world economy: A study of strategic themes in the internationalisation of Japanese industry.* Cheltenham: Edward Elgar.

Felix AR (2009) Do state corporate income taxes reduce wages? *Federal Reserve Bank of Kansas City Economic Review* 2009(Q II): 77–102.

Ferrão J and Vale M (1995) Multi-purpose vehicles, a new opportunity for the periphery? Lessons from the Ford/VW project (Portugal). In Hudson R and Schamp EW (eds.) *Towards a New map of automobile manufacturing in Europe? New production concepts and spatial restructuring.* Berlin: Springer, pp. 195–217.

Firn JR (1975) External control and regional development: The case of Scotland. *Environment and Planning A: Economy and Space* 7(4): 393–414.

Fischer AM (2015) The end of peripheries? On the enduring relevance of structuralism for understanding contemporary global development. *Development and Change* 46(4): 700–732.

Frank AG (2010 [1967]) Sociology of development and the underdevelopment of sociology. In Chew SC and Lauderdale P (eds.) *Theory and methodology of world development.* New York: Palgrave Macmillan, pp. 19–73.

Freyssenet M (2009) Wrong forecasts and unexpected changes: The world that changed the machine. In Freyssenet M (ed.)*The second automobile revolution: Trajectories of the world carmakers in the 21st century.* Houndmills, Basingstoke: Palgrave Macmillan, pp. 7–37.

Freyssenet M and Lung Y (2000) Between globalisation and regionalisation: What is the future of the motor industry? In Humphrey J, Lecler Y and Salerno MS (eds.) *Global strategies and local realities: The auto industry in emerging markets.* Houndmills, Basingstoke: Palgrave Macmillan, pp. 72–94.

Freyssenet M and Lung Y (2004) Multinational carmakers' regional strategies. In Carrillo J, Lung Y and van Tulder R (eds.) *Cars, carriers of regionalism?* Houndmills, Basingstoke: Palgrave Macmillan, pp. 42–54.

Freyssenet M, Shimizu K and Volpato G (2003a) Conclusion: Regionalization of the European automobile industry, more than globalization. In Freyssenet M, Shimizu K and Volpato G (eds.) *Globalization or regionalization of the European car industry?* Houndmills, Basingstoke: Palgrave Macmillan, pp. 241–263.

Freyssenet M, Shimizu K and Volpato G (2003b) *Globalization or regionalization of the European car industry?* Houndmills, Basingstoke: Palgrave Macmillan.

Friedmann J (1967) *A general theory of polarized development.* Santiago: The Ford Foundation, Urban and Regional Advisory Program in Chile.

Frigant V (2007) Between internationalisation and proximity: The internationalisation process of automotive first tier suppliers. *Cahiers du GREThA No. 2007-13.* Bordeaux: Université Montesquieu Bordeaux.

Frigant V (2009) Winners and losers in the auto parts industry: Trajectories followed by the main first tier suppliers over the past decade. In Freyssenet M (ed.) *The second automobile revolution: Trajectories of the world carmakers in the 21st century.* Houndmills, Basingstoke: Palgrave Macmillan, pp. 419–442.

Frigant V (2011a) Are carmakers on the wrong track? Too much outsourcing in an imperfect-modular industry can be harmful. *International Journal of Manufacturing Technology and Management* 22(4): 324–343.

Frigant V (2011b) *Egyptian pyramid or Aztec pyramid: How should we describe the industrial architecture of automotive supply chains in Europe?* Bordeaux: Université Montesquieu Bordeaux IV.

Frigant V (2013) Putting SMEs back at the heart of automotive supply chain analysis. *International Journal of Automotive Technology and Management* 13(4): 315–319.

Frigant V and Layan J-B (2009) Modular production and the new division of labour within Europe: The perspective of French automotive parts suppliers. *European Urban and Regional Studies* 16(1): 11–25.

Frigant V and Lung Y (2002) Geographical proximity and supplying relationships in modular production. *International Journal of Urban and Regional Research* 26(4): 742–755.

Frigant V and Miollan S (2014) The geographical restructuring of the European automobile industry in the 2000s. *MPRA Paper 53509*. Munich: MPRA.

Frigant V and Zumpe M (2017) Regionalisation or globalisation of automotive production networks? Lessons from import patterns of four European countries. *Growth and Change* 48(4): 661–681.

Fröbel F, Heinrichs J and Kreye O (1980) *The new international division of labour: Structural unemployment in industrialised countries and industrialisation in developing countries.* Cambridge: Cambridge University Press.

Fuller C and Phelps N (2004) Multinational enterprises, repeat investment and the role of aftercare services in Wales and Ireland. *Regional Studies* 38(7): 783–801.

Gallagher KP and Zarsky L (2007) *The enclave economy: Foreign investment and sustainable development in Mexico's Silicon Valley.* Cambridge, MA: The MIT Press.

Gatejel L (2017) A socialist–capitalist joint venture: Citroën in Romania during the 1980s. *The Journal of Transport History* 38(1): 70–87.

Gelb A, Ramachandran V, Meyer CJ, Wadhwa D and Navis K (2020) Can sub-Saharan Africa be a manufacturing destination? Labor costs, price levels, and the role of industrial policy. *Journal of Industry, Competition and Trade* 20(2): 335–357.

Gereffi G (1999) International trade and industrial upgrading in the apparel commodity chain. *Journal of International Economics* 48(1): 37–70.

Gereffi G (2005) The global economy: Organization, governance, and development. In Smelser NJ and Swedberg R (eds.) *The handbook of economic sociology*, 2nd ed. Princeton, NJ: Princeton University Press, pp. 160–182.

Gereffi G (2013) Global value chains in a post-Washington Consensus world. *Review of International Political Economy* 21(1): 9–37.

Gereffi G (2018) *Global value chains and development: Redefining the contours of 21st century capitalism.* Cambridge: Cambridge University Press.

Gereffi G (2020) What does the COVID-19 pandemic teach us about global value chains? The case of medical supplies. *Journal of International Business Policy* 3(3): 287–301.

Gereffi G, Humphrey J and Sturgeon T (2005) The governance of global value chains. *Review of International Political Economy* 12(1): 78–104.

Gereffi G and Korzeniewicz M (eds.) (1994) *Commodity chains and global capitalism.* Westport, CT: Praeger.

Gereffi G, Lim H-C and Lee J (2021) Trade policies, firm strategies, and adaptive reconfigurations of global value chains. *Journal of International Business Policy* 4(4): 506–522. DOI: 10.1057/s42214-021-00102-z.

Gersch I (2019) Foreign direct investment and local supplier upgrading: The case of grocery retail in Turkey. *Geografisk Tidsskrift-Danish Journal of Geography* 119(2): 108–120.

Gibbs N (2019a) Budget constraints. *Automotive News Europe*, March, 15–18.

Gibbs N (2019b) Vision of the future. *Automotive Manufacturing Solutions*, June 10.

Giroud A (2012) Mind the gap: How linkages strengthen understanding of spillovers. *European Journal of Development Research* 24(1): 20–25.

Giroud A, Jindra B and Marek P (2012) Heterogeneous FDI in transition economies: A novel approach to assess the developmental impact of backward linkages. *World Development* 40(11): 2206–2220.

Giroud A and Scott-Kennel J (2009) MNE linkages in international business: A framework for analysis. *International Business Review* 18(6): 555–566.

Glaeser EL and Kohlhase JE (2004) Cities, regions and the decline of transport costs. *Papers in Regional Science* 83(1): 197–228.

Görg H and Greenaway D (2004) Much ado about nothing? Do domestic firms really benefit from foreign direct investment? *World Bank Research Observer* 19(2): 171–197.

Görg H and Strobl E (2001) Multinational companies and productivity spillovers: A meta-analysis. *The Economic Journal* 111(475): 723–739.

Görg H and Strobl E (2005) Spillovers from foreign firms through worker mobility: An empirical investigation. *Scandinavian Journal of Economics* 107(4): 693–709.

Grabher G (1997) Adaptation at the cost of adaptability? Restructuring the eastern German regional economy. In Grabher G and Stark D (eds.) *Restructuring networks in post-socialism: Legacies, linkages, and localities.* Oxford: Oxford University Press, pp. 107–134.

Grzegorczyk M (2021) CEE risks being "left behind" in e-mobility race. *Emerging Europe*, June 29.

Guga Ş (2019) Automotive industry, which way? Global trends, peripheral perspectives. In Drahokoupil J, Guga Ş, Martišková M, Pícl M and Pogátsa Z (eds.) *The future of employment in the car sector: Four country perspectives from Central and Eastern Europe.* Prague: Friedrich Ebert Stiftung, pp. 60–97.

Gui-Diby SL and Renard M-F (2015) Foreign Direct investment inflows and the industrialization of African countries. *World Development* 74: 43–57.

Gunby P, Jin Y and Robert Reed W (2017) Did FDI really cause Chinese economic growth? A meta-analysis. *World Development* 90: 242–255.

Guzik R, Domański B and Gwosdz K (2020) Automotive industry dynamics in Central Europe. In Covarrubias VA and Ramírez Perez SM (eds.) *New frontiers of the automobile industry: Exploring geographies, technology, and institutional challenges.* Cham: Palgrave Macmillan, pp. 377–397.

Haberly D and Wójcik D (2015) Tax havens and the production of offshore FDI: An empirical analysis. *Journal of Economic Geography* 15(1): 75–101.

Haberly D and Wójcik D (2022) *Sticky power: Global financial networks in the world economy.* Oxford: Oxford University Press.

Hallin C and Lind CH (2012) Revisiting the external impact of MNCs: An empirical study of the mechanisms behind knowledge spillovers from MNC subsidiaries. *International Business Review* 21(2): 167–179.

Hampel C (2021) Czech Republic to grow charging stations with Skoda. electrive.com, October 13. Available at: www.electrive.com/2021/10/13/czech-republic-to-grow-charging-stations-with-skoda/ (accessed November 23, 2021).

Hampel C (2022a) Ford moves forward plans to convert German plant. electrive.com, October 10. Available at: www.electrive.com/2022/10/26/ford-moves-forward-plans-to-convert-german-plant/ (accessed November 6, 2023).

Hampel C (2022b) Geely licenses electric platform to Polish carmaker EMP. electrive.com, November 11. Available at: www.electrive.com/2022/10/26/ford-moves-forward-plans-to-convert-german-plant/ (accessed October 31, 2023).

Hampel C (2022c) Volvo will build electric cars at a new plant in Slovakia. electrive.com, July 2. Available at: www.electrive.com/2022/07/02/volvo-to-construct-new-plant-in-slovakia/ (accessed January 5, 2023).

Hansen MW, Pedersen T and Petersen B (2009) MNC strategies and linkage effects in developing countries. *Journal of World Business* 44(2): 121–130.

Harding T and Javorcik BS (2011) Roll out the red carpet and they will come: Investment promotion and FDI inflows. *Economic Journal* 121(557): 1445–1476.

Harrison D (2021) Electric vehicle battery supply chain analysis: How battery demand and production are reshaping the automotive industry. Automotive from Ultima Media, June. Available at: www.automotivemanufacturingsolutions.com/ev-battery-production/electric-vehicle-battery-supply-chain-analysis-2021-how-lithium-ion-battery-demand-and-production-are-reshaping-the-automotive-industry/41938.article (accessed October 3, 2022).

Harrison D (2022) Russia's invasion of Ukraine is a long-term risk for the automotive supply chain. *Automotive Logistics*, March 8.

Harvey D (1982) *The limits to capital*. Oxford: Basil Blackwell.

Harvey D (1987) Three myths in search of a reality in urban studies. *Environment and Planning D: Society and Space* 5(4): 367–376.

Harvey D (2001) *Spaces of capital: Towards a critical geography*. New York: Routledge.

Harvey D (2005a) *A brief history of neoliberalism*. Oxford: Oxford University Press.

Harvey D (2005b) *Spaces of neoliberalization: Towards a theory of uneven geographical development*. Munich: Franz Steiner Verlag.

Harvey D (2010) *The enigma of capital and the crises of capitalism*. Oxford: Oxford University Press.

Harvey D (2014) *Seventeen contradictions and the end of capitalism*. London: Profile Books.

Hatani F (2009) The logic of spillover interception: The impact of global supply chains in China. *Journal of World Business* 44(2): 158–166.

Havas A (1997) Foreign direct investment and intra-industry trade: The case of the automotive industry in Central Europe. In Dyker DA (ed.) *The technology of transition: Science and technology policies for transition countries*. Budapest: Central European University Press, pp. 211–240.

Havas A (2000) Changing patterns of inter- and intra-regional division of labour: Central Europe's long and winding road. In Humphrey J, Lecler Y and Salerno MS (eds.) *Global strategies and local realities: The auto industry in emerging markets*. Houndmills, Basingstoke: Palgrave Macmillan, pp. 234–262.

Hayter R (1982) Truncation, the international firm and regional policy. *Area* 14(4): 277–282.

Heines H (2022) *Battery atlas 2022: Shaping the European lithium-ion battery industry.* Aachen: RWTH Aachen University.

Henderson J (1989) *The globalisation of high technology production: Society, space and semiconductors in the restructuring of the modern world.* London: Routledge.

Henderson J, Dicken P, Hess M, Coe N and Yeung HWC (2002) Global production networks and the analysis of economic development. *Review of International Political Economy* 9(3): 436–464.

Henry I (2020) AMS on Africa: Part 4 – Morocco aims for a million. *Automotive Manufacturing Solutions*, February 11.

Hess M (2004) "Spatial" relationships? Towards a reconceptualization of embeddedness. *Progress in Human Geography* 28(2): 165–186.

HIPA (2020) *Automotive industry Hungary 2019: Automotive CEO survey.* Budapest: Hungarian Investment Promotion Agency.

Hirschman AO (1958) *The strategy of economic development.* New Haven, CT: Yale University Press.

HN (2019) ČEZ se dohodl s Australany na spolupráci při těžbě lithia, v těžařské firmě Geomet získá za 870 milionů většinu. *Hospodářské noviny*, November 20.

HN (2021) Česká gigafactory: Ročně by mohla vyrobit baterie až pro 800 tisíc aut. *Hospodářské noviny*, July 7.

HN (2023) Konečně se tu dá dýchat a mají se vrátit těžaři? Sever pochybuje o těžbě lithia, která má nastartovat Česko. *Hospodářské noviny*, September 9.

Hood N and Young S (1976) United States Investment in Scotland: Aspects of branch factory syndrome. *Scottish Journal of Political Economy* 23(3): 279–294.

Hopkins TK and Wallerstein I (1977) Patterns of development of the modern world-system. *Review (Fernand Braudel Center)* 1(2): 111–145.

Hopkins TK and Wallerstein I (1986) Commodity chains in the world-economy prior to 1800. *Review (Fernand Braudel Center)* 10(1): 157–170.

Horner R (2014) Strategic decoupling, recoupling and global production networks: India's pharmaceutical industry. *Journal of Economic Geography* 14(6): 1117–1140.

Horner R (2017) Beyond facilitator? State roles in global value chains and global production networks. *Geography Compass* 11(2): e12307.

Hovet J (2023) Volkswagen puts off east European gigafactory amid sluggish EV demand. Reuters, November 1. Available at: www.reuters.com/business/autos-transportation/volkswagen-not-planning-next-gigafactory-site-present-blume-2023-11-01/ (accessed X).

Howells J (1990) The location and organization of research and development: New horizons. *Research Policy* 19(2): 133–146.

Hudson R (2011) Spatial circuits of value. In Pike A, Rodriguez-Pose J and Tomaney J (eds.) *Handbook of local and regional development.* London: Routledge, pp. 109–118.

Hudson R and Schamp EW (1995a) Interdependent and uneven development in the spatial reorganisation of the automobile production systems in Europe. In Hudson R and Schamp EW (eds.) *Towards a new map of automobile manufacturing in Europe? New production concepts and spatial restructuring.* Berlin: Springer, pp. 219–243.

Hudson R and Schamp EW (1995b) *Towards a new map of automobile manufacturing in Europe? New production concepts and spatial restructuring.* Berlin: Springer.

Huizinga H and Laeven L (2008) International profit shifting within multinationals: A multi-country perspective. *Journal of Public Economics* 92(5–6): 1164–1182.

Humphrey J (2000) Assembler-supplier relations in the auto industry: Globalisation and national development. *Competition & Change* 4(3): 245–271.

Humphrey J (2003) Globalization and supply chain networks: The auto industry in Brazil and India. *Global Networks-a Journal of Transnational Affairs* 3(2): 121–141.

Humphrey J, Lecler Y and Salerno MS (eds.) (2000) *Global strategies and local realities: The auto industry in emerging markets.* Basingstoke: Palgrave Macmillan.

Humphrey J and Memedovic O (2003) *The global automotive industry value chain: What prospects for upgrading by developing countries.* Vienna: UNIDO.

Humphrey J and Oeter A (2000) Motor industry policies in emerging markets: Globalisation and the promotion of domestic industry. In Humphrey J, Lecler Y and Salerno MS (eds.) *Global strategies and local realities: The auto industry in emerging markets.* Houndmills, Basingstoke: Palgrave Macmillan, pp. 42–71.

Humphrey J and Schmitz H (2002) How does insertion in global value chains affect upgrading in industrial clusters? *Regional Studies* 36(9): 1017–1027.

Humphrey J and Schmitz H (2004) Governance in global value chains. In Schmitz H (ed.) *Local enterprises in the global economy: Issues of governance and upgrading.* Cheltenham: Edward Elgar, pp. 95–109.

Hungarian Insider (2021) Stellantis to produce new engine in Szentgotthárd. *Hungarian Insider*, March 1.

Hutzschenreuter T, Matt T and Kleindienst I (2020) Going subnational: A literature review and research agenda. *Journal of World Business* 55(4): 101076.

Hymer S (1970) The efficiency (contradictions) of multinational corporations. *American Economic Review* 60(2): 441–448.

Hymer S (1972) The multinational corporation and the law of uneven development. In Bhagwati JN (ed.) *Economics and world order.* London: Macmillan, pp. 113–140.

Hymer S (1976 [1960]) *The international operations of national firms: A study of direct foreign investment.* Cambridge, MA: The MIT Press.

Iammarino S (2018) FDI and regional development policy. *Journal of International Business Policy* 1(3-4): 157–183.

Iammarino S and McCann P (2013) *Multinationals and economic geography: Location, technology and innovation.* Cheltenham: Edward Elgar.

Iammarino S and McCann P (2018) Network geographies and geographical networks: Co-dependence and coevolution of multinational enterprises and space. In Clark GL, Feldman MP, Gertler MS and Wójcik D (eds.) *The new Oxford handbook of economic geography.* Oxford: Oxford University Press, pp. 1–20.

Iršová Z and Havránek T (2013) Determinants of horizontal spillovers from FDI: Evidence from a large meta-analysis. *World Development* 42: 1–15.

Irwin J (2022) Invasion of Ukraine cuts supply of neon, possibly impacting chip shortage. *Automotive News Europe*, March 5.

Isaksen A and Trippl M (2017) Innovation in space: The mosaic of regional innovation patterns. *Oxford Review of Economic Policy* 33(1): 122–140.

Ivarsson I and Alvstam CG (2005) The effect of spatial proximity on technology transfer from TNCs to local suppliers in developing countries: The case of AB Volvo in Asia and Latin America. *Economic Geography* 81(1): 83–111.

Jacobs AJ (2016) Automotive FDI and dependent development: The case of Slovakia's city-regions in the Bratislava-Zilina corridor. *Open Urban Studies and Demography Journal* 2(1): 1–19.

Jacobs AJ (2017) *Automotive FDI in emerging Europe: Shifting locales in the motor vehicle industry*. London: Palgrave Macmillan.

Jacobs AJ (2019) *The automotive industry and European integration: The divergent paths of Belgium and Spain*. London: Palgrave Macmillan.

Jakubiak M, Kolesar P, Izvorski I and Kurekova L (2008) *The automotive industry in the Slovak Republic: Recent developments and impact on growth. Working Paper No. 29, Commission on Growth and Development*. Washington, DC: The International Bank for Reconstruction and Development/The World Bank.

Javorcik BS (2004) Does foreign direct investment increase the productivity of domestic firms? In search of spillovers through backward linkages. *American Economic Review* 94(3): 605–627.

Jensen NM (2003) Democratic governance and multinational corporations: Political regimes and inflows of foreign direct investment. *International Organization* 57(3): 587–616.

Jessop B (2013) Revisiting the regulation approach: Critical reflections on the contradictions, dilemmas, fixes and crisis dynamics of growth regimes. *Capital & Class* 37(1): 5–24.

Jetin B (2020) Who will control the electric vehicle market? *International Journal of Automotive Technology and Management* 20(2): 156–177.

Jo HJ, Jeong JH and Kim C (2023) *Agile against lean: An inquiry into the production system of Hyundai motor*. Singapore: Palgrave Macmillan.

Jo T-H, Chester L and D'Ippoliti C (2018) *The Routledge handbook of heterodox economics: Theorizing, analyzing, and transforming capitalism*. London: Routledge.

Jones PN (1993) On defining a Western European automobile industry: Problems and potentials. *Erkunde* 47(1): 25–39.

Jordaan JA, Douw W and Qiang CZ (2020) *Multinational corporation affiliates, backward linkages, and productivity spillovers in developing and emerging economies: evidence and policy making. Policy Research Working Paper 9364*. Washington, DC: The World Bank.

Jürgens U and Krzywdzinski M (2009a) Changing East–West division of labour in the european automotive industry. *European Urban and Regional Studies* 16(1): 27–42.

Jürgens U and Krzywdzinski M (2009b) Work models in the Central Eastern European car industry: Towards the high road? *Industrial Relations Journal* 40(6): 471–490.

Jürgens U and Krzywdzinski M (2008) Relocation and East-West competition: The case of the European automotive industry. *International Journal of Automotive Technology and Management* 8(2): 145–169.

Kaneko J and Nojiri W (2008) The logistics of just-in-time between parts suppliers and car assemblers in Japan. *Journal of Transport Geography* 16(3): 155–173.

Kano L, Tsang EWK and Yeung HWC (2020) Global value chains: A review of the multi-disciplinary literature. *Journal of International Business Studies* 51(4): 577–622.

Kaplinsky R (1998) *Globalisation, industrialization and sustainable growth: The pursuit of the Nth rent.* Brighton: University of Sussex, Institute of Development Studies.

Kaplinsky R (2000) Globalisation and unequalisation: What can be learned from value chain analysis? *Journal of Development Studies* 37(2): 117–146.

Kaplinsky R and Morris M (2008) Value chain analysis: A tool for enhancing export supply policies. *International Journal of Technological Learning, Innovation and Development* 1(3): 283–308.

Kentor J (1998) The long-term effects of foreign investment dependence on economic growth, 1940–1990. *American Journal of Sociology* 103(4): 1024–1046.

Ketterer TD and Rodríguez-Pose A (2018) Institutions vs. "first-nature" geography: What drives economic growth in Europe's regions? *Papers in Regional Science* 97 (S1): S25–S62.

Kleibert JM (2014) Strategic coupling in "next wave cities": Local institutional actors and the offshore service sector in the Philippines. *Singapore Journal of Tropical Geography* 35(2): 245–260.

Kleibert JM (2016) Global production networks, offshore services and the branch-plant syndrome. *Regional Studies* 50(12): 1995–2009.

Klein M, Aaron C and Hadjimichael B (2001) *Foreign direct investment and poverty reduction. Policy Research Working Paper 2613.* Washington, DC: The World Bank, 41.

Kleinert J (2003) Growing trade in intermediate goods: Outsourcing, global sourcing, or increasing importance of MNE networks? *Review of International Economics* 11(3): 464–482.

Klier T and McMillen D (2015) Plant location patterns in the European automobile supplier industry. *Growth and Change* 46(4): 558–573.

Klier T and Rubenstein J (2008) *Who really made your car? Restructuring and geographic change in the auto industry.* Kalamazoo, MI: W.E. Upjohn Institute for Employment Research.

Klier T and Rubenstein J (2010) The changing geography of North American motor vehicle production. *Cambridge Journal of Regions Economy and Society* 3(3): 335–347.

Kohli A (2004) *State-directed development: Political power and industrialization in the global periphery.* Cambridge: Cambridge University Press.

Kowalski P (2020) *Will the post-COVID world be less open to foreign direct investment?* London: CEPR Press.

KPMG (2017) Corporate tax rates table. Available at: https://home.kpmg.com/xx/en/home/services/tax/tax-tools-and-resources/tax-rates-online/corporate-tax-rates-table.html (accessed December 4, 2017).

Krzywdzinski M (2014) How the EU's Eastern enlargement changed the German productive model: The case of the automotive industry. *Revue de la régulation* (15/spring): 1–20. DOI: 10.4000/regulation.10663.

Kuczynski P-P (2003) The financial system. In Kuczynski P-P and Williamson J (eds.) *After the Washington Consensus: Restarting growth and reform in Latin America.* Washington, DC: Institute for International Economics, pp. 102–121.

Kuemmerle W (1999) Foreign direct investment in industrial research in the pharmaceutical and electronics industries: Results from a survey of multinational firms. *Research Policy* 28(2–3): 179–193.

Kureková L (2012) Success against all odds? Determinants of sectoral rise and decline in Central Europe. *East European Politics and Societies* 26(3): 643–664.

Kureková Mýtna L (2018) The automotive industry in Central Europe: A success? *IZA World of Labor*. Available at: https://wol.iza.org/articles/the-automotive-industry-in-central-europe-a-success/long (accessed X).

Kurz C and Wittke V (1998) Using industrial capacities as a way of integrating the Central and East European economies. In Zysman J and Schwartz A (eds.) *Enlarging Europe: The industrial foundations of a new political reality*. Berkeley: University of California at Berkeley, pp. 63–95.

Lagendijk A (1995a) The foreign takeover of the Spanish automobile industry: A growth analysis of internationalization. *Regional Studies* 29(4): 381–393.

Lagendijk A (1995b) The impact of internationalization and rationalization of production on the Spanish automobile industry, 1950–90. *Environment and Planning A* 27(2): 321–343.

Lagendijk A (1997) Towards an integrated automotive industry in Europe: A "merging filiere" perspective. *European Urban and Regional Studies* 4(1): 5–18.

Lampón JF, Lago-Peñas S and Cabanelas P (2016) Can the periphery achieve core? The case of the automobile components industry in Spain. *Papers in Regional Science* 95(3): 595–612.

Lampón JF, Lago-Peñas S and González-Benito J (2015) International relocation and production geography in the European automobile components sector: The case of Spain. *International Journal of Production Research* 53(5): 1409–1424.

Larsson A (2002) The development and regional significance of the automotive industry: Supplier parks in Western Europe. *International Journal of Urban and Regional Research* 26(4): 767–784.

Laulajainen R and Stafford HA (1995) *Corporate geography: business location principles and cases*. Dordrecht: Springer Science+Business Media.

Layan J-B (2000) The integration of peripheral markets: A comparison of Spain and Mexico. In Humphrey J, Lecler Y and Salerno MS (eds.) *Global strategies and local realities: The auto industry in emerging markets*. Basingstoke: Palgrave Macmillan, pp. 16–41.

Layan J-B (2006) L'innovation péricentrale dans l'industrie automobile: une gestion territoriale du risque de résistance au changement. *Flux* 1(63–64): 42–53.

Layan J-B and Lung Y (2004) The dynamics of regional integration in the European car industry. In Carrillo J, Lung Y and van Tulder R (eds.) *Cars, carriers of regionalism?* Houndmills, Basingstoke: Palgrave Macmillan, pp. 57–74.

Layan J-B and Lung Y (2007) Les nouvelles configurations de l'espace automobile méditerranéen. *Région et Développement* (25): 157–175.

Lee K, Gao X and Li X (2017) Industrial catch-up in China: A sectoral systems of innovation perspective. *Cambridge Journal of Regions, Economy and Society* 10(1): 59–76.

Lee Y-S, Heo I and Kim H (2014) The role of the state as an inter-scalar mediator in globalizing liquid crystal display industry development in South Korea. *Review of International Political Economy* 21(1): 102–129.

Levinson M (2006) *The box: How the shipping container made the world smaller and the world economy bigger.* Princeton, NJ: Princeton University Press.

Lia Y and Cantwellb J (2021) Rapid FDI of emerging-market firms: Foreign participation and leapfrogging in the establishment chain. *Transnational Corporations* 28(1): 51–78.

Liebreich J (2021) Česko chce vyrábět baterie do elektromobilů. Mocně na to láká Volkswagen. *E15*, March 31.

Linares-Navarro E, Pedersen T and Pla-Barber J (2014) Fine slicing of the value chain and offshoring of essential activities: Empirical evidence from European multinationals. *Journal of Business Economics and Management* 15(1): 111–134.

Lloyd P and Shutt J (1985) Recession and restructuring in the North-West region, 1975–82: The implications of recent events. In Massey D and Meegan R (eds.) *Politics and method: Contrasting studies in industrial geography.* London: Methuen, pp. 15–56.

Lovering J (1999) Theory led by policy: The inadequacies of the "new regionalism" (illustrated from the case of Wales). *International Journal of Urban and Regional Research* 23(2): 379–395.

Lung Y (2000) Is the rise of emerging countries as automobile producers an irreversible phenomenon? In Humphrey J, Lecler Y and Salerno MS (eds.) *Global strategies and local realities: The auto industry in emerging markets.* Houndmills, Basingstoke: Palgrave Macmillan, pp. 16–41.

Lung Y (2004) The changing geography of the European automobile system. *International Journal of Automotive Technology and Management* 4(2/3): 137–165.

Lung Y and Volpato G (2002) Redesigning the automakers–suppliers relationships in the automotive industry. *International Journal of Automotive Technology and Management* 2(1): 3–9.

MacKinnon D (2012) Beyond strategic coupling: Reassessing the firm-region nexus in global production networks. *Journal of Economic Geography* 12(1): 227–245.

MacKinnon D, Cumbers A and Chapman K (2002) Learning, innovation and regional development: A critical appraisal of recent debates. *Progress in Human Geography* 26(3): 293–311.

MacKinnon D, Dawley S, Pike A and Cumbers A (2019) Rethinking path creation: A geographical political economy approach. *Economic Geography* 95(2): 113–135.

MacKinnon D and Phelps NA (2001a) Devolution and the territorial politics of foreign direct investment. *Political Geography* 20(3): 353–379.

MacKinnon D and Phelps NA (2001b) Regional governance and foreign direct investment: The dynamics of institutional change in Wales and North-East England. *Geoforum* 32(2): 255–269.

Mahutga MC (2014) Global models of networked organization, the positional power of nations and economic development. *Review of International Political Economy* 21(1): 157–194.

Mair A (1993) New growth poles? Just-in-time manufacturing and local economic development strategy. *Regional Studies* 27(3): 207–221.

Maiza A and Bustillo R (2018) Analysis of the relevance of China's development for main European automotive manufacturing countries. *Economia e Politica Industriale* 45(3): 403–424.

Malecki EJ (1980) Corporate organization of R and D and the location of technological activities. *Regional Studies* 14(3): 219–234.

Malmberg A, Sölvell Ö and Zander I (1996) Spatial clustering, local accumulation of knowledge and firm competitiveness. *Geografiska Annaler: Series B, Human Geography* 78(2): 85–97.

Manthey N (2019) Electric car battery line to be built in Slovakia. electrive.com, July 29. Available at: www.electrive.com/2019/07/29/electric-car-battery-line-to-be-build-in-slovakia/ (accessed November 5, 2021).

Manthey N (2021a) China's cheapest electric car coming to Europe. electrive.com, February 15. Available at: 2/15/chinas-cheapest-electric-car-coming-to-europe/ (accessed March 15, 2022).

Manthey N (2021b) Nidec is gearing up its electric motor business in Europe. electrive.com, April 9. Available at: www.electrive.com/2021/04/09/strategy-brief-nidec-gears-up-european-electric-motor-business/ (accessed March 15, 2022).

Markiewicz O (2020) Stuck in second gear? EU integration and the evolution of Poland's automotive industry. *Review of International Political Economy* 27(5): 1147–1169. DOI: 10.1080/09692290.2019.1681019.

Martin R (2000) Institutional approaches in economic geography. In Sheppard E and Barnes TJ (eds.) *A companion to economic geography*. Oxford: Blackwell, pp. 77–94.

Martin R and Sunley P (2006) Path dependence and regional economic evolution. *Journal of Economic Geography* 6(4): 395–437.

Martin WG (ed.) (1990) *Semiperipheral states in the world-economy*. Westport, CT: Greenwood Press.

Martínez-Noya A and Narula R (2018) What more can we learn from R&D alliances? A review and research agenda. *BRQ Business Research Quarterly* 21(3): 195–212.

Martišková M, Kahancová M and Kostolný J (2021) Negotiating wage (in)equality: Changing union strategies in high-wage and low-wage sectors in Czechia and Slovakia. *Transfer: European Review of Labour and Research* 27(1): 75–96.

Massey D (1979) In what sense a regional problem? *Regional Studies* 13(2): 233–243.

Massey D (1995 [1984]) *Spatial divisions of labour: Social structures and the geography of production*. London: Macmillan.

Massini S and Miozzo M (2012) Outsourcing and offshoring of business services: Challenges to theory, management and geography of innovation. *Regional Studies* 46(9): 1219–1242.

Maxton GP and Wormald J (2004) *Time for a model change: Re-engineering the global automotive industry*. Cambridge: Cambridge University Press.

McKinsey&Company (2021) *Why the automotive future is electric: Mainstream EVs will transform the automotive industry and help decarbonize the planet*. McKinsey Center for Future Mobility.

Melachroinos KA and Spence N (1999) Regional economic performance and sunk costs. *Regional Studies* 33(9): 843–855.

Mencinger J (2003) Does foreign direct investment always enhance economic growth? *Kyklos* 56(4): 491–508.

Meyer KE (2004) Perspectives on multinational enterprises in emerging economies. *Journal of International Business Studies* 35(4): 259–276.

Meyer KE and Sinani E (2009) When and where does foreign direct investment generate positive spillovers? A meta-analysis. *Journal of International Business Studies* 40(7): 1075–1094.

Micek G, Guzik R, Gwosdz K and Domański B (2021) Newcomers from the periphery: The international expansion of Polish automotive companies. *Energies* 14(9): 2617.

Midler C, Jullien B and Lung Y (2017) *Rethinking innovation and design for emerging markets: Inside the Renault Kwid project.* Boca Raton, FL: CRC Press.

MIEPO (2017) *Automotive components and industry overview: Republic of Moldova.* Chişinău: Moldovan Investment and Export Promotion Organization.

Milberg W and Winkler D (2011) Economic and social upgrading in global production networks: Problems of theory and measurement. *International Labour Review* 150 (3-4): 341–365.

Milberg W and Winkler D (2013) *Outsourcing economics: Global value chains in capitalist development.* Cambridge: Cambridge University Press.

Moran TH (1999) *Foreign direct investment and development: The new policy agenda for developing countries and economies in transition.* Washington, DC: Institute for International Economics.

Moran TH, Graham EM and Blomström M (eds.) (2005) *Does foreign direct investment promote development?* Washington, DC: Institute for International Economics, Center for Global Development.

Mordue G and Sweeney B (2020) Neither core nor periphery: The search for competitive advantage in the automotive semi-periphery. *Growth and Change* 51(1): 34–57.

Morgan K (1997) The learning region: Institutions, innovation and regional renewal. *Regional Studies* 31(5): 491–503.

Morris M, Kaplinsky R and Kaplan D (2011) *Commodities and linkages: Meeting the policy challenge.* MMCP Discussion Paper No. 14. Cape Town: University of Cape Town and Open University.

Morrissey O (2012) FDI in sub-Saharan Africa: Few linkages, fewer spillovers. *European Journal of Development Research* 24(1): 26–31.

Mudambi R (2008) Location, control and innovation in knowledge-intensive industries. *Journal of Economic Geography* 8(5): 699–725.

Munyi EN (2020) Africa's stalled structural transformation: The end of the flying geese? *Review of African Political Economy* 47(165): 474–483. DOI: 10.1080/ 03056244.2020.1789855.

Murphy JT (2019) Global production network dis/articulations in Zanzibar: Practices and conjunctures of exclusionary development in the tourism industry. *Journal of Economic Geography* 19(4): 943–971.

Narula R (2018) Multinational firms and the extractive sectors in the 21st century: Can they drive development? *Journal of World Business* 53(1): 85–91.

Narula R and Bellak C (2009) EU enlargement and consequences for FDI assisted industrial development. *Transnational Corporations* 18(2): 69–89.

Narula R and Driffield N (2012) Does FDI cause development? The ambiguity of the evidence and why it matters. *European Journal of Development Research* 24(1): 1–7.

Narula R and Dunning JH (2010) Multinational enterprises, development and globalization: Some clarifications and a research agenda. *Oxford Development Studies* 38(3): 263–287.

Nathan D and Sarkar S (2011) A note on profits, rents and wages in global production networks. *Economic & Political Weekly* 46(36): 53–57.

NC (2015) Angelika also fought for higher salary in front of PSA in Trnava: I will retire on €300 per month, which is shame. *Nový Čas*, March 7. Available at: www.cas.sk/

clanok/310061/za-vyssi-plat-pred-psa-v-trnave-bojovala-aj-angelika-do-dochodku-pojdem-s-300-eurami-to-je-hanba/ (accessed June 15, 2016).

Ndikumana L and Sarr M (2019) Capital flight, foreign direct investment and natural resources in Africa. *Resources Policy* 63: 101427.

Nestorović Č (1991) The automobile industry in the East: National and international strategies. *Eastern European Economics* 29(4): 34–85.

Nicolini M, Scarpa C and Valbonesi P (2017) Determinants of state aid to firms: The case of the European automotive industry. *Industrial and Corporate Change* 36(3): 399–420.

Nidec (2021) *Nidec holds groundbreaking ceremony to mark the construction of new factory in Serbia*. Nidec Corporation, December 10. Available at: www.nidec.com/en/corporate/news/2021/news1210-01/ (accessed March 15, 2022).

Nölke A and Vliegenthart A (2009) Enlarging the varieties of capitalism: The emergence of dependent market economies in East Central Europe. *World Politics* 61(4): 670–702.

Nunnenkamp P (2004) To what extent can foreign direct investment help achieve international development goals? *The World Economy* 27(5): 657–677.

Nunnenkamp P and Spatz J (2003) *Foreign direct investment and economic growth in developing countries: how relevant are host-country and industry characteristics?* *Kiel Working Paper, No. 1176.* Kiel: Kiel Institute for World Economics (IfW).

Oberhauser A (1987) Labour, production and the state: Decentralization of the French automobile industry. *Regional Studies* 21(5): 445–458.

OEC (2023) *The Observatory of Economic Complexity*. Available at: https://oec.world/en/ (accessed October 7, 2023).

OECD (2002) *Foreign Direct Investment for Development: Maximising Benefits, Minimising Costs*. Paris: OECD.

OECD (2020) *Global Outlook on Financing for Sustainable Development 2021*. Paris: OECD.

Oetzel J and Doh JP (2009) MNEs and development: A review and reconceptualization. *Journal of World Business* 44(2): 108–120.

OICA (2016) *World motor vehicle production by country and type, 1997–2015*. Paris: Organisation Internationale des Constructeurs d'Automobile.

OICA (2018) *World motor vehicle production by country and type, 1997–2017*. Paris: Organisation Internationale des Constructeurs d'Automobile.

OICA (2020) *World motor vehicle production by country and type, 1997–2019*. Paris: Organisation Internationale des Constructeurs d'Automobile.

OICA (2021) *World motor vehicle production by country and type, 1997–2020*. Paris: Organisation Internationale des Constructeurs d'Automobile.

OICA (2023) *World motor vehicle production by country and type, 1997–2022*. Paris: Organisation Internationale des Constructeurs d'Automobile.

Paprzycki R and Fukao K (2008) *Foreign direct investment in Japan: Multinationals' role in growth and globalization*. Cambridge: Cambridge University Press.

Pardi T (2020) Searching for industrial policy: The long decline of the French automotive industry. In Covarrubias V. A and Ramírez Perez SM (eds.) *New frontiers of the automobile industry: Exploring geographies, technology, and institutional challenges*. Cham: Palgrave Macmillan, pp. 113–135.

Pardi T (2021) Prospects and contradictions of the electrification of the European automotive industry: The role of European Union policy. *International Journal of Automotive Technology and Management* 21(3): 162–179.

Pavlínek P (1998) Foreign direct investment in the Czech Republic. *The Professional Geographer* 50(1): 71–85.

Pavlínek P (2000) Restructuring of the commercial vehicle industry in the Czech Republic. *Post-Soviet Geography and Economics* 41(4): 265–287.

Pavlínek P (2002a) Domestic privatisation and its effects on industrial enterprises in East-Central Europe: Evidence from the Czech motor component industry. *Europe-Asia Studies* 54(7): 1127–1150.

Pavlínek P (2002b) Restructuring the Central and Eastern European automobile industry: Legacies, trends, and effects of foreign direct investment. *Post-Soviet Geography and Economics* 43(1): 41–77.

Pavlínek P (2002c) The role of foreign direct investment in the privatisation and restructuring of the Czech motor industry. *Post-Communist Economies* 14(3): 359–379.

Pavlínek P (2002d) Transformation of the Central and East European passenger car industry: Selective peripheral integration through foreign direct investment. *Environment and Planning A* 34(9): 1685–1709.

Pavlínek P (2003) Transformation of the Czech automotive components industry through foreign direct investment. *Eurasian Geography and Economics* 44(3): 184–209.

Pavlínek P (2004) Regional development implications of foreign direct investment in Central Europe. *European Urban and Regional Studies* 11(1): 47–70.

Pavlínek P (2006) Restructuring of the Polish passenger car industry through foreign direct investment. *Eurasian Geography and Economics* 47(3): 353–377.

Pavlínek P (2008) *A successful transformation? Restructuring of the Czech automobile industry*. Heidelberg: Physica Verlag.

Pavlínek P (2012) The internationalization of corporate R&D and the automotive industry R&D of East-Central Europe. *Economic Geography* 88(3): 279–310.

Pavlínek P (2015a) The impact of the 2008–2009 crisis on the automotive industry: Global trends and firm-level effects in Central Europe. *European Urban and Regional Studies* 22(1): 20–40.

Pavlínek P (2015b) Škoda Auto: The transformation from a domestic to a Tier-two lead firm. In: Bryson JR, Clark J and Vanchan V (eds.) *Handbook of manufacturing industries in the world economy*. Cheltenham: Edward Elgar, pp. 345–361.

Pavlínek P (2016) Whose success? The state–foreign capital nexus and the development of the automotive industry in Slovakia. *European Urban and Regional Studies* 23(4): 571–593.

Pavlínek P (2017a) *Dependent growth: Foreign investment and the development of the automotive industry in East-Central Europe*. New York: Springer.

Pavlínek P (2017b) Truncated development in Eastern Europe. In Pavlínek P, Aláez-Aller R, Gil-Canaleta C Ullibarri-Arce M (eds.) *Foreign direct investment and the development of the automotive industry in Eastern and Southern Europe. Working Paper 2017.3*. Brussels: European Trade Union Institute, pp. 5–35.

Pavlínek P (2018) Global production networks, foreign direct investment, and supplier linkages in the integrated peripheries of the automotive industry. *Economic Geography* 94(2): 141–165.

Pavlínek P (2020) Restructuring and internationalization of the European automotive industry. *Journal of Economic Geography* 20(2): 509–541.

Pavlínek P (2022a) Relative positions of countries in the core–periphery structure of the European automotive industry. *European Urban and Regional Studies* 29(1): 59–84.

Pavlínek P (2022b) Revisiting economic geography and foreign direct investment in less developed regions. *Geography Compass* 16(4): e12617.

Pavlínek P (2024) Geopolitical decoupling in global production networks. *Economic Geography* 100(2): 138–169. DOI: 10.1007/978-3-7908-2040-9.

Pavlínek P, Domański B and Guzik R (2009) Industrial upgrading through foreign direct investment in Central European automotive manufacturing. *European Urban and Regional Studies* 16(1): 43–63.

Pavlínek P and Janák L (2007) Regional restructuring of the Škoda Auto supplier network in the Czech Republic. *European Urban and Regional Studies* 14(2): 133–155.

Pavlínek P and Smith A (1998) Internationalization and embeddedness in East-Central European transition: The contrasting geographies of inward investment in the Czech and Slovak Republics. *Regional Studies* 32(7): 619–638.

Pavlínek P and Ženka J (2010) The 2008–2009 automotive industry crisis and regional unemployment in Central Europe. *Cambridge Journal of Regions Economy and Society* 3(3): 349–365.

Pavlínek P and Ženka J (2011) Upgrading in the automotive industry: Firm-level evidence from Central Europe. *Journal of Economic Geography* 11(3): 559–586.

Pavlínek P and Ženka J (2016) Value creation and value capture in the automotive industry: Empirical evidence from Czechia. *Environment and Planning A* 48(5): 937–959.

Pavlínek P and Žížalová P (2016) Linkages and spillovers in global production networks: Firm-level analysis of the Czech automotive industry. *Journal of Economic Geography* 16(2): 331–363.

Peck J (2016) Macroeconomic geographies. *Area Development & Policy* 1(3): 305–322.

Peet R and Thrift N (eds.) (1989) *New models in geography: The political-economy perspective.* Winchester: Unwin Hyman.

Pennings E and Sleuwaegen L (2000) International relocation: Firm and industry determinants. *Economics Letters* 67(2): 179–186.

Perkmann M (2006) Extraregional linkages and the territorial embeddedness of multinational branch plants: Evidence from the South Tyrol region in northeast Italy. *Economic Geography* 82(4): 421–441.

Perrons DC (1981) The role of Ireland in the new international division of labour: A proposed framework for regional analysis. *Regional Studies* 15(2): 81–100.

Peteraf MA (1993) The cornerstones of competitive advantage: A resource-based view. *Strategic Management Journal* 14(3): 179–191.

Phelps NA (1993a) Branch plants and the evolving spatial division-of-labor: A study of material linkage change in the northern region of England. *Regional Studies* 27(2): 87–101.

Phelps NA (1993b) Contemporary industrial restructuring and linkage change in an older industrial region: Examples from the northeast of England. *Environment and Planning A* 25(6): 863–882.

Phelps NA (1996) Collaborative buyer-supplier relations and the formation of centralised networks. *Geoforum* 27(3): 393–407.

Phelps NA (2000) The locally embedded multinational and institutional capture. *Area* 32(2): 169–178.

Phelps NA (2008) Cluster or capture? Manufacturing foreign direct investment, external economies and agglomeration. *Regional Studies* 42(4): 457–473.

Phelps NA, Atienza M and Arias M (2015) Encore for the enclave: The changing nature of the industry enclave with illustrations from the mining industry in Chile. *Economic Geography* 91(2): 119–146.

Phelps NA, Atienza M and Arias M (2018) An invitation to the dark side of economic geography. *Environment and Planning A: Economy and Space* 50(1): 236–244.

Phelps NA and Fuller C (2000) Multinationals, intracorporate competition, and regional development. *Economic Geography* 76(3): 224–243.

Phelps NA, Mackinnon D, Stone I and Braidford P (2003) Embedding the multinationals? Institutions and the development of overseas manufacturing affiliates in Wales and North-East England. *Regional Studies* 37(1): 27–40.

Phelps NA, Morgan K and Fuller C (2000) Regions, governance and FDI: The case of Wales. In Hood N and Young S (eds.) *The globalization of multinational enterprise activity and economic development.* Houndmills, Basingstoke: Palgrave Macmillan, pp. 366–389.

Phelps NA and Wood A (2006) Lost in translation? Local interests, global actors and inward investment regimes. *Journal of Economic Geography* 6(4): 493–515.

Phelps NA and Wood A (2018a) The business of location: Site selection consultants and the mobilisation of knowledge in the location decision. *Journal of Economic Geography* 18(5): 1023–1044.

Phelps NA and Wood A (2018b) Promoting the global economy: The uneven development of the location consulting industry. *Environment and Planning A: Economy and Space* 50(6): 1336–1354.

Pickles J and Smith A (2016) *Articulations of capital: Global production networks and regional transformations.* Chichester: Wiley Blackwell.

Pike A (1998) Making performance plants from branch plants? In situ restructuring in the automobile industry in the United Kingdom. *Environment and Planning A: Economy and Space* 30(5): 881–900.

Pike A and Tomaney J (1999) The limits to localization in declining industrial regions? Trans-national corporations and economic development in Sedgefield borough. *European Planning Studies* 7(4): 407–428.

Pitelis C (2006) Stephen Herbert Hymer and/on the (theory of the) MNE and international business. *International Business Review* 15(2): 103–194.

Prague Morning (2021) Czech auto industry revving up for e-mobility transition. Prague Morning, September 7.

Pries L (1999) The dialectics of automobile assemblers and suppliers restructuring and globalization of the German "Big Three." *Actes du GERPISA.*(25): 77–91.

Pries L and Dehnen V (2009) Location tendencies of the international automotive industry: "Footless companies going east and south" or "regionalisation of value chain profiles"? *International Journal of Automotive Technology and Management* 9(4): 415–437.

Pries L and Wäcken N (2020) The 2015 Volkswagen "Diesel-Gate" and its impact on German carmakers. In Covarrubias V. A and Ramírez Perez SM (eds.) *New frontiers of the automobile industry: Exploring geographies, technology, and institutional challenges.* Cham: Palgrave Macmillan, pp. 89–111.

Prokeš J (2021) Zakazovat auta se spalovacími motory považuji za nesmysl, říká nový ministr dopravy Kupka. *Hospodářské noviny*, December 12.

PwC (2018) *Automotive supplier survey 2018.* Bratislava: PwC.

PwC (2019) *Automotive supplier survey 2019.* Bratislava: PwC.

Randall C (2021) Renault wants to prolong the fossil fuel era. electrive.com, September 9. Available at: www.electrive.com/2021/09/09/renault-wants-to-prolong-the-fossil-fuel-era/ (accessed February 11, 2022).

Randall C (2022a) InoBat to build battery gigafactory in western Europe. electrive.com, April 6. Available at: www.electrive.com/2022/04/06/inobat-to-build-battery-gigafactory-in-western-europe/ (accessed January 9, 2023).

Randall C (2022b) Serbia blocks lithium mining project. electrive.com, January 24. Available at: www.electrive.com/2022/01/24/serbia-blocks-lithium-mining-project/ (accessed March 19, 2022).

Randall C (2023a) ElectroMobility Poland postpones production of first model til 2025. electrive.com, January 20. Available at: www.electrive.com/2023/01/20/electromobility-poland-postpones-production-of-first-model-til-2025/ (accessed October 29, 2023).

Randall C (2023b) ElectroMobility Poland to utilize Pininfarina design. electrive.com, March 22. Available at: www.electrive.com/2023/03/22/electromobility-poland-to-utilize-pininfarina-design/ (accessed October 29, 2023).

Ravenhill J (2014) Global value chains and development. *Review of International Political Economy* 21(1): 264–274.

Rehnberg M and Ponte S (2018) From smiling to smirking? 3D printing, upgrading and the restructuring of global value chains. *Global Networks* 18(1): 57–80.

Revill J (2008) At risk: European car factories. *Automotive News Europe*, October 13.

Rodriguez-Clare A (1996) Multinationals, linkages, and economic development. *American Economic Review* 86(4): 852–873.

Rodríguez-De La Fuente M and Lampón JF (2020) Regional upgrading within the automobile industry global value chain: The role of the domestic firms and institutions. *International Journal of Automotive Technology and Management* 20(3): 319–340.

Rodríguez-Pose A (2013) Do institutions matter for regional development? *Regional Studies* 47(7): 1034–1047.

Rodríguez-Pose A and Di Cataldo M (2015) Quality of government and innovative performance in the regions of Europe. *Journal of Economic Geography* 15(4): 673–706.

Rodrik D (2011) *The globalization paradox: Democracy and the future of the world economy.* New York: W. W. Norton.

Rutherford T and Holmes J (2008) "The flea on the tail of the dog": Power in global production networks and the restructuring of Canadian automotive clusters. *Journal of Economic Geography* 8(4): 519–544.

Rutherford TD, Murray G, Almond P and Pelard M (2018) State accumulation projects and inward investment regimes strategies. *Regional Studies* 52(4): 572–584.

Rzentarzewska K and Cery J (2023) CEE attracting EV battery sector. CEE Macro and FI Daily, August 28. Available at: www.erstegroup.com/en/research/report/en/SR346396 (accessed October 15, 2023).

Sadler D (1995) National and international regulatory framework: The politics of European automobile production and trade. In Hudson R and Schamp EW (eds.) *Towards a new map of automobile manufacturing in Europe? New production concepts and spatial restructuring.* Berlin: Springer, pp. 21–37.

Sadler D, Swain A and Hudson R (1993) The automobile industry and Eastern Europe: New production strategies or old solutions? *Area* 25(4): 339–349.

Saggi K (2002) Trade, foreign direct investment, and international technology transfer: A survey. *World Bank Research Observer* 17(2): 191–235.

Saliola F and Zanfei A (2009) Multinational firms, global value chains and the organization of knowledge transfer. *Research Policy* 38(2): 369–381.

Santangelo GD (2009) MNCs and linkages creation: Evidence from a peripheral area. *Journal of World Business* 44(2): 192–205.

Santangelo GD (2018) The impact of FDI in land in agriculture in developing countries on host country food security. *Journal of World Business* 53(1): 75–84.

Sario (2016) *Automotive sector in Slovakia.* Bratislava: Slovak Investment and Trade Development Agency.

Sario (2022) *Automotive sector in Slovakia.* Bratislava: Slovak Investment and Trade Development Agency.

Sarkar P (2007) Does foreign direct investment promote growth? Panel data and time series: Evidence from less developed countries, 1970–2002. *MPRA Paper* (5176): 1–23.

Sass M and Szalavetz A (2013) Crisis and upgrading: The case of the Hungarian automotive and electronics sectors. *Europe-Asia Studies* 65(3): 489–507.

Schackmann-Fallis KP (1989) External control and regional development within the Federal Republic of Germany. *International Regional Science Review* 12(3): 245–261.

Schade W, Haug I and Berthold D (2022) The future of the automotive sector: Emerging battery value chains in Europe. In Galgóczi B (ed.) *The future of the automotive sector.* Brussels: ETUI.

Schmitt A and Van Biesebroeck J (2013) Proximity strategies in outsourcing relations: The role of geographical, cultural and relational proximity in the European automotive industry. *Journal of International Business Studies* 44(5): 475–503.

Schneider BR (2013) *Hierarchical capitalism in Latin America: Business, labor, and the challenges of equitable development.* Cambridge: Cambridge University Press.

Schneider BR (2017) Unfinished legacy: Understanding reciprocity, business groups and MNCs in Latin America. *Cambridge Journal of Regions, Economy and Society* 10(1): 111–125.

Schoenberger E (1988) Multinational corporations and the new international division of labor: A critical appraisal. *International Regional Science Review* 11(2): 105–119.

Schoenberger E (1991) The corporate interview as a research method in economic geography. *The Professional Geographer* 43(2): 180–189.

Schwabe J (2020a) From "obligated embeddedness" to "obligated Chineseness"? Bargaining processes and evolution of international automotive firms in China's new energy vehicle sector. *Growth and Change* 51(3): 1102–1123.

Schwabe J (2020b) Risk and counter-strategies: The impact of electric mobility on German automotive suppliers. *Geoforum* 110: 157–167.

Scott AJ (1987) The semiconductor industry in South-East Asia: Organization, location and the international division of labour. *Regional Studies* 21(2): 143–159.

Scott-Kennel J (2007) Foreign direct investment and local linkages: An empirical investigation. *Management International Review* 47(1): 51–77.

Seid SH (2018 [2002]) *Global regulation of foreign direct investment*. London: Routledge.

Seppälä T, Kenney M and Ali-Yrkko J (2014) Global supply chains and transfer pricing Insights from a case study. *Supply Chain Management: An International Journal* 19(4): 445–454.

Sheard P (1983) Auto-production systems in Japan: Organizational and locational features. *Australian Geographical Studies* 21(1): 49–68.

Shin N, Kraemer KL and Dedrick J (2012) Value capture in the global electronics industry: Empirical evidence for the "smiling curve" concept. *Industry and Innovation* 19(2): 89–107.

Shin N, Kraemer KL and Dedrick J (2013) Value capture in global production networks: Evidence from the Taiwanese electronics industry. *Journal of the Asia Pacific Economy* 19(1): 74–88.

SIEPA (2014) *Serbia: Automotive industry*. Belgrade: Serbia Investment and Export Promotion Agency.

Sigal P (2021) EV-only future looks closer than ever in Europe. *Automotive News Europe*, January 5.

Sigal P (2022a) Europe's combustion-engine factories at a crossroads. *Automotive News Europe*, October 4.

Sigal P (2022b) How Tesla is shaking up the European market, from the top down. *Automotive News Europe*, January 4.

Singer HW (1950) The distribution of gains between investing and borrowing countries. *American Economic Review* 40(2): 473–485.

Škoda Auto (2021a) Herbert Diess receives updates on the future of electromobility in the Czech Republic. October 11. Available at: www.skoda-storyboard.com/en/press-releases/herbert-diess-receives-updates-on-the-future-of-electromobility-in-the-czech-republic/ (accessed April 8, 2022).

Škoda Auto (2021b) Škoda Auto takes on worldwide responsibility for Volkswagen Group's MQB-A0 Global Platform. October 14. Available at: www.skoda-storyboard.com/en/press-releases/skoda-auto-takes-on-worldwide-responsibility-for-volkswagen-groups-mqb-a0-global-platform/ (accessed April 8, 2022).

Škoda Auto (2021c) *Škoda Auto: Annual report 2020*. Mladá Boleslav: Škoda Auto.

Slačík T (2022) The e-motion of car manufacturing in CESEE: The road ahead. *Focus on European Economic Integration* (Q3): 31–46.

Slowik P and Lutsey N (2018) *The continued transition to electric vehicles in US cities*. White Paper. Washington, DC: The International Council of Clean Transportation (ICCT).

Smeets R (2008) Collecting the pieces of the FDI knowledge spillovers puzzle. *World Bank Research Observer* 23(2): 107–138.

Smith A (2015) The state, institutional frameworks and the dynamics of capital in global production networks. *Progress in Human Geography* 39(3): 290–315.

Smith A, Rainnie A, Dunford M, et al. (2002) Networks of value, commodities and regions: Reworking divisions of labour in macro-regional economies. *Progress in Human Geography* 26(1): 41–63.

Smith N (1987) Dangers of the empirical turn: Some comments on the CURS initiative. *Antipode* 19(1): 59–68.

Smith N (1989) Uneven development and location theory: Towards a synthesis. In Peet R and Thrift N (eds.) *New models in geography: The political-economy perspective.* Winchester: Unwin Hyman, pp. 152–175.

Smith N (2008 [1984]) *Uneven development: Nature, Capital, and the production of space.* Athens: The University of Georgia Press.

Sonnenfeld J (2023) Yale CELI list of companies leaving and staying in Russia. Yale School of Management. Available at: www.yalerussianbusinessretreat.com (accessed November 26, 2023).

Sornarajah M (2017) *The international law on foreign investment.* Cambridge: Cambridge University Press.

South RB and Kim C (2019) Maquiladora mortality: Manufacturing plant closure in Mexico. *The Journal of Development Studies* 55(8): 1654–1669.

Spencer JW (2008) The impact of multinational enterprise strategy on indigenous enterprises: Horizontal spillovers and crowding out in developing countries. *Academy of Management Review* 33(2): 341–361.

Starosta G (2010) The outsourcing of manufacturing and the rise of giant global contractors: A Marxian approach to some recent transformations of global value chains. *New Political Economy* 15(4): 543–563.

Statistics Sweden (2020) *Research and development in Sweden.* Stockholm: Statistics Sweden.

Statistics Sweden (2023) *Research and development in Sweden.* Stockholm: Statistics Sweden.

Stewart JC (1976) Linkages and foreign direct investment. *Regional Studies* 10(2): 245–258.

Stöllinger R (2021) Testing the smile curve: Functional specialisation and value creation in GVCs. *Structural Change and Economic Dynamics* 56: 93–116.

Storper M and Walker R (1989) *The capitalist imperative: Territory, technology and industrial growth.* Oxford: Basil Blackwell.

Strzałkowski M (2021) Will Europe run on Polish lithium-ion batteries? Visegrad.info, January 29. Available at: https://visegradinfo.eu/index.php/national-policy-reports/609-will-europe-run-on-polish-lithium-ion-batteries (accessed October 4, 2022).

Sturgeon T and Florida R (2000) *Globalization and jobs in the automotive industry.* Cambridge, MA: The MIT Industrial Performance Center or the Massachusetts Institute of Technology.

Sturgeon T, Van Biesebroeck J and Gereffi G (2008) Value chains, networks and clusters: Reframing the global automotive industry. *Journal of Economic Geography* 8(3): 297–321.

Sturgeon TJ, Gereffi G, Rogers KB and Fernandez-Stark K (2010) The prospects for Mexico in the North American automotive industry: A global value chain perspective. *Actes du GERPISA* 42(June): 11–22.

Sturgeon TJ and Lester RK (2004) The new global supply base: New challenges for local suppliers in East Asia. In Yusuf S, Altaf MAA and Nabeshima K (eds.)*Global production networking and technological change in East Asia.* Washington, DC: The World Bank and Oxford University Press, pp. 35–87.

Sturgeon TJ and Van Biesebroeck J (2011) Global value chains in the automotive industry: An enhanced role for developing countries? *International Journal of Technological Learning, Innovation and Development* 4(1/2/3): 181–205.

Sultana N and Turkina E (2020) Foreign direct investment, technological advancement, and absorptive capacity: A network analysis. *International Business Review* 29(2): 101668.

Sunkel O (1972) Big business and "dependencia": A Latin American view. *Foreign Affairs* 50(3): 517–531.

Szabo J, Deák A, Szalavetz A and Túry G (2022) The future of the European automobile industry: Hungary. In Galgóczi B (ed.) *The future of the automotive sector*. Brussels: ETUI.

Szabo S (2020) *Transition to Industry 4.0 in the Visegrád Countries*. Luxembourg: Directorate General Economic and Financial Affairs (DG ECFIN), European Commission.

Szalavetz A (2005) Physical capital stock, technological upgrading and modernisation in Hungary. *Acta Oeconomica* 55(2): 201–221.

Szalavetz A (2015) Upgrading and subsidiary autonomy: Experience of Hungarian manufacturing companies. *Japanese Journal of Comparative Economics* 52(2): 1–19.

Szalavetz A (2019) Industry 4.0 and capability development in manufacturing subsidiaries. *Technological Forecasting and Social Change* 145: 384–395.

Szalavetz A (2022) Transition to electric vehicles in Hungary: A devastating crisis or business as usual? *Technological Forecasting and Social Change* 184: 122029.

Tavares AT and Young S (2006) Sourcing patterns of foreign-owned multinational subsidiaries in Europe. *Regional Studies* 40(6): 583–599.

Taylor I (2016) Dependency redux: Why Africa is not rising. *Review of African Political Economy* 43(147): 8–25.

Taylor I and Zajontz T (2020) In a fix: Africa's place in the Belt and Road Initiative and the reproduction of dependency. *South African Journal of International Affairs* 27(3): 277–295.

Thomas KP (2011) *Investment incentives and the global competition for capital*. New York: Palgrave Macmillan.

Tödtling F and Trippl M (2005) One size fits all? Towards a differentiated regional innovation policy approach. *Research Policy* 34(8): 1203–1219.

Townroe PM (1975) Branch plants and regional development. *The Town Planning Review* 46(1): 47–62.

Transport & Environment (2020) *Recharge EU: How many charge points will Europe and its member states need in the 2020s*. Brussels: European Federation for Transport and Environment.

Trippl M, Baumgartinger-Seiringer S, Goracinova E and Wolfe DA (2021) Automotive regions in transition: Preparing for connected and automated vehicles. *Environment and Planning A: Economy and Space* 53(5): 1158–1179. DOI: 10.1177/0308518X20987233. 0308518X20987233.

Turok I (1993) Inward investment and local linkages: How deeply embedded is "Silicon Glen"? *Regional Studies* 27(5): 401–417.

Turok I (1997) Linkages in the Scottish electronics industry: Further evidence. *Regional Studies* 31(7): 705–711.

Twomey MJ (2000) *A century of foreign investment in the Third World*. London: Routledge.

UN (1950) *Economic development of Latin America and its principal problems.* Santiago: United Nations.

UN (1992) *World investment report 1992: Transnational corporations as engines of growth.* New York: United Nations.

UNCTAD (2001) *World investment report 2001: Promoting linkages.* New York: United Nations.

UNCTAD (2005) *World investment report 2005: Transnational corporations and the internationalization of R&D.* New York: United Nations Conference on Trade and Development (UNCTAD).

UNCTAD (2007) *World investment report 2007: Transnational corporations, extractive industries and development.* New York: United Nations Conference on Trade and Development (UNCTAD).

UNCTAD (2009) *World investment report 2009: Transnational corporations, agricultural production and development.* New York: United Nations Conference on Trade and Development (UNCTAD).

UNCTAD (2012) *World investment report 2012: Towards a new generation of investment policies.* New York: United Nations Conference on Trade and Development (UNCTAD).

UNCTAD (2013) *World investment report 2013: Global value chains: Investment and trade for development.* New York: United Nations Conference on Trade and Development (UNCTAD).

UNCTAD (2015) *World investment report 2015: Reforming international investment governance.* New York: United Nations Conference on Trade and Development (UNCTAD).

UNCTAD (2016) *World investment report 2016: Investor nationality: Policy challenges.* New York: United Nations Conference on Trade and Development (UNCTAD).

UNCTAD (2017) *World investment report 2017: Investment and the digital economy.* New York: United Nations Conference on Trade and Development (UNCTAD).

UNCTAD (2020) *World investment report 2020: International production beyond the pandemic.* Geneva: United Nations Conference on Trade and Development (UNCTAD).

UNCTAD (2021) *World Investment Report 2021: Investing in sustainable recovery.* Geneva: United Nations Conference on Trade and Development (UNCTAD).

UNCTAD (2023) *World investment report 2023: Investing in sustainable energy for all.* Geneva: United Nations Conference on Trade and Development (UNCTAD).

USDT (2022) *National transportation statistics 2022.* Washington, DC: United States Department of Transportation, Bureau of Transportation Statistics.

Van Hamme G and Pion G (2012) The relevance of the world-system approach in the era of globalization of economic flows and networks. *Geografiska Annaler Series B-Human Geography* 94B(1): 65–82.

Van Tulder R and Ruigrok W (1998) *International production networks in the auto industry: Central and Eastern Europe as the low end of the West European car complexes.* Berkley, CA: Institute of International Studies University of California Berkeley.

Veloso F, Henry C, Roth R and Clark JP (2000) *Global strategies for the development of the Portuguese autoparts industry.* Lisbon: IAPMEI, MIT, INTELI and FEUP.

Veloso F and Kumar R (2002) *The automotive supply chain: global trends and Asian perspectives.* Manila

Vernon R (1966) International investment and international trade in the product cycle. *Quarterly Journal of Economics* 80(2): 190–207.

Vesić D and Vukša T (2021) Serbia: The automotive industry and the ecological transition. In Kropp M (ed.) *The need for transformation: Current challenges for the international automotive sector: Voices from unions, workers, climate movement, industry.* Brussels: Rosa-Luxemburg-Stiftung, pp. 208–256.

VW (2021) *2020 annual report: Na cestě k udržateľnosti (On the road to sustainability).* Bratislava: Volkswagen Slovakia.

Wade R (1990) *Governing the market: Economic theory and the role of government in East Asian industrialization.* Princeton, NJ: Princeton University Press.

Wade R (2018) The developmental state: Dead or alive? *Development and Change* 49(2): 518–546.

Walker R (1989) A requiem for corporate geography: New directions in industrial organization, the production of place and the uneven development. *Geografiska Annaler. Series B, Human Geography* 71(1): 43–68.

Wallerstein I (1974) *The modern world-system I: Capitalist agriculture and the origins of the European world-economy in the sixteenth century* New York: Academic Press.

Wallerstein I (1979) *The capitalist world-economy.* Cambridge: Cambridge University Press.

Ward MF (1982) Political economy, industrial location and the European motor car industry in the postwar period. *Regional Studies* 16(6): 443–453.

Ward's (2016) *Motor vehicle facts & figures, annual issues.* Southfield, MI: Ward's.

Wasti SN and Wasti SA (2008) Trust in buyer-supplier relations: The case of the Turkish automotive industry. *Journal of International Business Studies* 39(1): 118–131.

Watts HD (1981) *The branch plant economy: A study of external control.* London: Longman.

WBG (2019) *Retention and expansion of foreign direct investment: Political risk and policy responses.* Washington, DC: World Bank Group.

Weber A (1929) *Theory of the location of industries.* Chicago, IL: University of Chicago Press.

Werner M (2016) Global production networks and uneven development: Exploring geographies of devaluation, disinvestment, and exclusion. *Geography Compass* 10(11): 457–469.

Werner M (2018) Geographies of production I: Global production and uneven development. *Progress in Human Geography* 43(5): 948–958.

Werner M (2021) Geographies of production II: Thinking through the state. *Progress in Human Geography* 45(1): 178–189. DOI: 10.1177/0309132520911996.

Westerheide C (2024) BYD plans to open its Hungarian EV factory within three years. electrive.com, February 6. Available at: www.electrive.com/2024/02/06/byd-plans-to-open-its-hungarian-ev-factory-within-three-years/ (accessed March 1, 2024).

Williams D, McDonald F, Tuselmann HJ and Turner C (2008) Domestic sourcing by foreign-owned subsidiaries. *Environment and Planning C-Government and Policy* 26(1): 260–276.

Williams M (2021) VW to have 240 GWh of battery plants in Europe by 2030. *Automotive Manufacturing Solutions*, March 17.

Wionczek MS (1986) Industrialization, foreign capital and technology transfer: The Mexican experience 1930–85. *Development and Change* 17(2): 283–302.

Womack JP, Jones DT and Roos D (1990) *The machine that changed the world.* New York: Rawson Associates.

World Bank (2020) *World development report 2020: Trading for development in the age of global value chains.* Washington, DC: The World Bank.

Wren C and Jones J (2009) Re-investment and the survival of foreign-owned plants. *Regional Science and Urban Economics* 39(2): 214–223.

WTEx (2016) World's top exports: car exports by country. July 27. Available at: www .worldstopexports.com/car-exports-country/ (accessed July 27, 2016).

WTEx (2021) world's top exports: car exports by country. October 28. Available at: www.worldstopexports.com/car-exports-country/ (accessed October 28, 2021).

Yamin M and Nixson F (2016) New directions of foreign direct investment and industrial development. In Weiss J and Tribe M (eds.) *Routledge handbook of industry and development.* London: Routledge, pp. 166–183.

Yeung G (2019) "Made in China 2025": The development of a new energy vehicle industry in China. *Area Development and Policy* 4(1): 39–59.

Yeung HWC (2009) Regional development and the competitive dynamics of global production networks: An East Asian perspective. *Regional Studies* 43(3): 325–351.

Yeung HWC (2013) Governing the market in a globalizing era: Developmental states, global production networks and inter-firm dynamics in East Asia. *Review of International Political Economy* 21(1): 70–101.

Yeung HWC (2015) Regional development in the global economy: A dynamic perspective of strategic coupling in global production networks. *Regional Science Policy & Practice* 7(1): 1–23.

Yeung HWC (2016) *Strategic coupling: East Asian industrial transformation in the new global economy.* Ithaca, NY: Cornell University Press.

Young S, Hood N and Peters E (1994) Multinational enterprises and regional economic development. *Regional Studies* 28(7): 657–677.

Yülek MA, Lee KH, Kim J and Park D (2020) State capacity and the role of industrial policy in automobile industry: A comparative analysis of Turkey and South Korea. *Journal of Industry, Competition and Trade* 20(2): 307–331.

ZAP (2022) *Slovensko zaostáva v zelenej transformácii krajiny. Ako splniť záväzky EÚ?* Bratislava: The Automotive Industry Association of Slovakia.

Zdanowska N (2021) Central Eastern European cities within multi-level transnational company networks: Cores, peripheries and diffusion of innovation. *Environment and Planning B: Urban Analytics and City Science* 48(8): 2453–2465. DOI: 10.1177/2399808320977863.

Ženka J and Pavlínek P (2013) The Czech automotive industry in global production networks: Regional dimensions of upgrading between 1998 and 2008. *Geografie* 118(2): 116–137.

Zhan JX (2021) GVC transformation and a new investment landscape in the 2020s: Driving forces, directions, and a forward-looking research and policy agenda. *Journal of International Business Policy* 4: 206–220. DOI: 10.1057/s42214-020-00088-0.

Zhang J (2013) *Foreign direct investment, governance, and the environment in China: Regional dimensions.* Basingstoke: Palgrave Macmillan.

Zhao SXB, Wong DWH, Wong DWS and Jiang YP (2020) Ever-transient FDI and ever-polarizing regional development: Revisiting conventional theories of regional development in the context of China, Southeast and South Asia. *Growth and Change* 51(1): 338–361.

Index

Printed in the United States
by Baker & Taylor Publisher Services